New Towns

New Towns

Regional Planning and Development

PIERRE MERLIN

Directeur scientifique de l'Institut d'Aménagement et d'Urbanisme
de la Région Parisienne (IAURP)
and Professor at the University of Paris-Vincennes

Translated by Margaret Sparks

METHUEN & CO LTD

First published 1969 as *Les Villes Nouvelles*
by Presses Universitaires de France, Paris.
English language edition first published 1971
by Methuen & Co Ltd, 11 New Fetter Lane, London EC4
© 1971 Methuen & Co Ltd

Photoset by B A S Printers Ltd, Wallop, Hampshire
and printed in Great Britain
by Fletcher & Sons Ltd, Norwich

SBN 416 16810 8

Distributed in the USA by Barnes & Noble Inc

Contents

Figures

Preface to French edition

The term 'new town' becomes increasingly difficult to define. What is there in common between Tapiola, the model garden city outside Helsinki, and Brasilia, the new federal capital of Brazil? Between Montpazier or La Roche-sur-Yon, new towns of past ages, and the Le Vaudreuil project in Normandy? Between Welwyn Garden City, north of London, and the iron-working town of Dunaujvaros in Hungary?

Before embarking on the creation of new towns in France, either in the Paris region or the provinces, it is advisable to recognize the differences covered by this one term, to study the characteristics of each type of new town, the purpose for which it was built, the methods employed in its construction and the results obtained. A more complicated matter is the study of the relationship between the original purpose and the administrative, financial and other means employed and the successful functioning of the town, which does not always correspond exactly with the original concepts.

Each new town in another country, and even the small experience gained in France so far, can teach two lessons: the benefits acquired and also the pitfalls to be avoided.

England will impress one with the remarkable efficiency of the methods employed to create the new towns, even as early as 1946 after only a few months' study. Sweden or Finland will be particularly remembered for operations of high architectural quality at not much higher cost: if it is possible to combine building and beauty it is done here. The Netherlands will leave the impression that the provision of amenities to coincide with housing becomes easy when there is a single authority in charge. The United States or the countries of eastern Europe will show that the creation of a new framework of living can be the work of private promoters and state alike.

It was in order that French town planners might profit from the experience gained in the last few decades of practical town planning that I asked the Institut d'Aménagement et d'Urbanisme de la Région Parisienne some years ago to undertake detailed studies of new towns in other countries, within the framework of a regional planning policy. For this reason I warmly welcomed the request of the Délégation générale à la Recherche scientifique et technique for M. Pierre Merlin to undertake a synthesis and collection of these studies, under the auspices of the Institute.

The present work includes an account of French policy for new towns. How much ground has been covered between the *grand ensemble* and Évry or Le Vaudreuil! Even so, many questions have still to be answered: At what rate should a new town grow? What type of employment should be provided there? What will be its population structure? If the creation of new towns in France is to answer these questions, their development must be closely studied and redirected if necessary. Above all, each new town, developing its own personality, must stand apart from the rest.

Finally – though this criterion of success lies many years ahead – the difficulty of defining the term 'new town' will disappear when each new town succeeds in finding its own soul.

Paul Delouvrier

This study was originally made for the Délégation générale à la Recherche scientifique et technique. The information used in this study was gathered with the collaboration of MM. P. Guertin (Great Britain and Scandinavia), H. Nardin (USA), A. Fourquier (Poland) and D. Michaeli (Hungary), and Mlle B. Métayer and the Documentary Service of the IAURP (other countries).

Preface to English edition

During 1965, when my colleagues and I were working on the *South Hampshire Study*, we were visited by MM. Merlin and Guertin, who at that time were engaged on a study tour of the United Kingdom in order to gather material on British new towns. They had been asked to undertake this work by M. Paul Delouvrier, the Prefect of the Paris region, as part of a systematic analysis of the objectives and means of implementation of British new towns, their demographic, economic, social and physical structures; and their successes and their failures. This work was, in turn, part of a broader programme of research into new towns in many countries which was seen as an essential background to the development of the plan for the Paris region, on which l'Institut d'Aménagement et d'Urbanisme de la Région Parisienne was engaged. The results of the investigation of MM. Merlin and Guertin were later published as one of the supplementary volumes of the IAURP report, 'Urbanisme en région de Londres et aménagement du territoire', *Cahiers de l'IAURP*, vol. 8, June 1967. The volume was an extremely valuable addition to the restricted number of books dealing comprehensively with British new towns.

Now M. Merlin has written *Les Villes Nouvelles*, which draws on the IAURP volume but which, in addition, contains a similar analysis of new towns in the other countries. In his preface to the original French edition of the book, M. Delouvrier said that the work was undertaken in order that French planners could benefit from experience in other countries. In retrospect, this is perhaps too modest an objective, since the book has undoubtedly become a most useful document in the international planning scene. I have no doubt that the publication of this English edition will considerably strengthen that role.

In dealing with his subject, M. Merlin wisely sets a broader context of national and regional policies within which the new towns play their part. Furthermore he does not constrain the scope of his examination by writing only of what we in Britain come to think of as new towns. Instead he covers the whole field of new communities which, by diverse means, have been consciously designed and realized as such. Seen as a proportion of total urban development, these new communities represent a relatively small contribution. Their interest

lies in the fact that they are in many ways a unique social and technical phenomenon, a focus for new ideas, and, if we organize ourselves properly, a labora-
tory for monitoring the reaction of the people for whom they were built. The
satisfaction of their creators is of little importance. The satisfaction of their
inhabitants is the only true objective.

COLIN BUCHANAN

Introduction

The concept of new towns has been in existence since the end of the nineteenth century, when Ebenezer Howard was the first to propose the creation of Garden Cities in England.[1] If one excepts those towns created for political ends, of which Brasilia is the most notable example, the new towns built over the last few decades have been intended either to aid the industrialization of underdeveloped areas (particularly in eastern Europe and Siberia), to relieve the congestion of large built-up urban areas (especially the new towns around London) or to direct their growth, as in the case of Stockholm.

The term 'new town' means different things in different places. There is not a great deal in common between Brasilia and Tapiola, between the New Communities of the United States and the new surburban sectors of Stockholm, nor between the new towns of England and of Hungary. The differences stem from many causes: the planning of the towns, their size, pattern, site, system of development, main types of housing, etc; their social composition and their existence within or outside an urban region; their administration, the nature of the authority in charge and its relationship with local authorities; finance, etc.

But over and above these differences, what strikes one is the variety of aims and principles from which these new towns sprang. They rarely exist in isolation – with the exception of Tapiola – but are usually part of a regional planning policy or even of a national development policy.

At a time when the creation of new towns is being studied in many countries, it has seemed worthwhile to collect as much evidence as possible from those countries that built new towns some years ago, in order to pick out the main characteristics of these, to see to what extent they may be imitated, to indicate the pitfalls to avoid and the problems to anticipate. An attempt will also be made to show how a new towns policy reflects a national concept of urban life. The study of this new towns policy will in each case be set within the framework of regional planning policy and the national policy of land development.

It is obviously impossible to make an exhaustive survey of new towns all over

[1]Ebenezer Howard, *Garden Cities of Tomorrow* (London, Faber & Faber, new ed., 1965).

the world. This study will concentrate on some countries of western Europe, chosen for the importance of their new towns and the quality of their town planning tradition: Great Britain, homeland of the Garden City, where twenty or so new towns have been built over the last two decades; three Scandinavian countries (Denmark, Sweden and Finland), famed for the high quality of their town planning; the Netherlands, where land use is all the more important because of its scarcity and the unending struggle against the sea. French plans for large new urban developments within regional schemes have also been included. But it also seemed necessary to include examples from countries where the economic system and way of life are very different from those of western Europe. Ruling out the underdeveloped countries, for whom questions of town planning are very different and from whom little could be learned, it was decided to take some examples of new towns built by private promoters in the United States, land of free enterprise, the motor car and individual houses. Examples have also been taken from two countries of eastern Europe living under a communist regime: Poland and Hungary. The new towns of the USSR are of such importance that it seemed better to leave them for a later and more detailed study. Finally, an attempt will be made to list the main elements of these various undertakings, which may be of use to planners and builders of the new towns of the next decade.

1 : Town planning
in the London area and the new towns

Introduction

England is often quoted as an example by town planners in many countries, some of its plans – such as the Abercrombie Plan – and its new towns being world famous. The new towns, conceived as part of a national policy of land development (the Barlow Report of 1940) and a regional town planning policy deriving from this (the Abercrombie Plan of 1944), comprise one of the most remarkable achievements in town planning in the last twenty years, although they only represent one element of the strategy adopted immediately after the war, others being housing estates and town extensions. For some years now the problem has had to be faced again. The results of the 1961 census showed that, contrary to the forecasts of the Abercrombie Plan, the growth of the London area had not been checked. The same problems remained, the solution adopted twenty years before having proved inadequate in the face of changing circumstances. The resulting *South East Study* has become a guide for present development.

I   The formation of a policy 1937-1956[1]

On the eve of the Second World War the British were concerned with the formation of an overall policy of land development. The outlines of such a policy were formulated in the Barlow Report of 1940, presented by a Commission formed in 1937. Wartime conditions made its implementation impossible at that time but strengthened public and government opinion in favour of the need for the decongestion of London's built-up area, as proposed in the Barlow Report, as an essential element of national policy. It was in this mood that the Abercrombie Plan was received at the end of the war, with its proposals for a Green Belt round London and a ring of new towns beyond. As a result, the British government passed the New Towns Act in 1946, providing for a special system of finance and for development corporations in charge of each new town.

[1]P. Merlin and P. Guertin, 'Urbanisme en région de Londres et aménagement du territoire', *Cahiers de l'IAURP*, vol. 8, June 1967.

The outlines of the Barlow report

In 1937 a Royal Commission was set up under the chairmanship of Sir Montague Barlow to study the distribution of industrial population and the disadvantages of urban and economic over-concentration and to suggest solutions. These terms of study obviously prejudged the Commission's conclusions to some extent. After three years' work, the report was presented in January 1940.

First of all, it set out the first stage of a nationwide plan. After describing the development of urban and industrial concentration since the beginning of the nineteenth century and analysing its causes, the report lists the disadvantages of this concentration on strategic grounds (vulnerability to air or other attack), social grounds (poor housing conditions) and economic grounds (traffic congestion, lengthy commuting and the high cost of land).

After an examination of the solutions available under existing legislation comes the most interesting section of the report, setting out the Commission's proposals as follows:

The need for reorganization of congested urban areas.

The establishment of a policy of decentralization and deconcentration of industry.

The search for a balance between different regions with respect to the size and variety of industrial activity.

Furthermore, it recommends the creation of a national authority, outside Parliament, charged with putting these proposals into force and with working out the details of industrial decentralization and urban development. This body would also assume the task of co-ordinating planning on a regional or local scale.

The Commission laid particular stress on the problems of the London area, seeing it as the prototype of a congested and over-large built-up area. Some members of the Commission, however, considered that the measures should not be particularly concerned with the London area but with the country as a whole.

Following the Barlow Report, the Ministry of Works and Planning was created in 1942 and the Ministry of Town and Country Planning in 1943. After 1951 this became the Ministry of Housing and Local Government. This ministry, under its various titles, was to be in charge of the building of new towns and of the development plans prescribed for each county and county borough by the 1947 Act. The Board of Trade, however, retained the chief responsibility for the location of industry (according to the 1945 Act), so that the national authority envisaged by the Barlow Report became in fact split between two ministries.

The Abercrombie plan for Greater London[1]

The main themes of the Barlow Report were adopted and developed by Sir Patrick Abercrombie in the *Greater London Plan* on the following lines:

> No fresh industry was to be established in the County of London or its adjoining counties and regulations for controlling the increase of industrial employment were to be instituted.
>
> A number of industries and their personnel were to be dispersed.
>
> The total population of Greater London should be decreased.
>
> Part of the existing population was to be resettled outside the limits of the London area.
>
> The Port of London was to retain its important role.
>
> New planning organizations were to be set up to serve the London region.

The following are the main proposals of the *Greater London Plan*: zoning based on a system of concentric rings:

> The first corresponding with the central built-up area, whose high density made dispersal necessary. The maximum population densities for the different sectors of this zone, slightly larger than the County of London, were 185-250 per hectare.
>
> The second was formed by the suburbs, with spaced-out housing and low density. This zone was to remain stable in respect of housing and industry with a maximum of 125 people per hectare.
>
> The third was formed by the majority of the land defined in the Green Belt Act of 1938. Almost entirely agricultural at that time, it was to be used for recreational purposes but at the same time to keep its rural character. This zone was to be kept free from industrial development and the growth of existing towns and villages was to be strictly controlled. This zone, 25-35 km from the centre of London, was to absorb a maximum of 300 000 new inhabitants.
>
> The fourth, whose outer limit was less easily definable, would absorb the section of the London population dispersed from the centre. It was in this zone that the new towns would be built.

The policy of population dispersal aimed at reducing the population of

---

[1]Patrick Abercrombie, *Greater London Plan* 1944 (London, 1945). J. H. Forshaw and Patrick Abercrombie, *County of London Plan* (London, 1943).

central London to 340 per hectare. This would affect 1 033 000 people (618 000 in the County of London and 415 000 outside it), who would be rehoused through special building operations on the following lines:

Population in urban housing estates	125 000
Town extensions on the outskirts of the urban region	261 000
Town expansion outside the urban area (60–80 km)	164 000
Eight new towns	383 000
Dispersal outside the built-up area	100 000
Total	1 033 000

The Abercrombie Plan, with its concentric pattern, was based on the assumption, justifiable at the time, of the stabilization of the population of the built-up area. Its main aim was to ensure the dispersal of the population by the creation of moderate-sized new towns (with populations of about 50 000) comparable to the Garden Cities envisaged by Ebenezer Howard in the early days of the century. Two of these, Letchworth and Welwyn Garden City, had already been partly built. The plan was part of a national planning policy aimed at checking the growth of employment in London, particularly by a policy of dispersal.

These basic aims – stability of population and employment – have only been partly achieved and the Abercrombie Plan has been proved inadequate. Nevertheless, the creation of new towns has been the most interesting outcome of the Abercrombie Report.

The plan's policy was first put into force by the creation of a Royal Commission in 1946, presided over by Lord Reith, to study the general problems connected with the establishment, development, organization and administration of the new towns within the framework of a planned system of decentralization in congested urban areas. The Reith Report, published in 1946, the main points of which will be studied, was to guide the Labour government in its successful introduction of the New Towns Act of 1 August 1946 (see Section III, The New Towns).

II The implementation of a policy 1946-1961[1]

The New Towns Act of 1946 formed one of the main tools of the policy set out in the Barlow Report, developed in the Abercrombie Plan and now put into force. The legislation concerned with decentralization was, however, slow to

[1]P. Merlin and P. Guertin, op. cit.

take its final shape. At first, emphasis was laid only on industry and it was not until the end of 1964 that similar measures were taken in connection with office jobs. Meanwhile, the new towns had been built: eight around London and others in the rest of England, Wales and Scotland. But the new towns did not make up the only aspect of planning in the London area in the fifteen years following the passing of the New Towns Act: a policy of extension of small towns in south-east England was carried out in accordance with the Town Development Act of 1952 and large housing estates were also built.

The policy of decentralization

Immediately after the war the Board of Trade had employed a legislative clause to direct the siting of employment. Any firm wishing to establish or enlarge an industry had first of all to obtain a building permit (mainly technical), planning permission from the county (in the new towns this became the responsibility of the development corporation) and an industrial development certificate. The latter, instituted in 1947 for all new building or extensions exceeding 465 m^2, is granted by the Board of Trade on the advice of an interdepartmental committee dealing with building exceeding 7000 m^2 and by regional offices in the case of those of 465-7000 m^2. In 1965 the industrial development certificate was extended to include building in excess of 93 m^2 in south-east England and the Midlands (though this was raised to 280 m^2 in 1968) and any change in the use of premises.

On the other hand, positive incentives were created by the inauguration of six development areas in 1945. These now include Northern Ireland, the greater part of Scotland, north-east England (Newcastle-Durham), parts of the north-west, Merseyside and various parts of Wales and Cornwall.

In these development areas priority is given to the granting of industrial development certificates. Industrialists can also benefit from financial aid towards rent or purchase and advantageous conditions in premises built by industrial estate management corporations under the aegis of the Board of Trade and from subsidies of up to 25 per cent of the capital invested in premises and materials and from tax relief: the possibility of deducting total investments from profits, the rate of depreciation being left to the discretion of the head of the firm.

The continuing extension of these areas shows a progressive development of British planning policy. Whereas just after the war, in accordance with the proposals of the Barlow Report, the main emphasis was on the deconcentration or large urban areas and especially that of London, the accent is now more on the regional balance of employment and the battle against unemployment.

It seems that in future the causes rather than the effects of centralization will be tackled. This policy may be seen at the level of the Board of Trade's criteria for decisions: the search for a balance between employment and the working population of the area under investigation is the first consideration; the need for a balance between different regions is then carefully considered and the question of adapting existing premises and of regional or national aptitudes for different types of work follows later.

The results of this policy seem to be fairly successful. The floor area of new installations, extensions and alterations made by industrial or other firms has increased by more than 50 per cent compared with the period 1962-3 and has reached nearly 6 million m^2 per year. The London area and the south-east, which had a share of 10·5 per cent in 1963, still had an 8-9 per cent share in 1965, though even this decrease is a sign of success.

Office permits

Some of the measures adopted to encourage the decentralization of industry had repercussions on offices, though until recently the tendency for these to be concentrated in large towns and especially in London seemed, if anything, on the increase. In March 1962 the Town and Country Planning Association published an informative study of this subject.[1] The annual rate of growth of office jobs in the central area was about 15 000, or over 1 per cent total employment. However, since 1957, new buildings have not been able to exceed 10 per cent of the volume of buildings demolished. By juggling with ceiling heights, internal office arrangements, etc., the rebuilders actually succeeded in increasing the number of jobs considerably. Similarly, the reduction of indices of land occupation seems to have been wanting in efficiency.

It was for these reasons that the government proposed, on 4 November 1964, to introduce a system of office permits. These, which became law in 1965, under the Control of Office and Industrial Development Act, are needed for the construction of office premises of more than 280 m^2 in London and the London region (within a radius of 65 km of the centre). This permit, issued by the Board of Trade, plays the same role in relation to the construction and conversion of office premises as does the industrial development certificate in relation to factories. This legislation was extended to the Birmingham area in August 1965 and later, in July 1966, to the whole of the south-east and the Midlands (the rural areas of the Midlands and East Anglia being exempted from it in January

[1]Town and Country Planning Association, *The Paper Metropolis. A Study of London's Office Growth.*

1968). The 280 m^2 limit was increased to 930 m^2 outside the London area in 1967 and outside Greater London in 1968, with the purpose of encouraging office dispersal. Although the system has only been in force for a few years, it seems to be most strictly applied to building in London itself. However, as a temporary measure, the office permit is not required for offices whose building contracts were signed before 4 November 1964, while outside the central area it is only necessary to have obtained planning permission before that date, so that plenty of offices have been built since 1965.

But it is not at all certain that the methods of reaching decisions have proved as stringent as was intended. In the first year, 700 claims were made in the London area. Half of these were examined and, of these, two-thirds were awarded the coveted permit. In the majority of cases the offices were to be built outside the centre and very few (such as the new Stock Exchange) were on a large scale. In terms of floor area, only 20 per cent of the claims were successful. These totalled more than 200 000 m^2, representing a minimum of 10 000 jobs.

These first attempts confirm a well-known fact, observable in London, Paris and elsewhere: the difficulty of any policy of decentralization or dispersal of offices. Indeed, south-east England already contains, it is estimated, three-quarters of all new offices.

It appears that present official policy – though it is too soon to judge its effectiveness – is not adapted to regional development. The Town and Country Planning Association had proposed that the measures limiting office building should be accompanied by encouragement to establish offices in the new towns, expanding towns and new urban centres, mainly by means of a system of subsidies and rents comparable to that in force in the Paris region but on a higher scale. It seems that only the restrictive side of the policy has been put into practice so far.

Expanding towns

Alongside the new towns (see Section III), the Abercrombie Plan envisaged the creation of large housing estates with low population densities (with an average of somewhat over 270 per hectare on the outskirts of London) and the expansion of small towns. The Town Development Act of 1952 provided the administrative and financial framework of these extensions:

> The expansion of industrial areas should be accompanied by the creation of corresponding amenities and by the creation of industrial employ-ment, without finding it necessary to impose a strict balance of population and employment.

They were to permit the decrease of housing density in overpopulated cities (London and its suburbs and the county boroughs), without specifying the methods of selection of families to be rehoused.

The expansion project must be large in relation to the size and resources of the host community in order to qualify for Treasury aid.

The body in charge of the operation could be the county council concerned, the Greater London Council or the appropriate urban district council. An agreement should be reached between the authority in charge and the council of the host area, but the Ministry of Housing and Local Government could compel the host area to allow the planned expansion to be carried out. It was also considered desirable that the council of the host area should act as participating authority in any agreement between the authority in charge and the host area.

In the case of expansion carried out to relieve the overpopulation of Greater London, it is either the latter or the host area that has been in charge of the operation. In either case, however, the new tenants are from the Greater London waiting list, whereas the houses, once built, come under the host authority. Government financial aid takes the form of a subsidy granted to the authority in charge over a certain number of years for each dwelling built and sometimes assistance with the purchase and development of the land. The Greater London Council, whether or not it is in charge of the operation, gives financial assistance until the operation is self-supporting. The participating authority also contributes on a varying scale.

On the town planning level, these expansions assume the preservation and modernization of the original centre and addition of new residential and industrial zones, green spaces and new roads (especially ring roads linking the new residential areas to the newly created employment areas).

At the end of 1968, sixty-six town expansions were being carried out in England and almost as many in Scotland, mostly on a very small scale. Of those in England, half (thirty-two) were connected with Greater London and a quarter (fifteen) with Birmingham. The corresponding building programme had a target of 162 240 dwellings (56 669 already built and 10 253 under construction), more than half of these aimed at absorbing the London overspill (86 287 dwellings planned, of which 33 204 were built and 5671 under construction). Also, nearly 2·5 million m^2 of factory area had been built, two-thirds of this in the towns linked to Greater London.

The real importance of these town expansions is not their sum total but the experience gained through them since 1952. This undoubtedly influenced the government authorities in their recommendations since 1960 for large-scale expansion of medium-sized towns throughout south-east England to contain the growth of Greater London by delimiting demographic and urban overspill (see Section IV).

III The new towns[1]

The new towns remain the most important exercise in town planning in the twenty years following the Abercrombie Plan, since they have absorbed a population slightly larger than the 383 000 envisaged by the town planner in 1944. They form an achievement of undoubted interest in the field of town planning and of urban and community life, from the point of view of a balance between population and employment and of administrative and financial solutions, even though the solutions adopted could be improved in the light of experience.

The new towns: experiments in town planning

The new towns are part of an accepted English tradition − created by Ebenezer Howard about 1906 and carried on by the Town and Country Planning Association − of spacious residential areas, garden cities, two of which had been built to the north of London: Letchworth at the beginning of the century and Welwyn Garden City between the wars.

The general characteristics of these new towns were defined by the New Towns Committee set up at the beginning of 1946. This committee worked with remarkable speed, since the conclusions of its final report acted as a basis for the preparation of the New Towns Act of 1 August 1946, which established the legal foundations of the project.

The Reith Report proposed that the new towns should be sited round large built-up areas of great density to aid in the decrease of their population. Of the fourteen towns founded between 1946 and 1950, eight are in the London region, two in the north-east, two in the central lowlands of Scotland (Glasgow-Edinburgh), one near Cardiff and only one, Corby, at a distance from any large city. Later on, the link between the new town and an economic capital became looser and many new towns were established in the development areas (Fig. 1).

The Reith Report also recommended that the new towns should be sited not

---

[1]P. Merlin and P. Guertin, 'Villes nouvelles en Grande-Bretagne', *Cahiers de l'IAURP*, vol. 8, June 1967. See also P. Merlin, 'Les villes nouvelles en Grande-Bretagne', *Annales de Géographie*, May-June 1968.

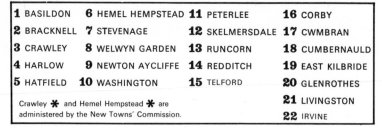

1 BASILDON	**6** HEMEL HEMPSTEAD	**11** PETERLEE	**16** CORBY
2 BRACKNELL	**7** STEVENAGE	**12** SKELMERSDALE	**17** CWMBRAN
3 CRAWLEY	**8** WELWYN GARDEN	**13** RUNCORN	**18** CUMBERNAULD
4 HARLOW	**9** NEWTON AYCLIFFE	**14** REDDITCH	**19** EAST KILBRIDE
5 HATFIELD	**10** WASHINGTON	**15** TELFORD	**20** GLENROTHES
			21 LIVINGSTON
			22 IRVINE

Crawley ✱ and Hemel Hempstead ✱ are
administered by the New Towns' Commission.

Fig. 1 New towns in Great Britain.

less than 40 km outside London, or 20 km outside the parent city in the other regions, to allow the development of a truly independent economic, social and cultural community. On the other hand, the need to attract employment, some of which needed to retain various contacts with the parent city, forbade too great a distance. The eight new towns round London are actually between 32 and 49 km from the centre, those in Scotland (apart from Glenrothes) 20 km from Glasgow (East Kilbride and Cumbernauld) or Edinburgh (Livingston). We shall see later on that the present tendency is towards the expansion of medium-sized towns at greater distances.

Another recommendation of the Reith Commission concerned the size of the new towns, suggesting populations of between 20 000 and 60 000. The upper limit, integral to the garden city tradition as conceived by Ebenezer Howard, tallies with the wish to create a social and physical community life with easy walking or cycling distances between residential areas and places of work on one hand and open country on the other. The lower limit was justified by the wish to ensure a satisfactory level of services, a good choice of jobs and a representative class structure. In the end, most of the new towns had a target fixed nearer the upper limit and this was often raised later, the arguments in favour of the lower limit having been found, in practice, to be less valid than had been expected.

The area of the new towns is largely determined by their predicted population. The Reith Commission recommended that the designated area of a new town should include a 1200 m wide green belt surrounding the town and that it should be further protected by a rural area beyond its administrative limits. In the area of construction, including parks and sports grounds but not the green belt, the overall planned density of population was 30 per hectare.

In a town with a population of 60 000, for instance, the area of construction would cover 2000 ha and the green belt 2400 ha, giving a town area of 4400 ha, not counting the rural protective area. Usually, however, an area of only about 2500 ha was reserved for the first new towns (and often even less later on) and the area of construction remained at about 700 ha (at Harlow and Crawley, for example) for a population of up to 80 000, giving a top density of 100 per hectare (and over 200 per hectare at Cumbernauld, with a denser pattern of housing). As for the total density of the towns, this varies from about 30 per hectare for the first towns to almost 50 per hectare for the latest ones.

After these decisions were made, how were the sites of the new towns chosen? First, one thing had to be settled: were they to be built on virgin sites – giving full scope to the town planners and avoiding the disruption of an existing community by the influx of a new population – or should the

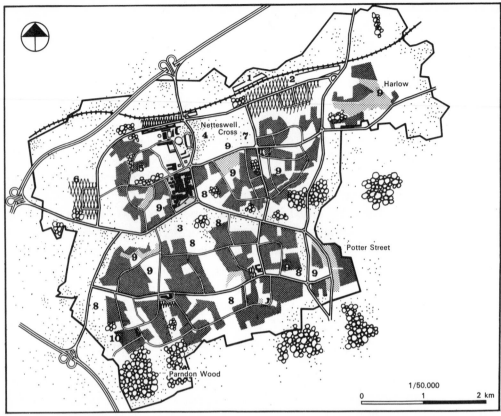

Harlow

Netteswell
Cross

Potter Street

Parndon Wood

1/50.000

0   1   2 km

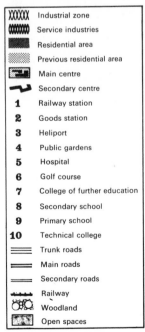

XXXXXXX	Industrial zone
	Service industries
	Residential area
	Previous residential area
	Main centre
	Secondary centre
1	Railway station
2	Goods station
3	Heliport
4	Public gardens
5	Hospital
6	Golf course
7	College of further education
8	Secondary school
9	Primary school
10	Technical college
	Trunk roads
	Main roads
	Secondary roads
	Railway
	Woodland
	Open spaces

Fig. 2   Harlow : overall plan 1952.

1	Offices	**7**	Public library	**12**	Bus station
2	Cinema	**8**	Church		Woodland
3	Bank	**9**	College of further education		Open spaces
4	Post Office				Car park
5	Supermarket	**10**	Police station		
6	Department store	**11**	Local government offices		Pedestrian precinct

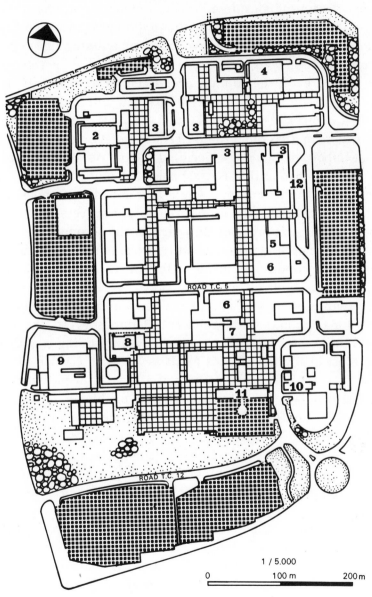

ROAD T.C. 5

ROAD T.C. 12

1 / 5.000

| 0 | 100 m | 200 m |

Fig. 3 The centre of Harlow.

initial nucleus be a small centre with enough amenities to begin with, able to provide or house manpower and containing a community life in embryo?

The Reith Commission favoured construction on virgin sites and was not in agreement with local authorities on this matter. In the event, many of the new towns benefited from the existence of a country town on their territory (previous populations of 5000 at Harlow, 9000 at Crawley and even 21 000 at Hemel Hempstead and 25 000 at Basildon), although this has not necessarily become the general rule. Technical considerations (water supply, drainage possibilities, the water level in the soil, land suitable for building) were taken into account in the choice of sites, as well as the avoidance of building on good farmland. This last factor, surprising to the observer who knows that this would only affect a very small area of the countryside, seems to have been a determining one in England – already a very densely built-up country – and to have caused the rejection of a number of sites proposed in the Abercrombie Plan. Simplicity in matters of ownership (in Cumbernauld 1200 out of the total 1600 ha had one owner) was an important but not a deciding factor. As for road and rail communications, there seemed at first two schools of thought on these, one holding that close links with the parent city would threaten the autonomy of the new town and the other thinking them essential to the success of the new town, especially in attracting employment. In practice, the second view has won the day and most of the new towns have had their communications improved as a result. Micro-climatic conditions can also affect the choice of site. Cumbernauld, for instance, which is built on a narrow ridge, receives the full force of the south-westerly winds along the axis of the town and needs belts of trees for protection. As for the countryside, the Reith Report suggests the avoidance of some areas and the preservation of other areas of outstanding beauty as regional leisure areas. Most of the new towns (such as Welwyn Garden City, Crawley, Harlow, Stevenage, Hatfield and Cumbernauld) are set in pleasant, undulating country. At Harlow (Fig. 3) the centre is built on higher ground, so that it catches the eye, and the town is enclosed by two woods and crossed by three streams flowing through valleys, which act as boundaries between the neighbourhood units and as green spaces and farmland in the very heart of the town. At Cumbernauld, the choice of rising ground led to the adaptation of the plan to the local topography (with the centre on the crest) and allowed extensive views (Fig. 4).

The recommendations of the Reith Commission are very precise in the matter of the type, size and siting of the new towns. They are equally precise about the preparation of plans: the master plan had to show the main amenities (especially communications) and the respective positions of the different zones (residential,

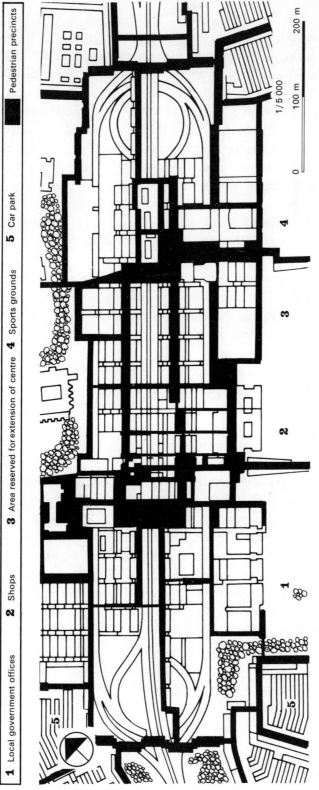

1 Local government offices   **2** Shops   **3** Area reserved for extension of centre   **4** Sports grounds   **5** Car park   ■ Pedestrian precincts

1/5 000

0   100 m   200 m

Fig. 4 The centre of Cumbernauld.

commercial, industrial, educational). Drawn up on a scale of 1:10 000, it is essentially short term, in preparation for immediate action, and precise in its recommendations, without losing the necessary flexibility. In most of the new towns, the only fundamental modification of the original master plan was the provision of extra sectors on the outskirts of the town and occasionally the extension of the centre to keep pace with the increased population level. Once the decision is made to create a new town, work begins on the master plan, which is often entrusted to a well-known architect (Frederick Gibberd at Harlow (Fig. 2), Wilson for Cumbernauld, etc.). The more detailed plans are customarily one of the tasks of the new town's own team of architects and town planners, unless this is decided against for some reason (sometimes, as at Harlow, being made competitive), either for cutting the costs or for ensuring a variety of urban landscape. The mass plans of quantities, areas, communications, densities and details of actual construction are drawn up according to building needs.

The zoning set out in the master plan establishes a functional but mainly commercial centre, offices, industrial areas, residential sectors, general amenities, communications and green spaces.

The size of the centre is calculated on the basis of 4 ha to 10 000 inhabitants, making 24 ha for a town with a population of 60 000. This will often mean 40 ha for a population of about 80 000. This rate of 1 ha to 2000 inhabitants is about that of ordinary towns.[1] It is usually sited at the geometric centre of the new town, often in juxtaposition to the old town centre (Crawley (Fig. 5), Hemel Hempstead). Though the essentially commercial nature of the centre is set out in the Reith Report, provision is also made for public buildings (Post Office, banks, etc.), administrative buildings (municipal offices and the headquarters of the development corporation), recreational and cultural facilities (sports rooms, meeting halls, etc.) and leisure facilities (cinema, restaurants, public gardens). In principle, there would also be a secondary centre for each neighbourhood unit and scattered shops in housing areas. On the question of offices, the Reith Commission suggested that they should be either above shops in the town centre or in special office blocks either in the industrial zone or, for some services, in the residential zone.

The industrial zones were to be close enough to the residential zones to be reached by foot or bicycle and also near the station. Their site also has to be decided according to the prevailing winds, in order to avoid polluting the air of

[1]'Caractéristiques du centre-ville à Grenoble, Nancy, Rennes, Strasbourg, Toulouse', *Cahiers de l'IAURP*, vol. 7, March 1967.

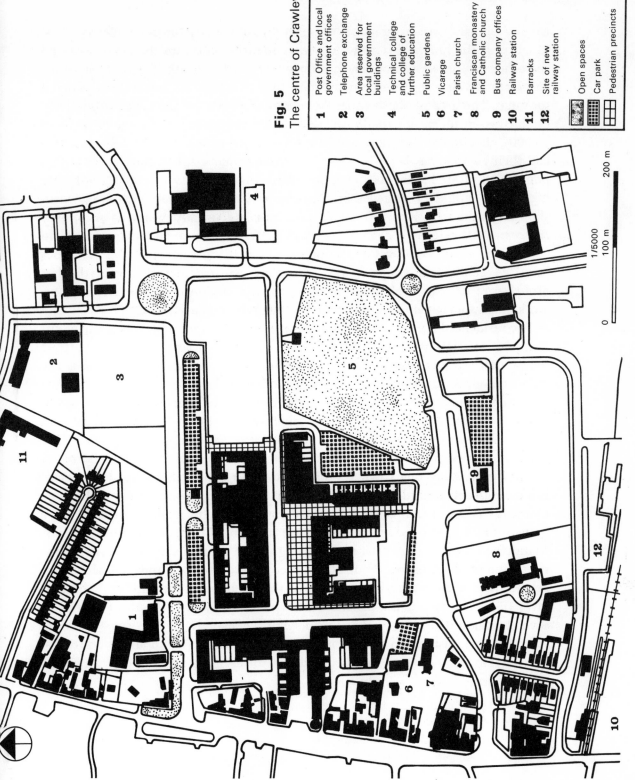

Fig. 5
The centre of Crawley.

1 Post Office and local
   government offices
2 Telephone exchange
3 Area reserved for
   local government
   buildings
4 Technical college
   and college of
   further education
5 Public gardens
6 Vicarage
7 Parish church
8 Franciscan monastery
   and Catholic church
9 Bus company offices
10 Railway station
11 Barracks
12 Site of new
   railway station

Open spaces
Car park
Pedestrian precincts

1/5000

0   100 m   200 m

the residential areas. In practice, these zones are usually on the outskirts of the town, near the railway. Harlow has two: one, the older, on the north-east and the other on the west; Crawley has only one, on the north, between the town and Gatwick airport; Cumbernauld had two to start with and others planned for later. The area of these zones obviously depends on the types of industry established in them, but the Reith Commission proposed an average of 40 ha to 10 000 inhabitants. The new towns have usually managed with less than this and their average has been 100-150 ha, in one or more zones, for a town with a population of 60 000-80 000, making a fairly high density of 100-120 jobs per hectare. It should be added that zones of service industries, including workshops, warehouses and craftsman's premises, are usually near the secondary centres. At Crawley, for example, a small 7 ha zone is near the main centre and another of 12 ha is near the station at Three Bridges and small 1 ha zones are sited behind the shops in the secondary centres. In the case of the last group, care has been taken to avoid any visual discontinuity between shops, workshops and housing by the choice of heights, materials, etc.

The residential areas are obviously of prime importance and, according to the Reith Commission, were to be planned to ensure the variety necessary to attract representatives of all social classes, including the higher executive classes. The organization is in neighbourhood units of 5000-12 000, each with its own amenities (shops, primary school, community centre, church, etc.). The neighbourhood unit, which struck the members of the Reith Commission as both natural and practicable, was not, however, to be completely isolated. The principle has been widely adopted, with the units generally separated by broad green spaces. Only one town – Cumbernauld, in Scotland, founded in 1956 – has disregarded this idea: its original plan provided for a continuous housing estate for a population of 50 000 but a revision of the plan to provide for a population of 70 000 led eventually to the addition of four neighbourhood units round the original residential nucleus (Fig. 6). In some places, such as Harlow, neighbourhood units for about 20 000 people are grouped round a secondary centre, with some amenities common to the neighbourhood unit and the new town (Fig. 7). The neighbourhood units themselves are made up of groups of several hundred dwellings developed comprehensively by the same building company and forming an architectural and social unity. The housing density of the new towns needs to be specified for different areas for it to have any significance.

Area	Density recommended by the Reith Commission (people per ha)	Present or expected density (people per ha)
The town as a whole (including the green belt)	about 15	
The town as a whole (excluding the green belt but including the industrial zones)	about 30	30-35 (Harlow 31) (exception Cumbernauld 42)
Residential areas (including roads and facilities)	42	about 50 (Crawley 58)
Neighbourhood unit (excluding facilities apart from access roads)	75	about 100 (Crawley 106, Harlow 117) (exception Cumbernauld 213)

The new towns (disregarding the exceptional case of Cumbernauld) therefore have a slightly higher density than was proposed by the Reith Commission. It is interesting to note that although there is a considerable difference at the neighbourhood unit level there is only a negligible difference at the level of the town as a whole (minus the green belt). Cumbernauld, whose residential density is higher than the original recommendations, is the only town to have a 40 per cent increase above the 30 residents per ha recommended. It should be added that the main break with the proposals of the Reith Commission lies in the greatly reduced area of the green belt.

This low density housing mainly conforms to the British tradition of individual houses. Flats usually only make up 15 per cent of the dwellings. Even at Cumbernauld, where more than 30 per cent was intended, the demand has reduced this to 20 per cent.

The road systems have conformed with a pattern laid out in the Reith Report:

A regional network linking the new town with the parent city and the rest of the region.
A network of ring roads and main radial roads in the town.
An intermediate network giving access to the neighbourhood units.
A network of local roads.

The road systems have nevertheless often proved inadequate for the unexpected amount of traffic. At Cumbernauld an important system of urban motorways has been planned, with a main road running below the town centre. In the earlier new towns the main roads have avoided the town centre (except

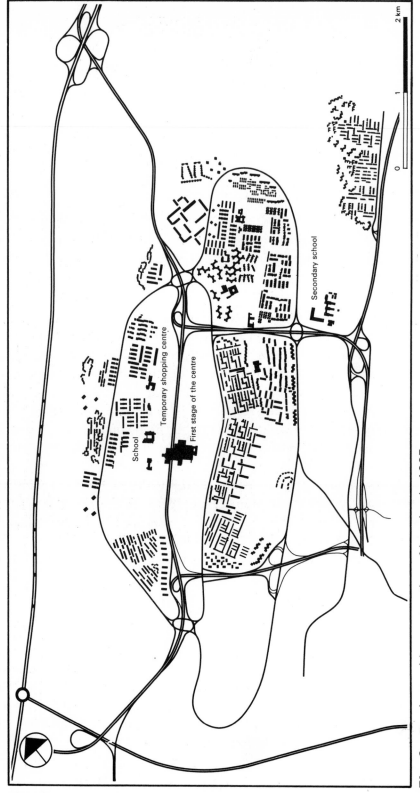

Fig. 6 Cumbernauld : construction of housing in 1965.

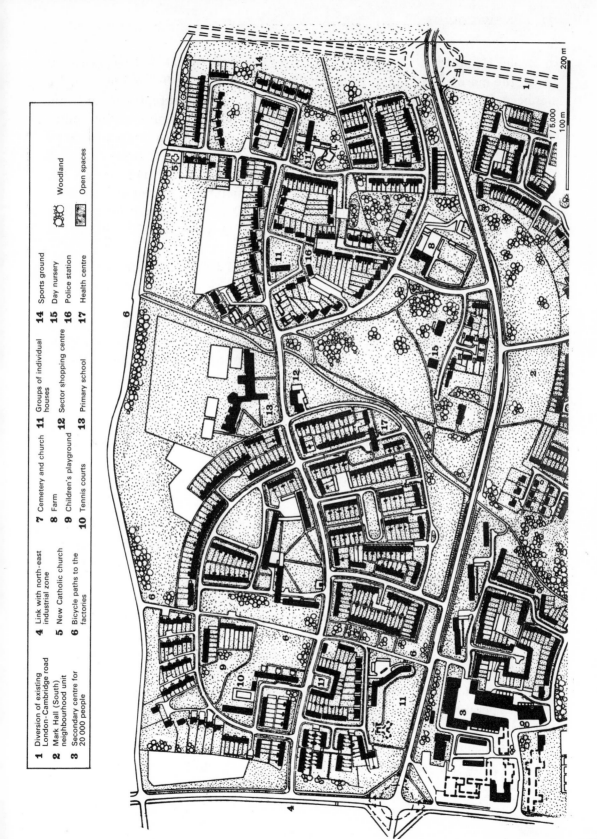

Fig. 7 Harlow: Mark Hall (North) neighbourhood unit.

at Hemel Hempstead, where it has been seen to be a mistake). The newer the town, the more attention has been paid to separation of traffic and much more has been achieved in this direction at Cumbernauld, for instance, than at Harlow.

Apart from the green belt, made up of woodland, sports grounds and culti-vated land, the Reith Commission recommended 4 ha of leisure area to every 1000 residents. This rate is rarely achieved in practice (Crawley has 2·8, Cumbernauld 2·1 and Harlow 0·8). The landscaping of the new towns has received a great deal of attention, though it is difficult to pinpoint any common element except perhaps the concern with planting trees right from the start (22 ha having been reserved for the planting of trees on the hill top at Cumbernauld).

The reservation of space for main amenities should also be mentioned: 1-2 ha to every 1000 residents for schools, for example (1 at Cumbernauld, 1·4 at Harlow, 2 at Crawley).

As we shall see, the development of the new town is the responsibility of the development corporation. This body is not in charge of the actual building operations but controls and oversees them in matters of architecture and town planning. The development corporation has to choose between various courses:

> Building for resale.
> Building premises to let.
> Renting the prepared land on a long lease to firms, individuals or local authorities to build on for their own use.
> Renting the prepared land to firms, individuals or local authorities to build premises for letting.

The decisions made vary according to the nature of the sites and from one town to another. The proportion of housing built by the development corpora-tions, for instance, has been around 85 per cent, the remaining 15 per cent being in the hands of a local authority (8·8 per cent of housing built before 1966) or a private company (6·2 per cent). The proportion built by the develop-ment corporation fell to 79 per cent at Crawley but, by the end of 1964, rose to 97 per cent at Cumbernauld. The amount built by local authorities (17 per cent before 1955) is decreasing while the amount built by private companies (1·8 per cent before 1955) is on the increase.

The policy followed for industrial premises, offices and shops is more varied. Some corporations (at Crawley, for instance) prefer to lease the prepared land to firms for building. Others (as at Harlow) consider that industry is their chief source of income and that it is preferable to build factories for letting (or some-times for selling). In all cases, the corporations have built shops to a module of about 7 m wide (or a multiple of this) by 10 m deep with access at the back. Similarly, factories of standard pattern and usually on a small scale (200-2000 m^2 of floor space) have been built for industries, either for temporary occupation or as permanent sites for small-scale light industries. The corporation may also build specialized factories for the needs of a particular firm, who will rent or buy them. Offices are usually built by private companies or by the firms themselves, though some corporations (at Harlow, for example) have themselves built office blocks in advance to attract future tenants.

The Reith Commission considered that infrastructures and the preparation of the land should be completely finished before building started, that this should be carried out according to a programme decided at the inception and that a steady rate of 2000 dwellings a year per town could be reached in three years. This rate has in fact only rarely been reached in some towns (1953-4 at Harlow; 1953 and 1957 at Crawley; while about 1000 a year have been built at Cumbernauld since 1964). Residential amenities (primary schools, scattered shops and neighbourhood centres) have kept pace with the housing.

In the matter of architectural control, the problem is to achieve a balance between architectural unity (with housing and shops built to the same pattern) and sufficient variety to give life to the urban landscape. This is the responsibility of the development corporation, which has complete control of styles of building, whether carried out by itself or other agencies either on rented or bought land. At Harlow, planning permission (granted by the corporation in the new towns) was even refused in a case where the style of roofing did not harmonize with adjacent buildings. However, this control is not usually too strictly imposed, because of the corporation's wish to see the businesses and amenities concerned established in the new town.

It will have been noticed that the recommendations of the Reith Commission favoured considerable conformity in the planning of the towns as a whole. The new towns were in fact mainly created according to the original plan over the course of twenty years, but inevitable changes had to be accepted with the modification of data, tastes and habits. At Crawley some roads that had become too narrow were able to be widened because reserves of land had been provided. The town centre has the greatest need for possible modification because of the accepted difficulty of exact planning *a priori*, especially in the earliest towns. The increase in the predicted population in some towns (Harlow and Stevenage in particular) raises the question of the actual size of the centre: at Harlow it has been decided to build six extra tower blocks on the edge of the centre, to modify the road system in order to achieve a better separation of pedestrian and motor traffic, to reserve some roads for pedestrians, to build extra car parks near the centre (giving 5600 spaces instead of 2600) and in particular to increase the area of shop space from 41 000 m^2 to 95 000 m^2, because of the increase in population and the wider attraction exercised by the town on its neighbourhood. Though easier than the redevelopment of an old town centre, this extension of Harlow's centre promises to be very costly.

As for the extension of the residential areas themselves, these are usually carried out at the expense of the green belt (already reduced by the standards of the Reith Commission).

As they stand, the new towns in Britain seem to have been successful ventures, especially compared with other building operations in Great Britain, France and elsewhere. There is a remarkable cohesion between the original plan and the final result, even though in some cases, as we shall see, some of the lines of policy could well be revised.

Administration

The success of the new towns would have been impossible without the passing of the New Towns Act in 1946, a few months after the delivery of the Reith Report and less than a year after the setting up of the Commission by Silkin, the first Minister of Town and Country Planning. The Act followed closely the recommendations of the Commission in creating the necessary administrative and financial machinery, with its own development corporation for each new town. The development corporation consisted of a committee of five to nine members, including the president and vice-president, nominated by the Minister of Town and Country Planning after consultation with the council of the locality concerned, whose task was to acquire land, install services and take charge of the town development. It would not supersede the function of existing councils but would be in charge of new administrative districts outside their areas. The financing of the operation was assured by Treasury loans, repayable over sixty years at the rate of interest in force for public loans at the time of issue, with a system of deferable payment. The committee, meeting once a month, nominated a director general whose task was to recruit personnel, with the agreement of the committee, whose role was that of a kind of administrative council. This personnel, usually chosen to be in charge of various branches (town planning and architecture, public works and civil engineering, finance, administration, external relations), might exceed 300 at the height of the operation (as at Harlow or Cumbernauld), not counting those working on the actual project.

The law was altered in 1959, with the creation of a New Towns Commission to take over the administration of existing or projected new towns from the development corporations. Hemel Hempstead and Crawley in 1962 and Welwyn Garden City and Hatfield in 1966 came under this administration but when the Labour government returned to power it was reluctant to extend a system that made the Treasury rather than local government responsible for excessive spending in the new towns. The members of the dissolved corporations helped to form the Commission, although this, being concerned only with administration, was on a smaller scale.

The development corporation possesses wide powers: in general, the planning and administration of the new town; in detail, the acquisition of land, by purchase or appropriation, the construction of dwellings, shops, offices, factories and public buildings, with the possibility, however, of delegating some of these tasks to local councils, companies or individuals. It is responsible for the designated area of the new town but can also function beyond this area in its planning capacity, as happened in the case of Livingston and its surrounding area. In the matter of housing, the corporation makes (or controls the making of) the general and detailed plans, invites estimates for groups of several hundred dwellings and supervises the work carried out by private contractors.

Problems could arise with the relationship between the corporation and the local councils. The latter were consulted before the final decision to build the new town was reached and if not actually hostile to the project could be sufficiently unsure of it to cause delay in settling the boundaries of the new area (as happened at Crawley with some private individuals). Relationships became easier when locals took an active part in the work of the development corporation. The local councils retained their own powers, especially in the matter of local rates, but the corporation could take over from them in case of difficulty or when the work in hand became too large for them to deal with alone. This needed the permission of the Ministry and made the corporation responsible for the work and for the necessary finance. It could also, in co-operation with the appropriate Ministry, grant subsidies to the local councils for carrying out the project in hand. This problem, however, was simplified by the size and importance of most of the town and county councils in Great Britain. The county councils are responsible for schools, health and housing, the police force and fire service, main roads, green spaces and large-scale sports and cultural facilities. The town councils are in charge of municipal buildings, the water supply, local roads and smaller-scale open spaces and sports and cultural facilities. The councils pay for these out of the local rates and with subsidies from the development corporations. Work carried out by the corporations was subsequently handed over to be administrated by the local council (especially where water supply and drainage were concerned). So the local councils were spared too great a financial burden, as can be seen at Harlow or Crawley, where the rise in rates over the last fifteen years is similar to that in the country as a whole. Collaboration between the local councils and the development corporations is essential to the prompt carrying out of any project and on the administrative level conflict is avoided by the councils' preservation of their own powers. They have, in fact, usually opened subsidiary council offices in the new towns.

Further complications are caused by the connection of new towns with rural district councils, or by a case like Crawley, which was connected with three different county councils. Modification of county boundaries (for Crawley in 1953) and of parish boundaries became a necessity. New urban district councils were created – at Harlow (25 000 inhabitants) in 1955 and at Crawley (30 000 inhabitants) in 1956 – with ordinary town council powers and later with some county council powers as well. In Britain, the size of the local councils and their willingness to co-operate have both helped to achieve satisfactory relationships with the development corporations.

Finance

The New Towns Act of 1946 provided for the financing of the new towns by a system of long-term Treasury loans, repayable over sixty years at varying rates of interest. These varied from 3 per cent in 1947 to 6 per cent or more over the last few years. On average, it stood at 5 per cent for the first wave of new towns and over 6 per cent for Cumbernauld. The total loans have by now exceeded £650 million and are increasing at the rate of about £35 million a year. To obtain a loan, the development corporation has to submit an estimated budget to its ministry and if this is approved the necessary money is soon available.

One of the first problems to confront the development corporation is the acquisition of land, which can either be purchased or taken over, if it is included in the designated area. If it is taken over, it was established in principle that the tribunals would not be able to take into account the future increase in value that the new town itself would give to the land, so that the price should change very little. In practice, it has increased twentyfold at Crawley, thirtyfold at Harlow (to more than £8500 per hectare) and tenfold at Cumbernauld in ten years. However, the corporations often find that private purchase improves their relations with the local people, and anyway represents only 1-3 per cent of the capital invested in the building of the new town (so that land is far less of a problem than would be expected in France, for instance).

Rents form the corporation's main source of income, enabling them to pay the interest and annual instalments of the Treasury loans. As a rule, rents from housing only cover the loans for that particular piece of land (including the expense of preparing the ground) and the building, and not for the town's facilities as a whole. The cost of these is borne by the shops, factories and offices. Housing rents are very low: at Crawley in 1967, they varied from £85 a year for a studio flat to about £170 for a seven-roomed house (not including a garage); while at Cumbernauld, where, because of the Scottish tradition of very low rents, the corporation had to subsidize housing for low or middle income families, they averaged only half that amount. In addition, the development corporation, like any other building concern, receives an annual government subsidy of £42 over sixty years for the new towns (the same length as for the loans), possibly made up by a subsidy from the parent city (Glasgow in the case of Cumbernauld, for example). To prevent rising building costs or rates of interest being reflected in the rents, the corporations have adopted a system of total perequation (as at Crawley) or partial perequation (as at Harlow).

The new town can also sell individual houses, or, which is becoming more common, grant a long-term lease (usually ninety-nine years) to firms who build and sell houses to private buyers who also pay ground rent. These houses are cheap: just over £4500 for a five-roomed house of about 80 m^2.

When it comes to commercial building, the corporation can follow one of two policies: either to build as much as possible itself to increase its resources, as it did at Harlow, or to rent out land fit for development to avoid taking unnecessary risks, as it did at Crawley. In the first instance, the rents are fixed about 3 per cent higher than the exact equivalent in costs, to allow for general development. At Harlow, for instance, commercial rents provide a third of the town's income (excluding rents from housing) and are calculated on the basis of a gross yield of 12 per cent. At Crawley, the rent for a moderate-sized shop of 73 m^2 with living quarters varies from £440 on the outskirts to £700 in the town centre. Industrial rents provide the largest part of the corporation's resources, in particular when, as at Harlow, a large number of factories have been built by the corporation itself. In 1965 the rents there were about £9 per m^2 for factories and about £15 per m^2 for offices.

The financial stability of a new town therefore depends largely on commercial rents, particularly from factories, although these only represent a small part of the money invested: a sixth at Harlow in 1965, even though that town had concentrated so much on factory building. Housing took 60 per cent, services (especially water supply) 13 per cent, the acquisition of land less than 2 per cent and its development nearly 10 per cent. However, by the end of twenty years the corporations have achieved financial stability, through the following process:

In the first phase (about ten years) the corporation borrows further from the Treasury to pay back part of the interest on the original agreed loans.

In the second phase (about another ten years) the corporation manages to pay back the interest on the loans and to pay arrears of interest.

In the third phase, the corporation has paid off arrears of interest and can begin to pay back the capital of the original loans.

This last phase has been reached at Harlow, whereas Cumbernauld is still in the first phase. The corporations naturally try hard to reach the third phase as soon as possible.

The machinery set in train by the 1946 Act can be held responsible for the successful creation of the new towns in Britain. Had it not been for Treasury loans on especially advantageous terms (long-term loans with varying redemption and moderate interest), it would have been impossible to build these towns according to plan and to house families from London and other large cities in satisfactory dwellings at very moderate rents. Above all, without the setting up of the development corporations any co-ordinated and effective system would have been an impossibility. In this field, Britain has much to teach.

Employment

A link between employment and housing was essential to the idea of the new towns, so that to obtain a house it is necessary to be able to give proof of a job in the new town. However, if the job is subsequently changed to one outside the town, the house does not necessarily have to be given up. This policy is in the interests of forming a stable and self-sufficient society with little movement of population and with an even distribution of workers, professional people and people of different income groups.

The original plans for the new towns were understandably undogmatic about types of employment, confining themselves to an overall programme covering basic requirements. In the new towns round London, for instance, one job in industry and one in tertiary employment (shops, services and offices) was allowed for every four inhabitants, corresponding to a level of employment slightly above average (the rate of employment in the new towns has averaged about 42 per cent) and to a rate of industrial employment higher than the London average. At Cumbernauld the eventual provision is for an employment rate of between 45 and 50 per cent, with 70 per cent of the jobs in industry, construction work and mining.

We have already seen that the industrial zones – one or more to a town and varying in density according to requirements but usually of about 100 jobs per hectare – were sited on the outskirts of the town, while small industrial service areas were sited in the town itself, near the shopping centres, railway stations, etc. While the new towns round London were being built, industrial employment remained at about 25 per cent of the total population, rising slightly (from 21 per cent at the beginning in about 1948 to 28 per cent in 1968). In the other towns, which were often in an industrial or mining area, the rate declined from 40 per cent at the start to 19 per cent in 1968, reflecting the difficulty of attracting workers to jobs outside London. In the country as a whole, however, and not without more initial problems in one town than in another, the number of industrial jobs (more than 200 000) has reached the proposed level.

The balance of employment requires both a variety of work and, if possible, different firms of similar type to give scope for changing jobs. Where certain towns are dominated by a very large firm (Ford at Basildon, de Havilland at Hatfield, etc.) this variety is practically ensured, at least in the towns round London. However, in some towns a particular type of work seems to predominate. Crawley, for instance, tends to have more of a concentration of light industry (electrical and electronic, pharmaceutical and plastic) than does Harlow. This can be explained by their positions relative to London (south and north-east respectively). Density of employment in the industrial zones is often very high. At Harlow it represents nearly 200 jobs per hectare, the coefficient of soil use reaching 42 per cent, an average rate, and the floor space per job not exceeding 21 m^2 (Fig. 8). In the other new towns around London the position is similar but over the remainder of the country the densities are lower, partly due to the different types of work carried out and partly because in a period of expansion the final level of employment has not yet been reached.

If, in the country as a whole, the progress of industrial employment in the new towns seems satisfactory, the same cannot be said for tertiary employment. This is especially true of office employment, which leads to a movement of workers away from the new towns. It is often argued by those in charge that the provision of office work is unnecessary for the first ten years or so in the life of the new town, since the original families are connected with the dispersed industrial firms and there will not be manpower for offices until the second generation has reached adulthood. This would seem a specious argument and shows the excessive importance given to industrial employment in the planning of the new towns, an error all too common until recently among town planners throughout Europe. For whatever reason, employment in office buildings is certainly very low: 16 500, or 1·8 per cent of the population in 1968 (2·8 per cent in the London area). This rate varies considerably from one town to

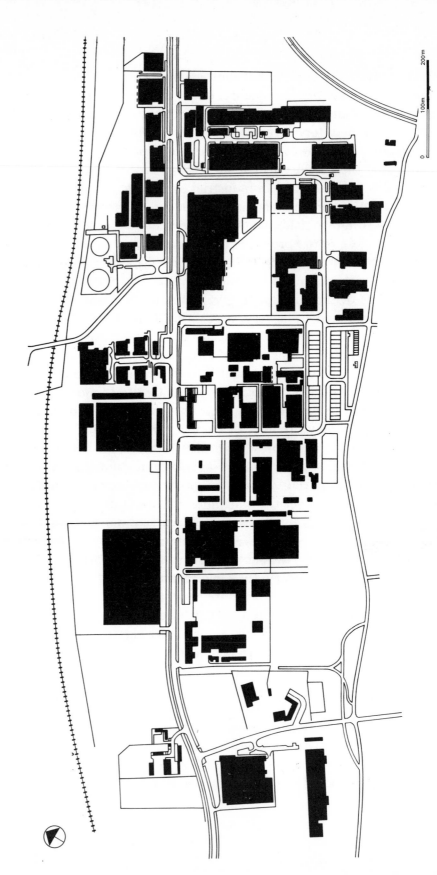

Fig. 8   Harlow : industrial zone, northern sector.

another. Bracknell, to the west of London, whose growth is more recent, and Crawley, to the south, have a higher rate than the towns to the north and east and elsewhere in England, particularly in Scotland. The type of employment also varies: the clerical departments of such large concerns as British Petroleum at Harlow, Lloyds Bank at Stevenage, the Rank Company at Harlow and government departments like the Meteorological Office at Bracknell, the Ministry of Transport at Hemel Hempstead and British Railways at Stevenage.

To these firms with their office blocks must, of course, be added jobs in administration and housing. The development corporations themselves employ some hundreds of workers and transport and telecommunications employ a considerable number (at Crawley 3450, or 10 per cent of the total manpower). The local councils are also important employers in administration, education, health, etc., employing 2150 at Crawley but only 403 at Cumbernauld, where local services are not yet up to strength. Lastly, construction and public works provide yet more jobs (1660 at Harlow in 1962; 1850 at Crawley in 1965) during the construction stage, with a number still required for maintenance later on.

Shops account for the highest proportion of tertiary employment, amounting to 3500 jobs at Crawley in 1965 (not including domestic service or service to businesses). They also have particular importance because the provision of shops has a direct effect on the inhabitants. To begin with, an average of one shop to 80 people over the area of the new town was allowed for. To this number was added one for every 200 more people (or one to 150 people in 1967). The total number of shops has not increased further, after an early rapid development in the town centre once half the projected population was installed (25 000, on average). While the development is under way, the residents have to find other shopping centres, either in the old town, if there is one (as at Crawley, Bracknell, Basildon and Hemel Hempstead), near which the new town centre was most often sited, or in a temporary shopping centre when other facilities are lacking, as at Cumbernauld, or in another town altogether. The floor area of shop premises is about 1 m^2, including selling and storage space, to each inhabitant, or a shop of 150 m^2 for 150 inhabitants. The development corporation assumes total control of the town's commercial premises by buying up the shops in the old centre, which it may redevelop in turn, as at Hemel Hempstead.

While the scattered shops provide daily needs, a wide variety of shops can be found in the secondary centres, especially if these serve an area at some distance from the main centre or a group of several neighbourhood units, as at Harlow. In Harlow's case, it was found that customers only did ordinary daily shopping in the secondary centres and that for this purpose one shop to 1000 inhabitants was sufficient. On the other hand, the main centre often contains more than half the shopping facilities and two-thirds of the shopping area (even more at Cumbernauld, which does not possess any secondary centre). This importance given to the main centre is not without its pitfalls when, for instance, delay in its development (as at Cumbernauld) means that the residents become accustomed to shopping elsewhere, even if in the end the new town is enabled to play the role of a secondary centre on a regional level (Harlow's shopping centre has become the focus for some 250 000 people from surrounding areas). Also, such a commercial flavour to the centre transgresses the original plans to some extent, even if administrative, social and cultural buildings have also been sited there. This gives a lively impression even if it means a reduction in the resident population of the centre (1000 people in Crawley) and an increase in the size of the area: 40 ha at Crawley, 34 ha (due to be at least doubled) at Harlow and 26 ha at Cumbernauld (possibly rising to 44), or an average of 0·6 ha to 1000 inhabitants.

So, in the country as a whole, the new towns show a fairly even balance of population and employment. While the lack of tertiary employment becomes daily more evident, employment in industry and construction accounts for about 60 per cent of total employment in the new towns round London and more elsewhere. Even this balance would not have been possible without special inducements to bring work into these areas. The link between employment and housing helped firms to become established and avoided an influx of residents attracted by new and roomy housing at moderate rents. Apart from this, the new towns have made contacts with employers and helped them with administrative formalities (especially with the obtaining of permits). Publicity campaigns, inaugurated by the Board of Trade, have been carried on for four or five years (except at Crawley, with its very favourable situation in an area of expansion mid-way between London and Brighton) and sometimes longer (in Scotland), demanding a specialized personnel. The offer of land ready for development or standard buildings is a further means of attracting firms. In the new towns the problem of employment is the main stumbling block. Some, like Crawley, have reached the point of selecting which industries will settle in their area.

Population

The new towns – or at least those around London – were built for the main part between 1950 and 1960, with resulting imbalances demographically as well as socially. The age structure is obviously a very young one at first but this will change as the first arrivals grow older, even if the change is slowed down by population movement. Twice as many young children are to be found in the new towns as in the population of the country as a whole, a considerably higher number of young adults but far fewer adolescents (half the normal proportion), middle aged people (one third to one quarter) and old people (one sixth).

Families tend to increase on first arriving in the new towns: a factor easily explicable by more spacious housing. But this phenomenon soon disappears, the birth rate remaining higher than the national average but the rate of fertility according to age being no different from that of the rest of the country. The death rate, on the other hand, is very low, owing to the youthful structure of the population.

Families are generally larger than average: 3·69 people to the family at Crawley (in 1965) and 3·52 at Harlow (in 1961). Satisfactory housing conditions are ensured by the size of the houses: 4·79 rooms (the living room counting as two) at Crawley in 1965 (1·30 rooms per person) and 4·57 at Harlow in 1961 (also 1·30 per person). Housing consisting of two or three rooms (four or five with a double living room) account for 85 per cent of the housing, very large or very small houses being rare (less than 10 per cent having three rooms or less).

The great majority of new town dwellers come from the parent city or its environs, in conformity with the arrangements made with the firms setting themselves up in the new town: 75-80 per cent in the new towns round London, nearly 80 per cent at Cumbernauld, etc., with the greatest number from the same side of the city as the site of the new town, a factor linked with the radial character of the dispersal of industry, which can also be seen in the Paris area.[1]

It would be a mistake to regard the population of the new towns as static, for movement of population continues to take place, with an outward movement of some 5 or 6 per cent a year. The number of families leaving the new towns round London leave in fairly equal numbers for London itself, other new towns, the remainder of Great Britain and abroad (including the Commonwealth). More than half these departures are due to a change of job, the other most frequent causes being family reasons and the wish to emigrate.

The class structure of the population has not been closely studied, though in Harlow a 10 per cent sample survey was carried out in 1961, furnishing this and other information. But the nature of the enquiry (a sample over-representative of employers and requiring a declaration of qualifications by the persons concerned) casts doubts on the results. These seemed to show a particular

---

[1] 'Mouvement des établissements industriels dans la région parisienne', *Cahiers de l'IAURP*, vol. 1, October 1964.

category of employment, in which three industrial wage-earners out of ten were managerial or clerical staff, five were skilled workers and two semi-skilled workers, with three managerial staff to two office workers in public services and industry alike. In fact, despite the great predominance of industrial employment, life in the new towns seems to a stranger essentially middle class.

Commuting and transport

The aim of reducing daily commuting to a negligible amount was too ambitious to be fully realized. In fact, a probable 20 per cent of residents of working age in the 'older' new towns are commuters. This proportion increases with the age of the town, both because of an unavoidable changing of jobs and because of the arrival at working age of a new generation, which may not choose the same jobs as the preceding generation and which feels in particular the shortage of office work in the new towns. More significant is the willingness of the development corporation to ignore a phenomenon that amounts to a definite setback. Harlow, for instance, published every year an estimate of its number of commuters, while the 1961 survey showed the actual amount to be four times larger. Even so, these figures remain lower than those observed in the townships about 40 km from Paris where the rate is 30-40 per cent. The commuters travel in various directions from Harlow, nearly half travel to London, nearly a quarter in the neighbourhood of the new town and the remainder (about 30 per cent) elsewhere.

Means of travel between home and work have not been closely studied. The 1961 survey at Harlow, however, showed the part played by private transport (80 per cent in the new town itself, 75 per cent in the immediate neighbourhood and 85 per cent to destinations other than London, the new town and its environs). The use of buses and coaches was limited to the town and its surroundings and that of trains to journeys to London.

Communications with the parent city have been considerably improved. In the rush hour, Crawley is served by four London-bound trains, two of them non-stop, calling at different parts of the town and with a new station planned near the town centre. Harlow has two trains an hour (three in the rush hour) and the length of the journey has been reduced to forty-five minutes (thirty minutes for non-stop trains), whereas the former village was served by only four trains a day. At Cumbernauld the length of journey has been reduced to twenty minutes and trains have become more frequent. Fares, however, even with season tickets, remain high. The new towns also have coach services but these, being so much slower, are mainly used for local journeys. And, as we have seen, the better its links with the parent city, the less independent the new town will be.

Internal transport is also necessary, due to the layout of the new town (its low residential density adding to distances and the concentration of work in the centre and in the industrial zones). The buses are run by large national companies and although they often run at a loss they are not subsidized by the local corporations. The increase in private motoring has helped to reduce their customers and thereby made their financial position more difficult. There is a close network of bus services (twenty routes in Crawley), but service is infrequent except in rush hours, when it is every ten minutes, but only once an hour at off-peak periods.

Parking problems, on the other hand, have become much greater. The increase in motoring had been underestimated: at Crawley 8000 vehicles had been expected and one garage had been allowed for every three dwellings. Later it became usual to allow one garage to each dwelling, with additional parking spaces where there was any spare ground, but this still did not meet the need. At Harlow the increase has been from 0·2 of a garage per dwelling to one garage and 0·5 of roadside parking to each house. At Cumbernauld the usual rate of one garage per dwelling and 0·4 of roadside parking spaces for visitors was accepted from the start, but for reasons of economy only half this number of garages was built at the same time as the housing. At the start, 2000 parking spaces were allowed for the centre of a new town of 60 000 inhabitants. Ten years later, 5000 were planned for Cumbernauld and a similar number is now aimed for the 'older' new towns. This underestimation is hardly surprising, for town planners all over Europe have made the same mistake in the last few decades.

The social life of the town

The most ambitious aim of the originators of the new towns was probably that of creating in them a true urban community. In the light of experience over the last twenty years, one can see the two main obstacles to be overcome: lack of facilities, especially in shopping centres, and the absence of a spontaneous social life.

Shopping centres have great importance in the creation of this social life. The largely commercial town centre is the liveliest part of the town and the recognized meeting place. In this respect, the 'older' new towns provided such a number and variety of shops in the main centre that they became commercially self-sufficient and even attracted customers from a wider area. At Harlow, it is reckoned that more than 25 per cent of the shops customers come from beyond the new town. However, it takes a long time for this favourable state of affairs to be reached and in the meantime shortage of shopping facilities (before the centre is completed) drives the residents elsewhere. This is what happened at Cumbernauld, with the townspeople shopping in Glasgow until their own shopping centre was opened.

Other facilities bring similar problems: some must keep pace with the growing population (primary schools, nursery schools, playing fields and churches) while others, which present a more difficult problem, cannot be justified until the population reaches a certain level. In this category are cultural centres (the one at Crawley cost more than £300 000), cinemas (and because of the state of the film industry many of the older new towns do not have one at all), bowling alleys (at Stevenage, Crawley, Harlow, etc.), dance halls, which are in particular demand by young people and have only lately been acquired in Crawley and Harlow, indoor swimming pools (the one at Crawley, opened in 1964, cost £300 000), golf courses and sports centres (both at Harlow). The adornment of public spaces by works of art commissioned from well-known artists has also given an individual flavour to towns like Harlow and Stevenage.

A true community spirit is not easy to create in towns with families of a young age group confined to their homes by children and television and with cars that enable them to get away from the town at the weekend. Provision of societies and meeting places by churches, brewers, local councils and youth clubs is insufficient. The local council may give financial help, through the rates, to the numerous clubs and societies (more than 300 at Harlow) that characterize British social life. All the same, there is something depressing about the new towns: the 'new town blues' expresses the feeling of isolation and apathy natural to a population that has undergone a process of uprooting and transplanting from a familiar to an unfamiliar environment.

Changes in the concept of the new towns in Britain

In the new towns, the original plans have been realized to a remarkable extent. Nevertheless, there are signs that a rethinking of theories of development has brought a slow but increasing change over the last few years (see Section IV below).

The Reith Commission had set a target of 20 000-60 000 for the eventual population of the new towns. The first master plans provided for 25 000-60 000 for the new towns around London (except for 80 000 at Basildon). In the event, all these totals were exceeded, especially after 1953 when the original targets had been reached, by amounts varying from 16 per cent at Hatfield to 140 per cent at Bracknell. At Cumbernauld the target of 50 000 was raised to 70 000 and at Telford the target became 220 000. Quite recently, when their targets were almost reached, it was proposed that the populations of Harlow, Stevenage and Basildon should be increased to about 130 000, more than double the original figure of 60 000, which had already been raised to 80 000. Such extensions obviously require available space and must avoid overloading the town centre and the road network. These changes stem from two separate causes: first, the size of the problem of urban growth, underestimated by the Abercrombie Plan, calls for larger towns; second, the towns need to be large enough to provide adequate amenities and tertiary employment.

There has also been a considerable change in the matter of population density. This, as we have seen, was higher in practice than in the recommendations of the Reith Commission. Cumbernauld (1956) and the Hook plan, dating from 1961,[1] intended slightly higher densities of about 200 people per hectare in neighbourhood units. But this did not prove very popular and later towns such as Livingston and Skelmersdale were planned with a lower density more to the British taste, even though this contradicted the avowed aim of increasing the urban nature of the new towns.

In the realm of town planning, the notion of neighbourhood units was revived at Cumbernauld and in the Hook plan. Later projects differ on this point: Livingston is to be divided into neighbourhood units but Skelmersdale is not. Cumbernauld wished to follow a new plan and house 30 per cent of its population in blocks of flats (and Hook 29 per cent), a logical solution to the proposed high density, but this proportion will have to be lowered in practice because of public feeling.

Traffic movement will become increasingly important in the future, both for commuters and for fast through traffic (as at Cumbernauld) while traffic-free areas will increase (as in the Hook plan and the centre of Cumbernauld) and parking facilities will have to be constantly increased. Planning of the town centre has now become more flexible: that of Cumbernauld, in a single linear block with traffic at different levels, allows for future expansion both outwards and upwards.

Summary

The new towns have achieved some but by no means all of their original aims. Over twenty years the new towns in Britain have absorbed more than 500 000 new residents, two-thirds of them in the London area, where the target in the

[1]London County Council, *The Planning of a New Town* (London, 1961).

Abercrombie Plan (383 000) has therefore almost been reached. On the other hand, the theory set out in the plan that the population of Greater London could be stabilized has been proved false. In fact, far from aiding in the reduction of Greater London's population, the new towns have absorbed little more than one sixth of its increase over twenty-two years (nearly 2 million).

In the economic field, a balance of employment and manpower has been achieved, at least in the towns round London. But the scarcity of tertiary employment (especially in office jobs) shows a serious lack of balance, which is proved by the increase in commuting to London and elsewhere. The new towns are obviously not large enough to attract this type of employment and it seems that the scale chosen twenty years ago was too small.

In contrast, the British experiment has been outstandingly successful in two respects: the development corporation in charge of the planning, building and maintenance of the new town, and the very helpful financial system – long-term loans (sixty years) at a moderate interest and varying rates of repayment. Both these have made possible the successful outcome – for such, despite the reservations noted, it must be called – of an experiment that must have seemed bold indeed at the time of its initiation.

IV Change of policy 1961-1965[1]

The weaknesses of the system of planning in Britain should have been all too apparent in the findings of the 1961 census, for ever since the end of the war the population of London, far from attaining the stability envisaged by Sir Patrick Abercrombie, had increased at an unprecedented rate, while the unpredicted increase of tertiary employment had undermined measures directed at industry only, in the realm of permits, subsidies, etc.

Administrative reform in the London area

One measure adopted, by an administrative regulation of 1964-5, was aimed at giving back autonomy to the different London councils by making them large enough for effective resources and administrative powers. On the other hand, major questions of planning, housing policy, traffic regulations and public transport were to be dealt with at government level. A system of sharing resources between different councils was instituted. So was created Greater London (population 8 500 000) administered by a council of 100 members

[1]P. Merlin and P. Guertin, 'Urbanisme en région de Londres et aménagement du territoire', *Cahiers de l'IAURP*, vol. 8, June 1967.

elected by universal suffrage, divided into thirty-two boroughs (plus the GLC, which preserved its own status) of 166 000-340 000 inhabitants each. This administrative regrouping was concerned only with the built-up area.

Studies in regional planning

At the same time, the policy of national development, whose slow growth since the war has already been noted (see Section II above), and the publication in September 1965 of a national economic plan up to 1970, led to the creation of a National Planning Council and of a regional planning council in each of the economic regions. In the south-east, a White Paper, *Employment-Housing-Land*, published in February 1963, was followed by the *South East Study*.[1] After this came studies for the Midlands and the north-west in 1965.[2] Thus a policy originally directed at limiting London's growth became a policy of national development.

The South East Study: *a general view*

The *South East Study*, looking ahead to 1981, began by restating, in the light of the 1961 findings, the problem of London's growth. The new towns had only absorbed about one sixth of this, while the increase of tertiary employment had largely compensated for the decrease in industrial employment in the centre of London (500 000 jobs in the former County of London). A probable natural increase of 6 million between 1961 and 1981 is estimated for the population of England and Wales, 40 per cent of this (2 400 000) in the south-east. Immigration would probably account for another 1 million throughout the country. Allowing for internal movement of population, the influx into the south-east is reckoned at about 1 100 000, giving a total increase of 3 500 000 over twenty years, bringing the population from 17·75 to 21·25 million. In the light of these conclusions, a fresh examination of the development of the region became necessary and was the main concern of the *South East Study*. This estimated that town planning operations could be extended to provide for 1 500 000 people, 250 000 of them in existing developments (by expanding the older new towns and other expanded towns).

A further 1 250 000 people had to be catered for over the next twenty years, requiring planning on a very different scale from that of the Abercrombie Plan. The authors of the study also saw the necessity of making provision for single

[1]Economic Affairs Department, *South East Study* (London, HMSO, February 1964).
[2]Economic Affairs Department, *The West Midlands, A Regional Study* and *The North-West. A Regional Study* (London, HMSO, 1965).

large-scale schemes for the attraction of tertiary employment and the creation of facilities for leisure, education and commerce, among others. However, various technical, economic and social considerations seemed to indicate that the rate of 1500 dwellings per year in each new development could not be much improved on: this naturally militated against any concentration on only a few large-scale operations. However, this line of reasoning has already been proved false, this rate having already been exceeded in the new towns (see Section III above), while social and economic problems linked with rapid growth have been on a larger scale, rather than of a different nature.

The South East Study: *development proposals*

The choice of sites for development must take account of existing facilities or of the need to build motorways, airports and road systems, water supplies etc. (though in the first new towns communications had been only a secondary consideration in the choice of site). They should be outside the existing urban area, which tends to expand rapidly outwards. This aim, repeating that of the Abercrombie Plan (separation of the new towns from the built-up area) on a different scale, can be criticized for aiming at destroying the unity of the region and limiting the benefits for firms and individuals alike. Lastly, the authors of the *South East Study* recommend linking development to an existing town of a reasonable size, mainly to take advantage of existing facilities in the early stages of development but also to have a ready supply of jobs and man-power. The chosen sites must be capable of absorbing at least 30 000 extra people over a period of fifteen years, as well as the natural increase of popula-tion, demanding towns of at least 50 000. The studies carried out at Ipswich and Peterborough (see Section V below) have confirmed the possibility of a 100 per cent increase in these medium-sized towns and have shown that this increase costs less per new inhabitant than would a 50 per cent increase, the chief outlay being in those places where the rebuilding of the town centre is necessary. Last, but not least, the chosen sites must be pleasant enough to attract newcomers.

These proposals – for this is all they were at this stage – concerned in the first instance three sizeable new towns, whose period of development would take until the end of the century: one between Portsmouth and Southampton, another at Bletchley, on the M1 halfway between London and Birmingham, and the third at Newbury-Hungerford, on the M4 halfway between London and Bristol. The first of these could accommodate a population of 250 000 and the two others populations of 150 000 (about half before 1981) (Fig. 9).

Large-scale expansions concerned towns about 100 km from London with

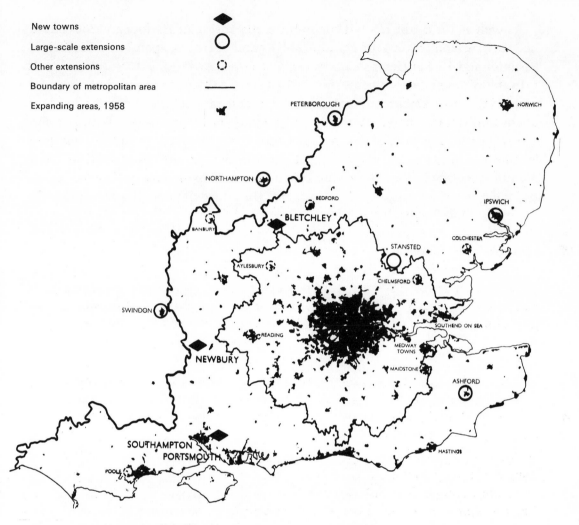

Fig. 9   The *South East Study*: development proposals.

populations of about 100 000 (Ipswich, Northampton, Peterborough, Swindon). Only Stanstead, with its proposed international airport, and Ashford, on the route to the future Channel Tunnel, were smaller. Additional populations of about 100 000 were envisaged for all these towns.

Further expansion was suggested for other, smaller towns at similar distances from London, chosen for their connection with the capital and their own facilities (three of them possessing a university), with a proposed increase of at least 30 000 people each: Aylesbury, Banbury, Bedford, Chelmsford, Colchester, Hastings, Maidstone, the Medway Towns, Norwich, Poole, Reading and Southend.

As well as these, the study proposed the expansion of Harlow and Stevenage new towns from 80 000 to about 130 000 and further expansion at Crawley, Basildon and Hemel Hempstead.

In the realm of employment, the authors stressed the need to provide for new centres of employment on the edge of London, as well as those in the new towns and the expanded towns, for those firms closely connected with London affairs, suggesting such places as Ilford, Romford, Dartford, Bromley, Croydon, Surbiton, Kingston, Uxbridge and Watford. Also, as an alternative to commuting, it seemed wise to provide for increased employment in smaller towns beyond the urban area, such as Reigate, Guildford, Maidenhead, Tonbridge, Sevenoaks and Tunbridge Wells.

Proposed sites for development

	Population 1961	Natural increase 1961–1981	Possible increase (in excess of natural increase)	Increase before 1981 (in excess of natural increase)
1 New towns				
Southampton-Portsmouth	750 000	144 000	250 000	150 000
Bletchley	17 000	4 000	150 000	75 000
Newbury	20 000	3 000	150 000	75 000
2 Major expansions				
Stansted			100 000	75 000
Ashford	28 000	3 000	100 000	75 000
Ipswich	120 000	19 000	60 000+	60 000
Northampton	100 000	7 000	100 000	50 000
Swindon	90 000	14 000	50 000–75 000	50 000
Peterborough	60 000	7 000	50 000+	50 000
3 Other expansion				
Aylesbury	27 000	6 000	At least 30 000	
Banbury	21 000	3 000	—	
Bedford	65 000	8 000	—	
Chelmsford	50 000	7 000	—	
Colchester	60 000	8 000	—	
Hastings	65 000	2 000	—	
Maidstone	60 000	8 000	—	
Medway Towns	170 000	24 000	—	
Norwich	120 000	14 000	—	
Poole	90 000	9 000	—	
Reading	120 000	16 000	—	
Southend	165 000	8 000	—	

The study further concerned itself with those areas not scheduled for future development, affecting more than 2 million people, county by county. According to their calculations, the outer zones of the urban area would have a normal population increase of 870 000 and a further increase of 515 000 from London and other areas. The remainder of the south-east would see a natural population increase of 475 000 and an additional 375 000 newcomers, not including any development schemes.

To resolve the problem of the Green Belt, the authors rejected the drastic solution of permitting development along certain axes and routes of communication with empty spaces between, as it seemed to them too late to make so radical an alteration of the policy pursued so far. Instead, they proposed to keep the Green Belt as already planned, extending it from 2000 to 5000 km² or even more. Without concealing the comparative failure of the original Green Belt (which had suffered a good deal of building, starting with some of the new towns), they proposed concentrating on the use to which these areas could be put without rejecting *a priori* the notion of limited building in this protected zone.

The South East Study: *criticisms*

From its first appearance, the *South East Study* has been studied and criticized. The target of 1981 seemed too close, since, after the publication of the study in 1964 and subsequent discussion of its contents, its proposals could not begin to be implemented before 1970. In fact, the proposal was for a ten-year plan in the first instance, a short time in the face of London's problems, especially when one considers that at the time local authorities[1] and private research[2] were carrying out studies aimed at the end of the century.

The question of population aroused differing reactions. The public as a whole, which had been led to believe in the possibility of stabilizing London's population, was naturally alarmed, while some experts, in view of the data on the increasing birth rate, thought that too conservative a view had been taken of the situation. Its treatment of the subject of employment – not fully dealt with in the study – was also criticized, calling attention to the discrepancy between regional and national planning. Stricter measures to limit the growth of employment in the London area were called for. We have already seen (see Section II above) that office permits had been a welcome innovation, but not wholly

---

[1]Standing Conference on London Regional Planning, *Population, Employment and Transport in the London Region* (London, 25 November 1964).

[2]Peter Hall, *London 2000* (London, Faber & Faber, 1963).

successful in their aim. What is certain is that British public opinion, as well as that of the experts themselves, does not take kindly to the inescapable fact of the growth of the London region.

Development proposals came in for less criticism, being only proposals. The concentric pattern of development was criticized by the Standing Conference on London Regional Planning (now called the Standing Conference on London and the South East Regional Planning), which provided evidence that, since the war, the built-up area had continued to develop outwards into the Green Belt and claimed that the proposals of the *South East Study*, which allowed for a spontaneous increase in population of 2 million, would only exacerbate the situation. The favouring of expanded towns of medium size rather than the creation of large-scale new towns was also criticized. Lastly, it seemed contradictory to some critics, including Professor Self, to assist people and firms to get out of London and at the same time to subsidize suburban railways and encourage commuting over a radius of 100 km.

If the *South East Study* displayed a certain boldness in recognizing the impossibility of controlling population growth altogether, in giving a new character to the region and proposing development at a higher level than that of the older new towns, it nevertheless seemed hesitant on some other matters, such as its proposals for large-scale town planning, which only catered for a third of the expected growth. The fear of creating very large new towns (of more than 250 000 inhabitants) is rather surprising, as well as the wish to avoid too rapid an expansion of towns scheduled for development.

Various other points were not clearly dealt with. The theory of population growth – half the whole country's increase in the south-east – does not seem to tally with the employment theory, according to which all new employment would be sited in the south-east. It can also be asked how the tendency of heads of firms to wish to become established in the centre of London can be redirected to medium-sized towns 100 km from the capital without recourse to undesirable methods of regulation and whether the relatively slow growth of these towns will give them the qualities necessary to create a powerful enough rival attraction to London. The question of optimum size and the number of secondary centres to be developed has not been dealt with.

Finally, it is doubtful whether it is reasonable to retain the Abercrombie scheme of concentric development, when the theory of a stable urban region of which it was a part has since been abandoned. The difficulty of preserving the Green Belt has proved the inadequacy of such a scheme along with continued, even if slow, growth.

A strategy for the south-east

The *South East Study* was, in fact, soon revised. In the first place, the Secretary of State for Economic Affairs detailed the South East Economic Planning Council, a consultative body of experts, to draw up, in collaboration with government departments, local authorities and workers' and employers' associations, a 'strategy for the south-east'. A first report was published in 1967[1] (the economic planning councils of the other regions were charged with a similar task).

Dealing, as had the *South East Study*, with the future of the London region (the south-east, not including East Anglia) but bringing the proposals of the study up to date by extending them not to 1980 but to the end of the century, this report outlined an overall plan with a general scheme of development, with the siting of activities and facilities, dealing with the main sections of the region (Greater London, the suburbs and the rest of the region).

Population figures were lower than those contained in the *South East Study*, partly because of the exclusion of East Anglia, which contains some of the large-scale developments aimed at absorbing London's overspill (Ipswich and Peterborough in particular), because of the exclusion of other developments outside the south-east (such as Northampton and Swindon), the fall in birth rate since 1964 and also the aim of slowing or even halting altogether the movement to the south-east. This hope, based on population estimates by the General Register Office, seems dubious, even allowing for the evidence from electoral rolls. It would result in a population of 18 970 000 in 1981 in this limited area of the south-east, or 2 620 000 more than in 1961. Greater London would maintain its present population of 8 million, with the increase shared between the outer suburbs and the rest of the area (not allowing for proposed developments outside the south-east). Between 1981 and the end of the century an increase of 4 million people was expected. A considerable change in the make-up of the population was entailed, with a larger proportion of children and old people, with the result that a smaller proportion of people of working age could bring problems of shortage of manpower.

The overall scheme of development proposed (Fig. 10) largely repeats the main proposals of the *South East Study*. The new town between Portsmouth and Southampton is given first priority and that of Milton Keynes (the former Bletchley project) second, with the expansion of Northampton and of Ipswich

[1] *A Strategy for the South East. A First Report by the South East Planning Council* (London, HMSO, 1967).

third.[1] The plan for a new town at Newbury was rejected, but those at Swindon, Peterborough and Ashford were retained, subject to government approval. On the other hand, the authors evinced a definite hostility towards the proposal for a third international airport (for supersonic airliners) at Stansted, 50 km from the centre of London, and towards the urban development necessary for housing the airport workers. They also wished to limit the number of small-scale developments proposed for the suburbs, which could not be properly integrated and would increase commuting, with resultant transport problems to and within the centre. The only ones to be retained were those already accepted, especially the extensions to the older new towns: Harlow, Basildon, Stevenage, Bracknell. But the real originality of the *Strategy for the South East* lies in its complete break with tradition in patterns of town planning in the London area. With the need to preserve a widened Green Belt, urban development could be confined to specific axes, arranged in pairs (one of the pair being the principal):

> To the north-west: the principal axis towards Milton Keynes and Northampton, the secondary axis towards Peterborough.
>
> To the east and south-east: the principal axis towards Ashford and the secondary axis along the Thames estuary.
>
> To the south-west: the principal axis towards the new town of South Hampshire and the secondary axis towards Swindon.

One reason for the decision to develop along these axes is the best use of existing or proposed lines of communication and another is the desire to preserve large open spaces between these corridors for agriculture and recreation. An important point is that, in the authors' view, urban development should begin at the outer ends of the corridors and work towards London. This may sound unrealistic but, even if this should be found to be true, the chief aim of corridor development would remain.

Another innovation in the *Strategy for the South East* is the position it adopts towards employment. While approving the official policy of decentralization, the authors stress the difficulties this can cause in the balance of employment and hint that it should be applied with discretion in the future. It was pointless, for instance, to discourage every kind of industry automatically from setting up in the south-east: on the contrary, a balanced scheme was essential for the success of the plan as a whole. Similarly, office permits should be available to firms that would form an integral part of the strategy for the south-east. Small

[1]To reduce the cost to the state, provision was made for 50 per cent of the new housing to be put up for sale. Similarly, tenants in existing new towns were to be encouraged to become owner-occupiers.

firms of up to 1000 m² of floor space would not need permits to build in the suburbs. Lastly, a minimum of office building in London itself was desirable, to allow the capital to play its traditional role and to encourage foreign business concerns.

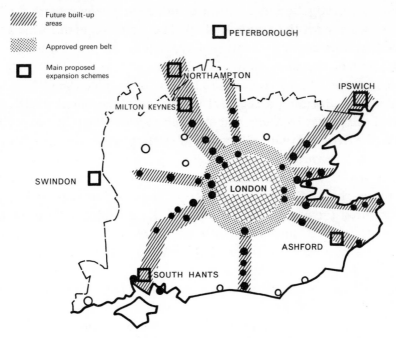

Fig. 10   *A Strategy for the South East*: proposed plan of development.

This report, then, though looked upon as only a first stage, breaks with earlier policies on two main points: the idea of urban development along special corridors (perhaps too many) and a discreet but definite relaxation of national policy in the siting of industry and offices. The report is undergoing examination by the government, whose view will be subsequently published. It has been submitted for perusal to experts and local authorities and so far its reception has been remarkably favourable, though the majority of the local authorities concerned have not yet pronounced upon it.

V   Current studies in town planning 1965-1968[1]

Even before the publication of the *South East Study*, other studies in town planning had appeared. One of these was a plan for the newly created Greater London and other plans were commissioned for new towns or town expansions.

[1]P. Merlin and P. Guertin, 'Urbanisme en région de Londres et aménagement du territoire', *Cahiers de l'IAURP*, vol. 8, June 1967.

The Greater London plan

This study was undertaken at the instigation of the Greater London Council, in conjunction with the councils of the new London boroughs (who, for instance, carried out an investigation into land use and drew up town plans for their own districts in accord with the regional plan). The resulting plan forms a species of master plan establishing a general framework (overall picture, main infrastructures, etc.) and at the same time gives details of the plans of each authority connected with the GLC. It consists, therefore, of a collection of local plans in a larger framework, forming a regional plan. The government itself carried out the *London Transportation Study* and also had the responsibility of giving formal approval to the Greater London Plan and of settling any disputes arising between the GLC and the boroughs.

The thirty-three boroughs concerned took part on four separate levels. In the first place, the GLC indicated the type of plan that was to be drawn up, then it presented them with the outlines of the planning policy for the whole built-up area; next, it consulted with them about their own local plans and finally, when a provisional plan for Greater London had been drawn up (1969), this was passed to them for their opinion.

This provisional document, which was allowed for *a posteriori* in the Act of 1968, which prescribed the preparation of structure maps, aimed at providing a general framework into which the plans of the thirty-three boroughs could be fitted. Apart from the structure maps themselves, a road plan and a relevant report were submitted to the government, together with a broad canvas that placed Greater London in a national setting. The plan looked ahead twenty years but provided for modifications, which have already been taking place, when the boroughs' own plans should be drawn up or in particular operations (especially in the case of infrastructures).

The Greater London Plan followed generally accepted lines: the decrease of the 8 million population (one sixth of the whole country's population) to 7 million by the end of the century (which would represent only a tenth); the decrease of jobs from 4·5 million to 4·2 million, by dispersal beyond the Green Belt or decentralization into the provinces. However, the central administration, banks, colleges, centres of research and leisure facilities would remain in London, helping to retain its role of capital city and its individual character, while improving living conditions and the quality of the environment, ensuring a closer balance between housing and employment and improved accessibility by different means of transport. The GLC would be responsible for co-ordinating the transport system: underground trains, buses and roads. Extensions to the

London Underground were provided for (the completion of the north-south Victoria Line, the building of the east-west Fleet Line and extensions towards south London), but particular importance was given to the construction of motorways, with provision for three ring roads and thirteen approach roads.

The carrying out of this plan, which did not demand any new and widespread operation on the scale of the new towns or expanded towns, will require a task of renewing the whole fabric of the city life all the more difficult because it concerns the poorer boroughs. The reconstruction of the suburbs envisages six secondary centres, each serving about 750 000 people, and twenty-two tertiary centres serving about 200 000 people. Some authorities have been loath to adopt these plans for reconstruction, especially where the limitation of population is concerned, something whose need is recognized as a general principal but not so readily at the local level. The GLC will have the responsibility for development of regional importance and the local authorities for development on a local scale: this division of responsibility will need to be worked out in detail.

Preliminary studies for schemes of development

The Ministry of Housing and Local Government, without waiting for official approval of the proposals of the *South East Study*, commissioned a feasibility study of its suggested plans. The question of an extension of Ipswich, for instance, was studied by the firm of Vincent & Gorbing.[1] This geographical, economic and social study of the town and its environment, of its facilities (the town centre, drainage, water supply, sewerage system and transport) and of the quality and suitability for development of its surrounding farmland led to the suggestion of four possible lines of extension. The land required was calculated on the basis of 150 people per hectare for the new development, a figure that seemed more in keeping with modern notions of town planning than the 85 per hectare suggested by the town authorities, and other standards were laid down for industrial zones, road systems, car parks and open spaces. Four distinct schemes were eventually proposed: two of them allowed for a 50 per cent increase in two particular directions; the third provided for a 100 per cent increase to the south-west and east, retaining the present town centre, which covers 40 ha; the fourth provided for a 100 per cent increase in a continuous linear development including a new centre covering 50 ha. The study also deals with the possibilities of modernizing the present town centre and gives an outline plan for a future new centre.

[1]Ipswich County Borough, *A Planning Study for Town Development* (London, HMSO, 1964).

Another typical preliminary study is that for the Portsmouth-Southampton region, where a new town of some hundreds of thousands of inhabitants is proposed between the two great ports, 125 km from London.[1]

This study deals with the natural expansion of an urban region already containing 800 000 people, dominated at present by the existence of the two large towns, with an increase to a population of 1 500 000 by the end of the century. The study, which took eighteen months to complete, was undertaken by a firm of town planners consisting of six architects, one geographer, two town planners, three engineers and a mathematician, working in collaboration with economists and other experts. The actual method of work was original: one third of the time was given to a study of existing conditions and their potentialities and one third to theoretic schemes of urban development, leaving only one third to practical consideration of the scheme of extension that seemed the best choice.

The voluminous report resulting from this work is of great interest for its methods as well as for its proposals. A thorough geographical, economic and demographic analysis describes in minutest detail not only the proposed corridor of development but also a far wider area, so that the influence of the proposed development could be fully investigated. Various dates for the completion of the scheme were suggested, but only a normal increase of population from outside the area was allowed for up to 1971. In particular, the study contains a detailed analysis of the pattern of employment and its possibilities of growth – with stress on its essential dependence on political decisions – and of the population structure and its future, so that any proposals have a solid foundation of fact. Technical problems – water supply, sewage system, drainage, power and transport (in great detail) – and social questions of shopping and leisure facilities are also treated in detail.

The most original section of the report is undoubtedly the analysis of different theoretic schemes of urban development, made with the aim of selecting those which were most suitable. The authors of the report finally reduced these to three: the concentric pattern made up of hexagonal units; the linear pattern; and the rectangular grill pattern (Fig. 11). The chosen criteria were:

Freedom of choice, communication and association for the population.

Reasonable facilities during the period of development.

Scope for later expansion.

Adaptability and variety within the pattern, especially for housing and transport.

[1]Colin Buchanan & Partners, *South Hampshire Study*, a report to the Ministry of Housing & Local Government (London, HMSO, 1966), 3 vols.

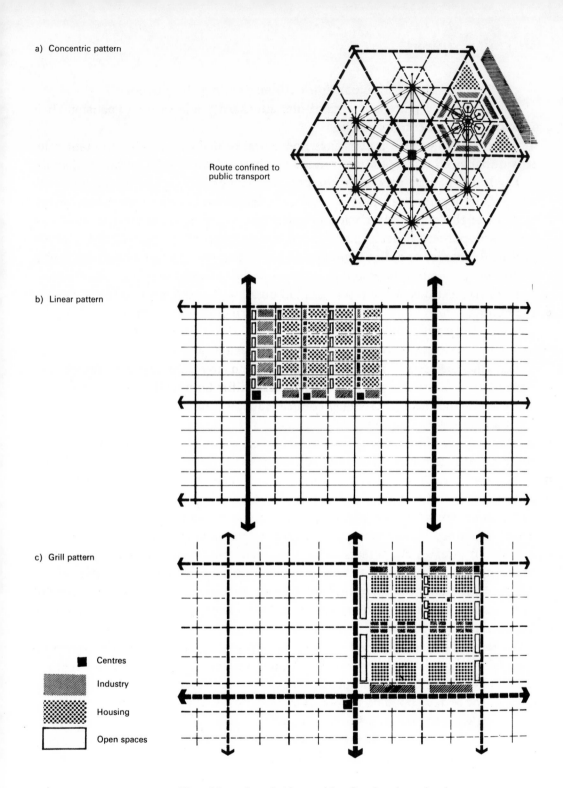

a) Concentric pattern

Route confined to
public transport

b) Linear pattern

c) Grill pattern

Centres

Industry

Housing

Open spaces

Fig. 11 *South Hampshire Study*: three basic patterns.

The possibility of expansion without spoiling the pattern.

The concentric pattern is a rigid one and hardly allows for expansion. It is inflexible and essentially static.

The rectangular grill pattern has no natural centre to act in a dominant role; it is unbalanced and does not provide the best conditions for public transport.

The linear pattern was voted the best, with its greater flexibility, adaptability and suitability for transport schemes. It therefore became the choice of the authors of the study, after various experiments aimed at testing the results of various hypothetical decisions. It nevertheless must be stated that the analysis of the advantages and disadvantages of these different patterns was not carried out on very scientific lines and that the hypothetical tests were qualitative only.

The final sections of the report deal in detail with the possibilities of adapting the chosen scheme to the particular area of urban development (Fig. 12) under consideration, allowing for various time limits and for the effects of the scheme on communications, shopping centres, employment and transport.

The financial side was not treated in any detail. The authors denied any attempt to produce a rigid grill pattern for South Hampshire, showing how in many ways the theoretic scheme could be adapted to the actualities of the site.

As a result of this study, a tripartite organization was formed by the county of Hampshire and the county boroughs of Portsmouth and Southampton to make a fresh examination of this plan for providing for London's overspill and to suggest a definite plan. In consequence, there is promise of the scheme materializing and of a development corporation being set up.

A similar study, concerned with the large expansion planned for the small town of Ashford,[1] was recently carried out by the same firm. Employing a similar method, it stresses the effects of expansion on the existing town and its surroundings and deals with the costs and length of time needed for the undertaking. In the end, the town of Ashford and the GLC reached a joint agreement (the usual procedure for expanded towns) of an expansion limited to an increase in population of 30 000.

Other studies were carried out by town planning consultants for Swindon, Peterborough and Northampton. Swindon is already an example of an extended town. In the case of Peterborough, a new town system was followed, with the creation of a development corporation in January 1968, working in close cooperation with the local authority. The town's population of 70 000 is due to be doubled. Likewise at Northampton, a proposed doubling of the population is to be carried out under the auspices of the development corporation created in August 1968.

[1]Colin Buchanan & Partners, *Ashford Study. Consultants' Proposals for Designation*, a report to the Ministry of Housing & Local Government (London, HMSO, 1967).

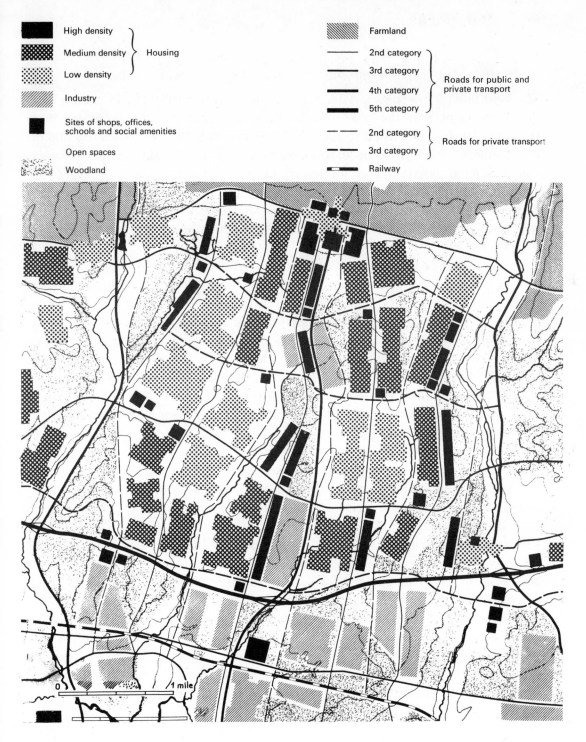

Fig. 12 *South Hampshire Study*: application of the linear pattern to a section of the corridor scheme.

High density ⎫

Medium density ⎬ Housing

Low density ⎭

Industry

Sites of shops, offices, schools and social amenities

Open spaces

Woodland

Farmland

2nd category ⎫

3rd category ⎪

4th category ⎬ Roads for public and private transport

5th category ⎭

2nd category ⎫ Roads for private transport

3rd category ⎭

Railway

0 _____ 1 mile

Plans for new developments

The next move after these preliminary studies was naturally the formation of a development plan on the same lines as the master plan for the new towns. The Ipswich plan was entrusted to the firm of Shankland, Cox & Associates, one of the foremost private concerns in town planning in Great Britain. The preliminary study, started in 1965 and published in the following year, envisaged an additional 70 000 population before 1981, which, allowing for natural increase in the existing population and among the newcomers, would raise the total population of the town from its existing 121 000 to 219 000 by 1981 and to 274 000 by 2001.[1]

In the course of this study, the planners first of all sought the most suitable scheme of expansion, basing their investigations on a geographical and economic analysis of the town, its population, activities and environment. A concentric pattern with its recognized disadvantages was rejected in favour of a linear pattern of development, which would be more economic for transport, allow easy access between town and country and allow for future growth, only modifying it by concentrating development in nuclei along an axis of communication. This section of the study is undoubtedly the most interesting, although the various schemes proposed are analysed purely qualitatively, leaving their conclusions somewhat vague.

The main directions of the extension – towards the north-west and south-west – were decided on because of their facilities, particularly of transport, for economic reasons and from the wish to preserve coastal areas. The only argument against the plan – and this was discounted by its authors – was the quality of agricultural land.

The final plan was not exactly on these lines. In addition to linear development towards the north-west, two areas of expansion immediately to the south-west and west of the town allowed for an additional 50 000 population each. This decision was justified by economic considerations, particularly with regard to the period of transition. Each of these two zones would be served by a district centre, the sole subregional centre remaining that of the town of Ipswich itself, whose size and number of workers did not admit an increase but whose role would change with the town's expansion.

The report also studied the impact of the plan in various fields: population

[1]Shankland, Cox & Associates, *Expansion of Ipswich Designation Proposals. Consultants' Study of the Town into Sub-region*, a report to the Ministry of Housing & Local Government (London, HMSO, 1966).

structure, employment, transport, road systems, etc., but in particular the effects of such a rapid expansion on the town's environment. The authors of the report made provision for out-of-door leisure activities but were especially concerned with the preservation of the surrounding villages and with the creation of new ones.

It is too soon to tell whether these proposals will be accepted by the ministry concerned, whose decision should shortly be published. They were accepted by the County Borough of Ipswich but met with opposition from the East Suffolk County Council, into whose territory the north-eastern development would intrude. The conclusions of the study were also fundamentally opposed to those of the preliminary study carried out by the firm of Vincent & Gorbing, which makes one question the value of two successive studies.

Further studies in town planning

There are some studies outside the scope of the *South East Study*, one of these being the development study of the county of Buckinghamshire and studies concerned with a new town of 250 000 inhabitants proposed in this county in the area of Bletchley and Newport Pagnell, halfway between London and Birmingham. Here, a new town with a population of 250 000 is planned, to be developed over a period of thirty years.

The town's general pattern and the distribution of its different zones are as follows: a main centre laid out on a linear pattern; four series of small, compact residential nuclei on a linear pattern parallel to that of the centre; four main industrial zones sited at the ends of the lines of residential development; ample planned green spaces and farmland; the whole linked by a system of public transport and a road network. Pedestrian ways would be separated from traffic routes.

The centre would be built on the line of the main railway and above the A5 and a main road at right angles to the A5 linking it to the M1, the London-Birmingham motorway. This centre could be entirely a pedestrian precinct on a higher level, while parking, service access and public and private transport systems would be at a lower level.

One of the novel aspects of this project lies in the siting of the residential areas at a distance from the centre but linked to it, to each other and to the industrial zones by a free public system of overhead transport. The system would be in four sections, corresponding to the four lines of residential development, sited between the groups of housing and the green spaces so that no house would be more than seven minutes from the station, with 1·2 km between

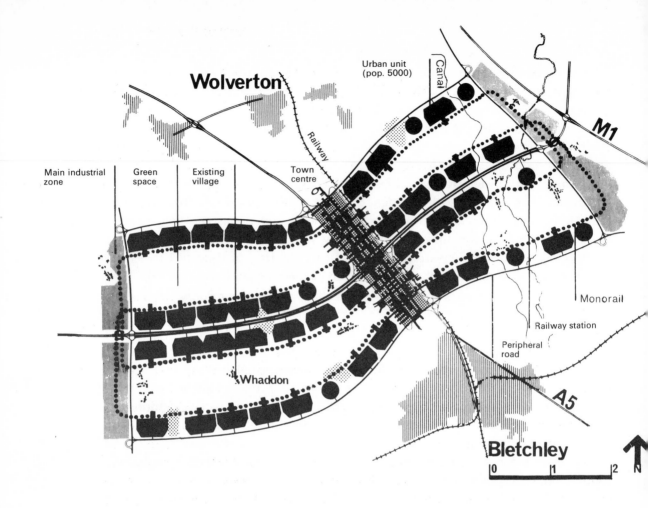

Fig. 13 North Bucks (Bletchley) : proposed pattern.

stations. The reason given for the choice of an elevated railway of the monorail type is to give easy access to the green spaces from any part of the residential areas and to avoid any crossing of the public transport system and the road network. The residential areas would be developed on a linear pattern parallel to the public transport system. They would be small, compact, varied and separated from each other by screens of trees. Each section would be planned by a different architect to allow for individuality and to avoid monotony. They would vary in density but their average population would be about 5000, with an average of 125 people per hectare (Fig. 13).

After a series of studies carried out by the firm of Llewelyn Davies, these proposals were accepted by the government and a development corporation created in 1967 for the town, now to be known as Milton Keynes. A regional study was commissioned by the government for the new town and also for the proposed large-scale extension of Nottingham.

Later studies were carried out for areas with particular problems: Bourne-mouth, Poole, Betchworth and its surroundings, for instance, and, apart from the south-east, there are plans for large new towns in Wales, near Cardiff at Llantrisant, for a population of 140 000,[1] and in mid Lancashire in the area of Preston, Leyland and Chorley, where the present population of 250 000 is to be doubled.[2]

Conclusion

In Britain, the policy of town planning for the London region was formulated immediately after the war, with the Abercrombie Plan, the Reith Commission and the New Towns Act. Despite some errors of foresight in the realm of population increase and the part played by tertiary employment, the policy has achieved some notable successes: the first wave of new towns, now almost completed.

These have nevertheless shown some failings: they have not absorbed more than a sixth of the region's population growth and have not succeeded in attracting enough diversity of employment and enough regional facilities to create truly balanced communities. With the 1960s the need to redefine the policy in the light of current conditions and recent findings became clear. Two successive regional studies – the *South East Study* and the *Strategy for the South East* – laid stress on the need for large-scale operations and the need to break with the traditional concentric pattern of expansion for the London area. It has taken more than five years' work before developments 100 km from London have finally been embarked on. There has not, however, been a complete break with former policy: the organization of the development corporations and the methods of financing the new towns, both instituted by the New Towns Act of 1946, have remained the cornerstones of later development.

[1] A study entrusted to Colin Buchanan & Partners, with a choice of six possible develop-ment schemes.
[2] A study carried out by R. Matthew, Johnson-Marshall & Partners, who pay particular attention to the foreseeable influence of the new town on its environment.

2: Town planning
and new towns in the Scandinavian capitals[1]

Introduction

The Scandinavian capitals have made a considerable reputation for themselves in the realm of town planning. This is partly due to the drawing up, over the last few decades, of excellent regional plans (particularly in Denmark and Sweden), but mainly to the quality of the new towns that have been built. Outstanding among these are new suburbs of Stockholm and the creation of the garden city of Tapiola near Helsinki. These differ from each other more than do the regional plans of which they are a part, but they nevertheless have much in common and much to teach town planners elsewhere. For this reason, it seemed best to study them together, having first of all placed them in their appropriate settings of regional planning.

I Planning policies in Copenhagen, Stockholm and Helsinki[2]

Before attempting a synthesis of the main outlines of town planning policy in the Scandinavian capitals, a short summary will be given of the history of this policy as it affects the chief plans drawn up and the main practical steps taken to put them into practice, such as a land policy and modernization of existing centres.

The development of planning in Copenhagen

Copenhagen, a capital with a long history, had no planned growth before 1936 and still shows little visible sign of it, though since before the war, and particularly after it, planning machinery has been put in motion to aid the task of the authorities. A plan of zoning laid down general principles on a country-wide scale and master plans outlined the development for individual districts and towns. The detailed plans that followed these could only be applied in a third of the cases and legislation for the Copenhagen area failed to be carried, partly

[1]Oslo is not dealt with in this chapter, but Helsinki is treated as a Scandinavian capital for the purposes of this study.
[2]P. Merlin with P. Guertin, 'Urbanisme à Copenhague, Stockholm, Helsinki', *Cahiers de l'IAURP*, vol. 9, October 1967.

due to an absence of official backing and partly due to a general opposition to any form of coercion.

The 'finger plan' of 1947 was the first main regional plan for Copenhagen. It was instigated by an official body, with the aim of checking Copenhagen's growth and channelling its natural development along axes served by suburban railways and separated by guaranteed green spaces. Travelling times to the town centre would in no place exceed forty-five minutes (Fig. 14). An improved balance of employment would be sought without creating any official link between housing and place of work. In practice, this 'finger plan', which only consisted of a general outline, met with many difficulties, with delays in the construction of the railways and a lack of co-ordinated regional planning.

The 'preliminary scheme' of 1961 was also drawn up by an official body (Fig. 15). It consisted of bolder plans, looking ahead to the year 2000, envisaging an increase of 67 per cent in thirty-nine years and a particularly rapid development of tertiary employment. In a constant search for a reduction in commuting, a lessening of traffic congestion in the centre and better communications between housing and leisure facilities, the plan proposed development to the west – towards the country's principal towns and the continent of Europe – the preservation of areas to the north and the gradual creation of new town sectors with populations of about 250 000, each absorbing regional urban growth over a decade. These new sectors, built along the main axes of development, would be capable of attracting the tertiary employment and the facilities necessary for forming stable communities. These town sectors, the first of which would be built adjacent to the existing town, would not, however, be self-sufficient, as one of the aims of the plan was to preserve freedom of choice for the inhabitants in the realm of employment, leisure, etc. (Fig. 16).

The preliminary scheme was submitted to a committee of experts for examination and was strongly criticized by transport officials, who had not previously been consulted. The only agreement reached was for plans for the current decade and apart from that nothing has been settled. Plans for the first town sector are under way, but differences of aim persist, exemplified by Copenhagen's desire to develop the island of Amager, next to the international airport, in complete opposition to the regional plan.

The development of planning in Stockholm

Stockholm, though a more modern city, has undergone town planning since as long ago as the seventeenth century and still exhibits many signs of planning. This is largely thanks to the foresight of her local councillors in acquiring land over the last sixty years, thus avoiding all the problems of speculation, so that

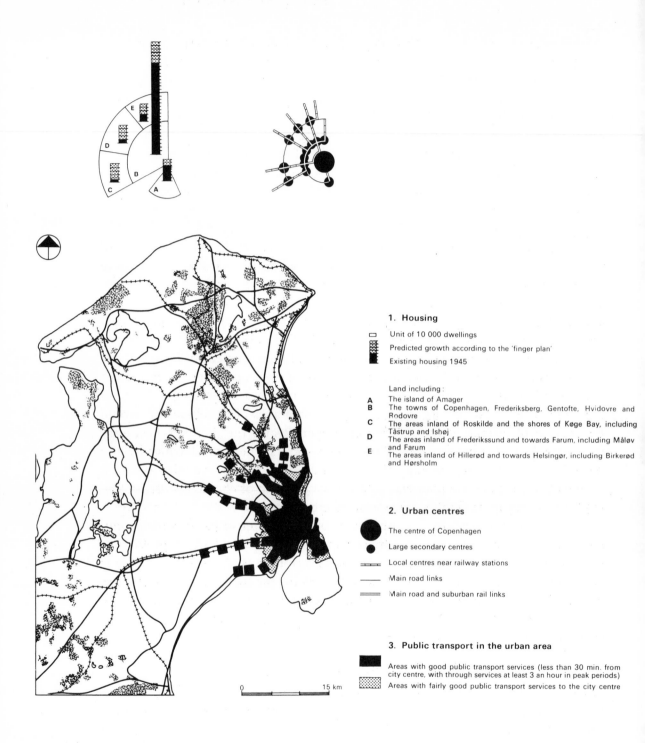

1. Housing

☐   Unit of 10 000 dwellings

▨   Predicted growth according to the 'finger plan'

■   Existing housing 1945

Land including :

A   The island of Amager
B   The towns of Copenhagen, Frederiksberg, Gentofte, Hvidovre and Rodovre
C   The areas inland of Roskilde and the shores of Køge Bay, including Tåstrup and Ishøj
D   The areas inland of Frederikssund and towards Farum, including Måløv and Farum
E   The areas inland of Hillerød and towards Helsingør, including Birkerød and Hørsholm

2. Urban centres

●   The centre of Copenhagen

•   Large secondary centres

╪╪╪   Local centres near railway stations

──   Main road links

═══   Main road and suburban rail links

3. Public transport in the urban area

■   Areas with good public transport services (less than 30 min. from city centre, with through services at least 3 an hour in peak periods)

▨   Areas with fairly good public transport services to the city centre

0   15 km

Fig. 14   Copenhagen : finger plan 1947.

the town already possessed the land necessary for expansion and was able to draw up detailed plans to be carried out by municipal or private bodies.

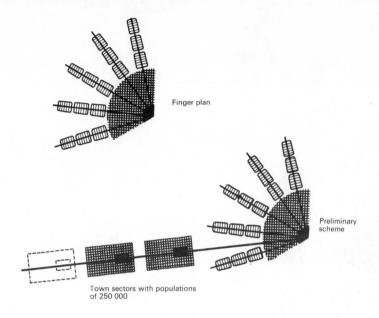

Fig. 15 Copenhagen : finger plan (1947) and preliminary scheme (1961).

The 1952 plan for Greater Stockholm was thus assured of success from the start. The policy proposed was for lines of satellite towns linked to the underground railway system already under construction, consisting of neighbourhood units with populations of 10 000-20 000 grouped within a radius of 500 m of the stations, with housing mainly in flats and an outer ring at a radius of 500-1000 m for individual houses, with a small shopping centre near the station and a main shopping centre for the whole satellite town. The construction of the underground railway decided the order of priority for these new urban developments and resulted in varying neighbourhood units grouped into whole new towns, among which the most complete are those centred on Vällingby and Farsta and one under construction centred on Skärholmen.

The growth of the Stockholm region led to the need for a regional plan. A Planning Commission for Greater Stockholm was formed to study a regional plan whose first version was published in 1958, with a revised version in 1967. Rejecting the limited proposals of the 1952 plan and even of the regional plan

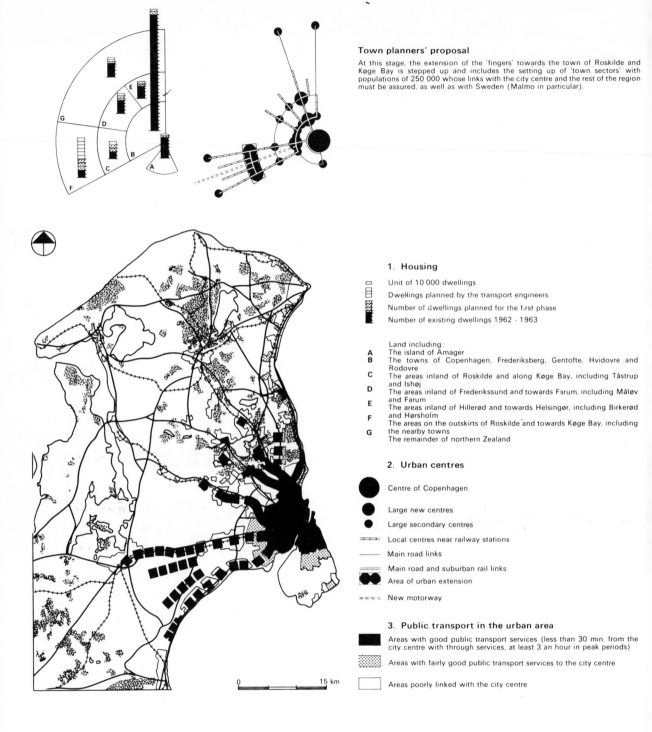

Town planners' proposal

At this stage, the extension of the 'fingers' towards the town of Roskilde and Køge Bay is stepped up and includes the setting up of 'town sectors' with populations of 250 000 whose links with the city centre and the rest of the region must be assured, as well as with Sweden (Malmo in particular).

1. Housing

☐ Unit of 10 000 dwellings

▤ Dwellings planned by the transport engineers

▨ Number of dwellings planned for the first phase

■ Number of existing dwellings 1962 - 1963

Land including :

A The island of Amager

B The towns of Copenhagen, Frederiksberg, Gentofte, Hvidovre and Rodovre

C The areas inland of Roskilde and along Køge Bay, including Tåstrup and Ishøj

D The areas inland of Frederikssund and towards Farum, including Måløv and Farum

E The areas inland of Hillerød and towards Helsingør, including Birkerød and Hørsholm

F The areas on the outskirts of Roskilde and towards Køge Bay, including the nearby towns

G The remainder of northern Zealand

2. Urban centres

● Centre of Copenhagen

● Large new centres

● Large secondary centres

▭▭▭ Local centres near railway stations

──── Main road links

══ Main road and suburban rail links

◼◼ Area of urban extension

==== New motorway

3. Public transport in the urban area

■ Areas with good public transport services (less than 30 min. from the city centre with through services, at least 3 an hour in peak periods)

▨ Areas with fairly good public transport services to the city centre

☐ Areas poorly linked with the city centre

0   15 km

Fig. 16 Copenhagen : preliminary scheme adopted by the consultative committee. Town planners' proposal.

of 1958, the 1967 plan envisaged a far greater population growth (to 2 100 000 by the year 2000). The rise in standards of living also demanded increased facilities, particularly in transport, leisure activities and housing (with an expected 2·2 rooms per person by the year 2000).

While the regional plan adopted the idea of satellite towns, though on a different scale – grouped along the fast suburban railway and made up of units of nearly 40 000 people outside the existing built-up area – it also made several new proposals. For one thing, development would be in particular directions – to the north-west, along the line linking the capital to the north of the country, and to the south-west, along the line linking it to the other chief towns and to the European continent – thus preserving the lakes and coast for leisure activities (Fig. 17). For another, the need for good centralized organization, at least for Stockholm itself, was stressed. Included in the plan was the complete modernization of the centre of Stockholm, with a concentration of commercial and financial interests there, based on the theory – not yet tested – that the advantages of such centralization, with easier exchange of information and freer choice, would outweigh the disadvantages (distance of travel, traffic congestion, etc.). This forms the most original aspect of planning for the Stockholm region.

The development of planning in Helsinki

Helsinki, though possessing a town plan since 1911, seems less advanced than her Swedish neighbour and has legal problems avoided by Stockholm's far-seeing policy of acquiring land.

Her 1960 plan resembles Stockholm's 1952 plan, with fairly dense neighbourhood units grouped along axes of transport and with a main regional centre for each group of units.

This plan has been partially applied (with the one really original creation, the garden city of Tapiola, standing apart from the plan) but is being superseded by a new regional plan, or, to be exact, by one of two plans now under consideration. The official plan, prepared by Helsinki's Development Association, proposes satellite towns of the Tapiola pattern and a dispersal of the capital's functions into secondary centres. The Housing Institute's plan is more ambitious, aiming at a demographic equilibrium for the whole region, the plan for Helsinki itself being treated only as a means to this end. Independent new towns would absorb the capital's overspill population, but, instead of being built around Helsinki, as envisaged in the official plan, they would be strung out along the coast. Two of these new towns are already under discussion.

Fig. 17 Regional plan of Stockholm: proposed scheme.

II The main characteristics of town planning in the
Scandinavian capitals[1]

A study of planning policy in Copenhagen, Stockholm and Helsinki reveals a number of common characteristics. It is interesting to attempt a synthesis of these elements and to see whether they represent a typically Scandinavian view of the problems of town planning and whether it would be profitable to apply them elsewhere. One of the first, or indeed basic, elements is the role of the capital itself. The theories of town planners on this vital subject revolve round large-scale patterns of population and employment and their attitude to the question of decentralization lies at the heart of the matter.

In the area of the capital itself, the respective roles played by the main centre and future secondary centres, existing or planned, dictate the policy of the localization of employment.

Within this framework the town planner must translate the main points of his scheme (notably the chief axes of development and leisure areas) into practical terms. A necessarily important part is played by the transport system, with its effects on type and density of housing.

The role of the capital within a development scheme

A town plan may be defined as a scheme for the organization of an urban area for a given population with a particular standard of living. The time limit of the scheme is a secondary consideration but may influence the scheme in two ways. First, by the fact that economic growth may bring a rise in the standard of living and, second, by the need for complementary studies where the time limit of the plan is concerned. Apart from this limit, the plan presupposes – implicitly or explicitly – a particular increase of population on a national scale and the division of this increase between different regions, and especially between the capital and other areas. It is of interest, therefore, to study the aims that have been achieved in these capitals, to see whether they have been adhered to in the course of time and whether they have proved effective or not. This question needs to be looked at in two different ways. In the realm of theory, the advantages and disadvantages must be weighed up – something that has not been fully done – and in the realm of practice the effectiveness of the scheme must be tested by contrasting official policy with actual results.

It is possible to distinguish two major elements in the plans for the

[1]P. Merlin with P. Guertin, op. cit.

Scandinavian capitals. On one hand, the town planners are not obsessed by the need for decentralization and sometimes even regard it as undesirable. On the other, their attitude, evolving over the last twenty years, has become more favourable to high concentrations of population. In practice, however, it is only in Stockholm that the size of the problem has been fully realized and has been reflected in collaboration between the planners and the university departments.

The disadvantages of urban concentration are well known and are touched on in all Scandinavian plans. They will only be mentioned here briefly: traffic congestion, distance and time of commuting, atmospheric pollution, mental strain among the city dwellers and so on.

Its advantages are less often mentioned. Copenhagen's preliminary scheme states clearly that the expected growth of international trade would mean an increase of employment in the wholesale business and that Copenhagen alone could become an important international trading centre. On a local scale, it also states that centralization would permit a larger fund of manpower to be drawn on, a larger market of consumers and better opportunities for contacts and exchange of information.

It was this last point that seemed the most important to Professor Ahlberg's team in charge of Stockholm's regional plan and to the group of economists, led by Professor Kristensson, which has carried out studies on this subject.[1] It also forms one of the bases of a new draft of the regional plan.[2]

Admittedly, official national policy is one of decentralization. Parliament has granted over 800 million kroner (£65 million) in five years to assist decentralization towards the north and this sum will probably have to be increased. This assistance takes the form of interest-free loans but has only been applied half-heartedly. Official circles do not disguise the fact that they regard the policy as a political manoeuvre, linked to the fact that provincial members of parliament are in the majority, and they put little faith in its long-term effectiveness.

It seems that the problem cannot be seen in the same terms for Sweden or Denmark as for Great Britain or France, for Stockholm or Copenhagen as for London or Paris. Many consider that the Scandinavian capitals are so unimportant in Europe as a whole that an increase in their size would strengthen their position. Copenhagen, for instance, is anxious not to suffer in comparison with Hamburg as an important seaport.

[1] Folke Kristensson, *People, Firms and Regions. A Structural Economic Analysis* (Stockholm, 1967).
[2] *Skiss 1966 till regionplan för Stockholmstrakten* (Stockholm, 1967).

In theory, Kristensson's team reckon that transport costs – one of the disadvantages of centralization – are small in comparison with the benefits accruing from such centralization. Only a large city can make fullest use of the exchange of economic information, administrative services, centres of study, etc., and these benefits would increase with time. The team's task is to collect the facts concerned with the advantages of centralization and to compare them with the disadvantages. A study has been made of the frequency and importance of communications between workers in various firms. The question of dispersed firms has also been studied in an attempt to balance extra expenses, such as transport, postage, telephones and telegrams, against saving in rent, etc., and the importance of communications before and after decentralization. Another study deals with the normal economic effects of centralization. The same economists have collected information about the level of public services demanded by the Swedes and their consequent reluctance to live in very small or very isolated communities.

It would appear that this attitude of planners in Scandinavia – and particularly in Sweden – towards decentralization is comparatively recent. The 'finger plan' of 1947 assumed a voluntary reduction in commuting to the capital, while the preliminary scheme of 1961 allowed for a continuation of earlier practices. Similarly, the 1952 plan for Stockholm itself assumed a reduction in commuting, as did the regional plan of 1958, whereas the new regional plan, drawn up by the same firm, retains the notion of the continued growth of the Stockholm area on the present scale.

Although it sets out the advantages of decentralization, the plan drawn up for Helsinki by a regional body also allows for the continuation of present tendencies.

It would seem that the change in outlook on this problem is partly due to the reasons already set out and partly to an acknowledgement of the setbacks suffered by the official policy of decentralization so far in force. Despite measures taken by the governments concerned to check the growth of their capital cities, these have increased at an unparalleled rate (with a population increase per year of 18 000 in Stockholm, about 20 000 in Copenhagen and 15 000 in Helsinki): a reflection of the situation in London and Paris. Moreover, experts in regional economics have proved that the most dynamic industries, especially those with skilled activities employing a majority of highly qualified labour, are those to be found in the region of the capital, so that to check their growth or to force dispersal upon them would make economic nonsense.

A general pattern

A general pattern of population, employment, land and so on can be assumed from these theories of the role of the capital and can be found to give a true picture of the situation. Where the Scandinavian plans are concerned, these patterns have changed with the changing role given to the capital.

The earliest post-war plans were based on a policy of decentralization and therefore contained conservative estimates of population increase. Hence Copenhagen's 'finger plan' maintained an upper population limit of 1 500 000, a limit which has already been exceeded. No limit was set for the country as a whole, so no comparison can be made here. Stockholm's 1952 plan assumed almost a halving of the existing rate of growth.

Later regional plans allow for far higher limits, especially in Copenhagen, where a 67 per cent population increase over forty years is expected (from 1 500 000 to 2 500 000). Stockholm's regional plan, drawn up in 1958, was somewhat more conservative, assuming a total population of 1 570 000 by 1990, or an increase of 36 per cent over thirty-two years from a population of about 1 150 000 in 1958. The 1967 plan, with limits of 1 900 000 by 1990 and 2 100 000 by 2000, assumed a population growth of 68 per cent over thirty-five years (from about 1 250 000 in 1965), or nearly double the previous rate. The plan for Helsinki drawn up by the Society for Finland's Towns provided for a doubling of the population over thirty years, from 600 000 to 1 200 000. The proposals of Mr Heikki Van Hertzen were, by contrast, more modest.

The raising of these limits is partly a result of a nationwide population increase in the immediate post-war years. In Sweden, for example, the expected population level for the year 2000 has had to be raised from 9·5 to 10·5 million (7·6 million in 1966).

Patterns of employment are necessarily linked to patterns of population. The Scandinavian plans, however, do not lay stress on levels of employment and at times figures for employment and population do not seem to tally (in the 1952 Stockholm plan, for example). In modern planning, influenced by the economists, the tendency is, on the contrary, towards a preliminary forecast of employment and a resulting forecast of population, which can be equally fallible. Population and employment and their respective growths are closely linked and it is useless to try to decide which determines the other. In the new detailed regional plan of Stockholm, much attention has been given to the question of the growth of employment, studied in its various branches.

One consideration in housing is the space required for a given number of dwellings and another the changes in density of occupation. The plan for

Copenhagen allowed for an average of 2·5 persons per dwelling by the year 2000, while the new plan for Stockholm contains the more ambitious aim of 2·2 rooms per person (1·2 in 1966).[1] This, although the authors of the plan do not deal with the matter, necessitates the modernization of many existing small dwellings.

The plans also provide for greater space requirements for housing, with added facilities due to the expected rise in the standard of living, increase of leisure and of motoring. As in Great Britain and France and throughout Europe in general, post-war plans seriously underestimated the need for parking space. Present plans estimate a rise of 400 per cent by the year 2000 (333 per cent by 1975 in Stockholm) almost identical to the figure given in the master plan for the Paris region (360 per cent by 2000). The present rate in Stockholm (220 per cent) is near to that of Paris and the rate in Copenhagen (133 per cent in 1960, about 200 per cent in 1965) to that of London.

The main background of the Scandinavian plans appears to be the result of the decision made about the role of the capital in the development of the country as a whole. The question of centralization must be seen in this context and it remains an open question throughout Scandinavia and in Sweden in particular.

The importance of urban centres

Modern town planning for large built-up areas usually provides for the establishment of various centres with varying functions and at various levels, in existing suburbs or *a fortiori* in future extensions. Apart from their various functions, the first question, inseparable from that of decentralization, is of their relationship with the main centre. But the creation of these new centres is of great significance in one particular respect: the ability of the town planner to offer a sufficient choice of employment, shopping facilities, leisure activities, etc.

The problem of dispersal is similar to that of decentralization, but on a different scale – that of the urban area and not of the country as a whole. What activities should remain at the centre and which can (or should) be transferred to the outskirts? The advantages of dispersal for industry are well known, particularly with its possibilities of expansion. The disadvantages lie mainly in less direct communications and the question of distance between home and

[1] In Sweden, the kitchen counts as one room. These figures may be compared with those of Paris (0·93 in 1962) and of London (0·88 in the centre, 1·39 throughout the remainder of the London area in 1962, and about 1·30 in the new towns).

work, which may grow less in future. In Paris, for instance, industries have tended to lessen the disadvantages of dispersal by moving less far away and mainly concentrating on one chief sector.[1]

This dispersal policy has been widely adopted by town planners in Scandinavia, with some modifications. Copenhagen's 'finger plan' proposed a concentration of industry in the nearest urban ring to the centre, where there were already a number of industries and where communications would be improved by the new transport network. This policy of limited dispersal became more ambitious in the preliminary scheme, in which it was considered that the proposed town sectors should possess centres that, while not rivalling the centre of Copenhagen itself, would provide various facilities, particularly department stores, wholesale business and administrative services. These centres would provide a variety of amenities and activities comparable to those of large provicial towns (such as Odense, Århus and Ålborg), which would demand an active policy of dispersal. The centre of Copenhagen would, however, retain its present functions in relation to the existing built-up area and to the country as a whole and as a centre of activities demanding frequent and important contacts.

In the Stockholm area the 1952 plan stressed the need for a balance between employment and the working population in the new neighbourhood units. At the same time it advocated the modernization of the existing centre, which would entail, if only for ensuring a financial balance, a concentration of commercial and administrative affairs and of services in the modernized centre, without any ordinary housing.

The result of this policy might be expected to be the enlargement of an intermediate zone – equivalent to the existing suburbs – without any industry, between a balanced zone (the new town areas) and a zone of excess (the centre). The relative modification of the policy of the dispersal of industry has brought a somewhat different result. The dispersal policy remains the official goal but it is hardly compatible, at least in the realm of tertiary activities, with the current modernization of the centre. Important commercial centres (Vällingby and Farsta) have been built or are under construction (Skärholmen) but examples of the dispersal of offices, such as the dispersal of 1500 jobs to Råcksta near Vällingby, are rare. The experts in charge of the regional plan express doubts of the possibility of large-scale office dispersal and do not seem persuaded of its expediency. However, an important project will serve as a test, as a huge employment area is to be developed on land recently handed over by the army

[1]'Mouvement des établissements industriels dans la région parisienne', *Cahiers de l'IAURP*, vol. 1, October 1964.

at Järvafältet, less than 10 km from the commercial centre. This area, at present only served by suburban railways, will eventually be bordered by two sections of the underground railway. Proposals include the provision of 50 000 office jobs – a very large number for Stockholm – 13 000 jobs in industry, 2000 jobs in research and 16 000 jobs of various kinds including services. The project also provides for housing, with a total of 100 000 rooms. The three towns affected, including Stockholm itself, have formed a co-ordinating committee and taken steps to further the project, which is supported by the planning services of Stockholm. The size of the project should attract industry, as should the expected dispersal of 10 000 government jobs not directly concerned with decision-making (forestry, agriculture, insurance, etc.).

It can thus be seen that although the policy of dispersal is officially promulgated in the Scandinavian capitals, results are so far on a modest scale. The present tendency is towards the creation of secondary centres of sufficient size to exert effective attraction.

In Helsinki the plan drawn up by the Society for Finland's Towns, like the projects of Van Hertzen, stresses the idea of dispersal but so far there is little sign of any concrete measures being undertaken. It will also undoubtedly be compromised by the plan for modernizing the centre, with a trebling of the area of office building.

Freedom of choice

All the Scandinavian plans stress that an important element in the amenities of the new towns is the freedom of choice offered to their citizens, something that must be preserved. This freedom of choice concerns housing as much as place of work, shopping and recreation, with the result that the new towns conceived in these plans must on the one hand be as balanced as possible, to give maximum satisfaction to the needs of the local inhabitants, but on the other hand cannot be treated as completely independent units. This particularly implies the absence of any link between the choice of job and the allocation of housing and is in complete contrast to the system prevailing in the new towns in England, for example:

This freedom of choice can only be implemented where communications allow easy travel throughout the built-up area and, especially, where full employment and the rate of house-building have attained a state of stability.

Shape in planning

Any town plan must provide for the final shape of the proposed development. Many towns have adopted a concentric pattern modified only by transport infrastructure. This pattern is often aimed at in plans that seek a stability based on the lessening importance of the built-up area in the country as a whole and the encouragement of decentralization. This principle is explicit in Sir Patrick Abercrombie's plan for Greater London.[1] It appears implicit in the PADOG established for the Paris region.[2] These plans, on the contrary, assume a growth of the built-up area, which does not easily accommodate itself to a concentric pattern. For one thing, this growth demands a consumption of space, which means an alteration in the roles of the different rings. This is very apparent in Paris and also in London, where the theory of stabilization has not been borne out by the facts. For another, the growth of the built-up area usually requires new infrastructures of transport, which give preference to new districts and break the concentric pattern. The sites of these districts, served by new transport systems, must be decided by voluntary and deliberate choice and are known to planners as preferential directions.

The Scandinavian plans do, in fact, provide a good illustration of this point. The plans drawn up about 1950, when a reduction in the rate of growth was expected, were more or less concentric in pattern. Copenhagen's 'finger plan' assumed the development of radiating lines of rail transport with town development along these lines and preserved green spaces between the 'fingers'. This cannot properly be called a concentric pattern, but all the new districts played a similar role in relation to Copenhagen. The 1952 plan for Stockholm likewise assumed town planning in neighbourhood units grouped round the stations on the new underground railway. Here again the pattern was concentric, but varied to keep pace with the building of different branches of the railway. Helsinki's plan, in 1960, is also concentric in pattern, without assuming a reduction in the rate of growth.

The regional plans drawn up since 1960 mark a complete break with this line of thought. We have seen that after the check to the policy of decentralization the size of planning units increased. The concentric pattern was abandoned almost everywhere, remaining only in the plan prepared by the Society for Finland's Towns, in opposition to Van Hertzen's scheme, in a concentric pattern similar to that in the 1952 plan for Stockholm.

The choice of preferential directions depends mainly on two considerations. One is the fact that the development of the capital cannot be undertaken without placing it in a far larger framework, that of the main economic development of

[1] Patrick Abercrombie, *Greater London Plan* 1944 (London, 1945). See P. Merlin and P. Guertin, 'Villes nouvelles en Grande-Bretagne', *Cahiers de l'IAURP*, vol. 8, June 1967.

[2] SARP, *Plan d'aménagement et d'organisation générale de la région parisienne* (Paris, 1960).

the whole country. Another is the fact that the scheme, depending on a small number of directions, allows the inhabitants easy access to the recreation areas enclosed between the lines of development and that the determination of preferential directions depends largely on the choice of protected areas.

The preliminary scheme for the Copenhagen area affirms that the most important direction of development economically is without doubt that which links Copenhagen to Odense and Jutland (in an east-west line) and proposes to give that priority. Such a conjunction of the main axes of development on a local, national and international scale would also be advantageous in assuring the most profitable use of transport facilities in serving the new towns (main line railways in particular).

In the regional plan for Stockholm – the first draft of which appeared in 1958 and the second in 1967 – the two directions that seemed most deserving of priority to those responsible for the national plan were those to the north-west and south-west. The first of these corresponds to the route of the railway linking the capital to the north of the country and the second is in the direction of the two chief provincial towns, Göteborg and Malmö, and especially in the direction of the European continent. It should be added that the choice of the Swedish planners in the matter of preferential directions is less exclusive than that of their Danish counterparts. In Finland Van Hertzen proposes a preferential development along the coast, on both sides of Helsinki.

The preservation of large areas devoted to recreational purposes is another common characteristic of recent Scandinavian plans. The importance of anything connected with nature to the Nordic races is well known and may have some connection with their severe climate. A small example highlights this tendency: in a very tiny group of two or three local shops can be found a florist even before a grocer, this being all the more remarkable when one considers that its contents are imported and therefore expensive.

The preliminary scheme for the Copenhagen region states that the lovely countryside in the north of Zealand is threatened by widespread development and by the growing unrestricted habit of acquiring second holiday houses. Laws for the protection of nature have indeed granted free access to all to the woods, river banks and lakesides, but unrestricted building threatens to ravage the countryside beyond repair. The desire to turn this area into a vast reserve of green spaces and recreational facilities is probably the authors' main reason for proposing preferential development towards the west and south-west, where the countryside is less beautiful. The existence of an undeveloped coastline is another argument brought forward in favour of preferential development in the direction of Køge and Roskilde.

The regional plan for Stockholm uses similar arguments, aiming at preserving from development the region of the islands of Lake Mälar to the west, that of Lakes Lilla Värtan and Stora Värtan to the north-east and, to a lesser extent, the Erstaviken area to the east-south-east and the lakes to the south and north.

The proposals of Van Hertzen rest on a similar basis but the official plan proposes only the protection of islands and open spaces at a distance from Helsinki.

Although these questions seem less clear-cut in Stockholm than in Copenhagen – where the division between the west to be developed and the north to be protected seems an oversimplification – they seem to be more acceptable and more likely to be put into force in the Swedish capital, through the influence of public opinion and official action. In Copenhagen, on the other hand, the very reason that leads the planners to demand the protection of the north – the beauty of the countryside – is the one that encourages speculators to exploit it.

Transport and housing

Although the amount of motor traffic in Scandinavia is among the highest in Europe, the planners have paid it relatively small attention and this is reflected in housing arrangements.

This would hardly have been surprising in the plans drawn up fifteen or twenty years ago. The 1947 'finger plan', for instance, underestimating the future need for car parking, relied essentially on the scheme for a new suburban rail network. Development was planned along these routes, grouped at walking distance from the stations. This required housing in the form of blocks of flats, with only 35 per cent of housing as individual dwellings. The plan of 1952 for Greater Stockholm is comparable in this respect with the new underground railway system forming the framework and neighbourhood units built round the stations in a string of groups of buildings of diminishing size. Tower blocks of more than ten storeys surround the stations and nothing but blocks of flats are to be found for a radius of 500 m. Beyond this are individual houses, though not as many as the 20 per cent originally planned.

It is more surprising to find that the role of public transport remains uppermost in recent plans, which also assume a rapid rise in the amount of motor traffic. Though the preliminary scheme for the Copenhagen region takes account of a motorway system planned by the Roads Commission for Greater Copenhagen, in particular for a ring road round the lakes in the city centre, it still leaves the main role, at least for transport from the centre outwards, to the railway. The completion of the rail system proposed in the 'finger plan' is demanded, as well as the construction of a new infrastructure bringing a fast service, with a few stations, to the different sectors of the town. Access from these to the centre by road is provided for, with a choice of motorway or fast rail service. In the centre itself it is considered that the building of a ring road will not be sufficient to solve the problems of communications and the earlier plan for an underground railway is retained. The question of individual houses is ignored in the preliminary scheme, but the planners provide for an increase in their number, up to 50 per cent for the Køge Bay scheme.

The Greater Stockholm plan includes similar proposals. The underground railway is by no means regarded as outdated and its completion is planned. But, as development spreads beyond the present limits (a circle 15 km in radius, corresponding to a half hour journey by rail to the centre), a more extensive and more rapid service is envisaged. This, comparable to the Paris regional express system, would be based on existing suburban railway lines and run on two tracks across the city centre, needing some modification of the layout there. Two north-south regional lines are planned over the next ten years, at a cost of 400 million kroner (£32 million). The rolling stock would consist of trains of eight to ten carriages 20 m long with two decks of seats (the Stockholm underground railway only has one deck, which is considered insufficient nowadays). Apart from these two lines more or less on the present layout, a third line is proposed in the regional plan. Stopping places would be far enough apart (3 km at least) to allow a working speed of 60 km/h, or double that of the underground railway. This would enable town development to be extended to a radius of 30 km. The service would be improved, with two trains an hour at off-peak times and four an hour at peak times. Urban units of a larger scale than the present neighbourhood units would be built round the new stations and would not have to adhere to earlier criteria, whereby all the housing blocks were built within a radius of 500 m from the station, without alternative means of transport. These are now planned and will mean that more individual houses can be built. Road transport has not been neglected. Urban motorways are being built in the modernized centre and a 25 km long ring road encircling the 'city of stone', which should be completed by 1980, is in course of construction, with the first section already opened. Ten radial motorways are also planned, of which one, linking the city to its international airport, is already in use, three are partly built and two are under construction. But, contrary to long-cherished hopes, calculations have shown that even this ambitious motorway network will not be able to ensure easy access to the city centre by car. Transport experts estimate that, by 1980, 25 per cent of peak hour commuters will be able to get as far as the ring road and only 10 per cent will be able to reach the city centre, where 20 000 meter parking spaces are planned.

In Helsinki the official regional plan relies upon a similar scheme: the construction of a new suburban rail system by the use and combination of existing lines and the building of satellite towns round the main stations of this fast line, with alternative means of transport.

Scandinavian town planning, hinging as it does on public transport and providing for relatively concentrated housing, has more in common with planning in France than in the Anglo-Saxon countries, where low-storey housing in terraces (in Great Britain) or separated (in the USA) and, especially, a garden hold undisputed sway.

Particularly notable in Scandinavia are the happy results of planning where, as in Stockholm, the infrastructures, particularly of transport systems, can be prepared before the erection of the buildings that they are there to serve.

III The new towns[1]

With an annual increase in population of 15 000-20 000, the Scandinavian new towns do not need to be on the scale of those around London or Paris, short of concentrating on a single site, which has been done in some places. Other problems also have to be seen in different terms: the balance between population and employment, so difficult qualitatively, is not of overriding importance in new moderate-sized areas near their parent city.

The pattern of the Scandinavian new towns

The small scale of the operations already carried out exemplifies the different areas of decision: siting, commercial framework, employment. The new areas are all near the original built-up area without any gap. The Scandinavian plans usually fix a desirable time-distance limit (forty-five minutes from the centre of Copenhagen according to the 'finger plan', thirty minutes from Stockholm according to the 1952 plan, thirty minutes from Helsinki according to the regional plan. The distances involved can be doubled with a good rail service: even with more extended development the link with the centre can be rapid, as in the case of the town sectors planned for Copenhagen and the new areas planned for Stockholm. The earliest new developments, however, were near the centre: Albertslund at 15 km from the centre of Copenhagen, Tapiola 10 km from the centre of Helsinki and the new areas of Stockholm between 10 and 15 km from the central station. The small distance and size involved made it

[1]P. Merlin with P. Guertin, 'Ville nouvelles en Scandinavie', *Cahiers de l'IAURP*, vol. 9, October 1967.

unnecessary to attach them to existing communities.

The first prerequisite for a choice of site is a good transport system. If Albertslund is so far the only part of the 'finger plan' put into practice, on a fast railway line (twenty minutes from the central station), it is due to the slowness in implementing the programme of rapid public transport. Tapiola, linked to Helsinki by bus only, is the sole exception to this rule. The new parts of Stockholm, on the other hand, have been sited along the line of the underground railway and built as the railway has been extended, with the new development ringed round the stations. Even their internal organization depends upon the railway: first comes the commercial centre, then tall blocks of flats, decreasing in height, up to 500 m from the station (satisfactory walking distance even in a country with severe winters), then separate houses in an outer ring from 500 to 900 m. The new town itself consists of a collection of such units (each with a population of about 15 000) grouped along the same stretch of line.

The chosen sites often have great natural beauty, with forests and rocks, sometimes on the sea or lake shore (Tapiola, Hässelby Strand, Farsta Strand). When the site itself lacks variety, an artificial relief and landscape may be created, as at Albertslund. Great attention is also paid to conserving the countryside, including the protection of river banks and of trees near buildings.

The new sections built round the Scandinavian capitals are comparatively small in size: units of 15 000 in population (sometimes more in the newest sections) for the suburbs of Stockholm, forming groups of units with populations of about 60 000, served by a main centre sited in one of the units (Vällingby: Fig. 18 – Farsta, Skärholmen: Fig. 19). A population of about 30 000 is planned for Albertslund, but the first completed section only provides for 7000. In Tapiola the population intended is 17 000, nearly all already installed, allowing a density of 65 per hectare (whereas the Swedish units often exceed 80 per hectare). But the tendency is towards the creation of larger and larger units (40 000-50 000, according to the new plan for the Stockholm area, forming groups of 200 000; 250 000 in the new town sectors in Denmark, etc.).

It is only in Stockholm that planning is carried out systematically, though Albertslund and Tapiola are isolated examples in Denmark and Finland respectively. The plan for Albertslund was entrusted to a well-known town planner, Professor P. Bredsdorff, and later taken over by a former colleague of his, K. Svensson (Fig. 20). In Tapiola a plan had been drawn up by Professor Meurman even before the acquisition of land by the Housing Foundation (the Asuntosäätiö) responsible for the building of the town and for modifying the plans considerably at later stages (Fig. 21). A competition was held (and won by Aarne Ervi) for plans for the centre as well as for the third neighbourhood unit.

Fig. 18   Sweden: the new town of Vällingby. A series of sectors round the underground railway stations.

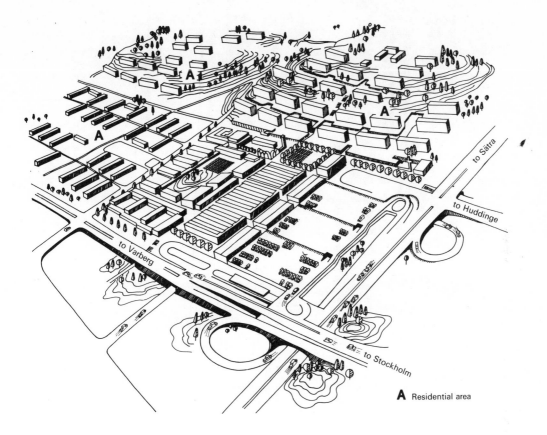

to Sätra

to Huddinge

to Varberg

to Stockholm

A Residential area

Fig. 19 Sweden: Skärholmen. Distribution of buildings and details of the centre.

In Stockholm the city itself owns the land and is in charge of all planning. A planning department with a staff of a hundred first draws up master plans and the authorities then distribute the actual work of construction among different firms, mainly municipal or co-operative. These firms next draw up blueprints, in close co-operation with the city's planning services, who often leave them only small scope for initiative, mainly concerned with the architecture of the buildings rather than their general layout: their role, in fact, is limited to the practical application of the plans.

These plans, often empirical in nature, have one common characteristic: they all pay great attention to zoning, which, when rigidly applied to units as small as those of the Scandinavian new towns, produces an excess of uniformity throughout the different areas of the town. This makes for a certain visual monotony when not tempered, as in Tapiola, by the richness and variety of the

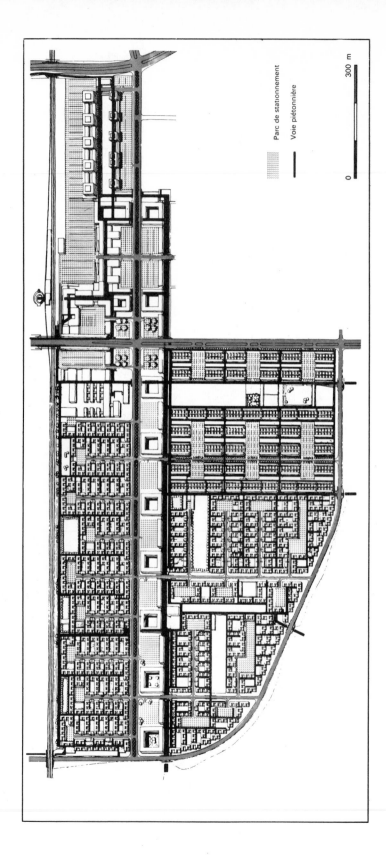

Parc de stationnement
Voie piétonnière

0   300 m

Fig. 20 Denmark: plan of Albertslund South.

Fig. 21 Finland : plan of Tapiola.

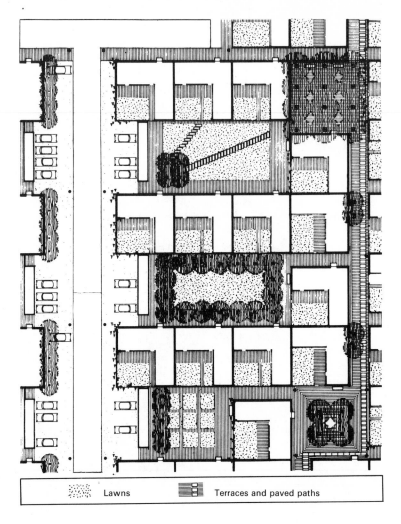

<table>
<tr><td>Lawns</td><td>Terraces and paved paths</td></tr>
</table>

Fig. 22 Denmark : Albertslund. Patio dwellings.

architecture and a combination of buildings of different heights. This criticism is especially valid in the case of Albertslund, where so far only two styles of individual house have been built. Less separation of residential zones of different densities would no doubt produce a happier effect.

In other respects, there seems to be no system of residential zoning similar to that of the new towns in Britain (see Chapter 1). The densities, the types of housing and the grouping and arrangement of the residential units are extremely variable. Albertslund was conceived in terms of the use of prefabricated housing units and consists of four different groups: two zones of bungalows with patios, one zone of terraced two-storey houses and one of three-storey flats. This makes for visual monotony and quite a high density of population (45 per hectare overall, 58 per hectare for the residential areas alone), despite the predominance (79 per cent) of individual housing (Fig. 22).

In Tapiola the population density is scarcely higher (65 per hectare for the town as a whole, 78 per hectare not counting the centre), despite the predominance (80 per cent) of collective housing. This makes for an impression of low density of building, which, together with the variety of types of building and the quality of the landscaping, produces a very happy result. The housing is grouped in three neighbourhood units, each grouped round a secondary commercial centre and an education centre.

Around Stockholm the new areas are planned in conjunction with the underground railway system, which implies fairly high densities and a high proportion (85 per cent) of flats, so that other transport can be dispensed with. Densities vary from 40 to 100 people per hectare (50 to 120 in the housing zones alone). The units of 15 000 inhabitants around 1950 (20 000 or 25 000 after 1960) are themselves divided according to topography and the transport system into groups of about 1000 dwellings with a number of shops, a primary school and a day nursery.

But the chief energies of planners in the secondary new towns have been concentrated on the centres. These 'towns' were never intended to be self-sufficient, so that their centres exist only for consumer goods and services. As a result, their size is reduced, at any rate around Stockholm: 6·8 ha in Vällingby (serving a population of 60 000 directly and of 150 000 indirectly), 8 ha in Farsta, which plays a similar role, and 16 ha in Skärholmen (Fig. 23), serving a population of 250 000. The solely commercial centres of the neighbourhood units occupy only 1-2 ha. On the other hand, the centres of Albertslund (26 ha) and of Tapiola (30 ha) are much larger, although their zones of influence are more limited. These areas, however, include lakes and other recreational areas, cinemas and cultural centres, swimming pools, office buildings and places of higher learning.

Since the planners were not primarily concerned with the creation of employment, business activities play a small part except in the centre itself. The industrial zones are separated from the housing zones by roads or railways (as at Johannelund near Vällingby) or by woodland, sometimes planted as at Albertslund. They need good transport services (Johannelund having its own underground railway station). Blocks of offices are rare and are mostly to be found in the main centres (Vällingby, Farsta, Skärholmen, Tapiola). An exception to

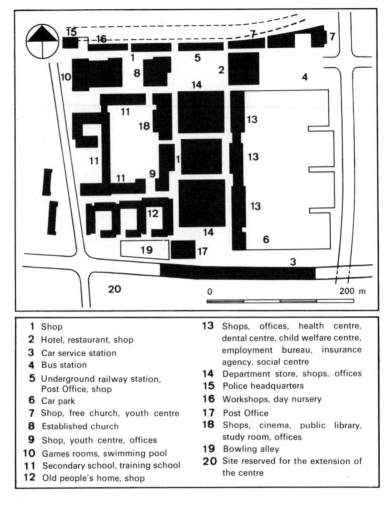

1 Shop
2 Hotel, restaurant, shop
3 Car service station
4 Bus station
5 Underground railway station, Post Office, shop
6 Car park
7 Shop, free church, youth centre
8 Established church
9 Shop, youth centre, offices
10 Games rooms, swimming pool
11 Secondary school, training school
12 Old people's home, shop
13 Shops, offices, health centre, dental centre, child welfare centre, employment bureau, insurance agency, social centre
14 Department store, shops, offices
15 Police headquarters
16 Workshops, day nursery
17 Post Office
18 Shops, cinema, public library, study room, offices
19 Bowling alley
20 Site reserved for the extension of the centre

Fig. 23 Sweden: Skärholmen. Town centre.

this is Råcksta, near Vällingby, which has three office blocks next to the railway station.

Nothing very new has been achieved in the field of traffic systems. Motor and pedestrian routes have been separated where possible and without undue expense and pedestrian ways lead to schools and shopping centres.

The building of the Scandinavian new towns

When the new towns were built around the Scandinavian capitals, special attention was paid to the main centres. To ensure the control and unity of the plan and its composition, general and detailed plans were entrusted to the same

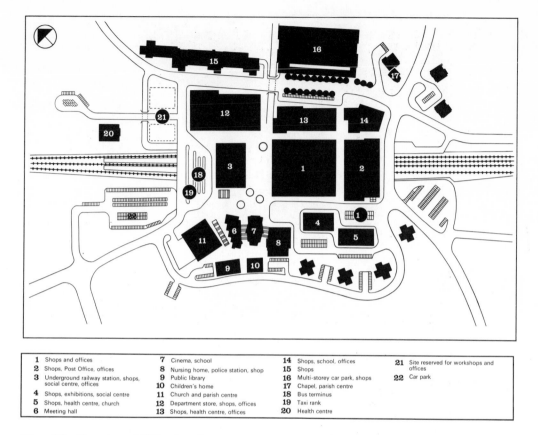

1	Shops and offices	7	Cinema, school	14	Shops, school, offices	21	Site reserved for workshops and
2	Shops, Post Office, offices	8	Nursing home, police station, shop	15	Shops		offices
3	Underground railway station, shops, social centre, offices	9	Public library	16	Multi-storey car park, shops	22	Car park
		10	Children's home	17	Chapel, parish centre		
4	Shops, exhibitions, social centre	11	Church and parish centre	18	Bus terminus		
5	Shops, health centre, church	12	Department store, shops, offices	19	Taxi rank		
6	Meeting hall	13	Shops, health centre, offices	20	Health centre		

Fig. 24   Sweden : Vällingby. Town centre.

firm of architects. As well as this, the actual work of construction was entrusted to a single firm, either a non-profit-making co-operative firm (Vällingby and Skärholmen were built by the Svenska Bostäder) or a private firm (Farsta Centrum was formed by six private firms to build the centre of Farsta). Sometimes the town itself is in charge: the centre of Albertslund was built by the commune of Hestederne and that of Tapiola by the Housing Foundation. The authority in charge retains the ownership of the new buildings in order to keep control of the development of the centre in finance and planning. Where the latter is concerned, the new Scandinavian centres have several characteristics in common: they are reserved for pedestrians, traffic routes being underground or on the perimeter. Some have an elongated pattern, with the buildings distributed so that the pedestrian ways continue the line of the roads, as in Vällingby (Fig. 24) and in the renovated centre of Stockholm, where the main pedestrian route, bordered by five skyscrapers, links two squares with different

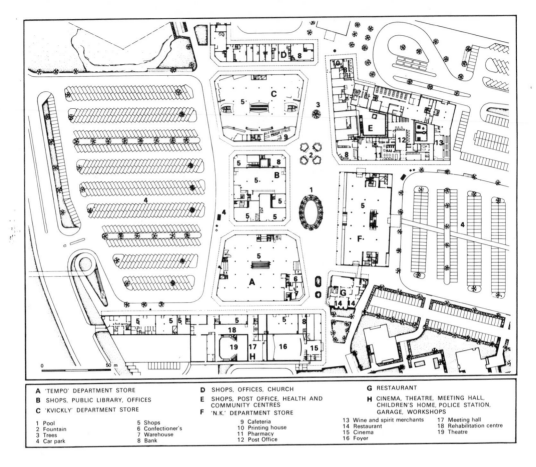

Fig. 25   Sweden: Farsta. Ground level plan of the centre.

characters and functions, 300 m apart, and in the restored centre of Copenhagen, where the famous Strøget pedestrian way links two squares 1200 m apart. Others are planned round a central square, as in Farsta, where its oval shape and the details of its layout give a pleasing impression of variety (Fig. 25), or round a lake, as in Tapiola (Fig. 26), while the centre of Albertslund includes all three: square, lake and straight avenues (Fig. 27).

Throughout the residential areas great care has been taken to create a pleasant and varied landscape, with natural beauties of rock, tree and water to decorate the outskirts of Stockholm or Tapiola. In an area devoid of natural beauties, such as Albertslund, an artificial landscape has been created by cutting a canal, planting woodland, building an artificial ski slope and so on. The buildings are also sited to make the most of the natural advantages of the locality, with

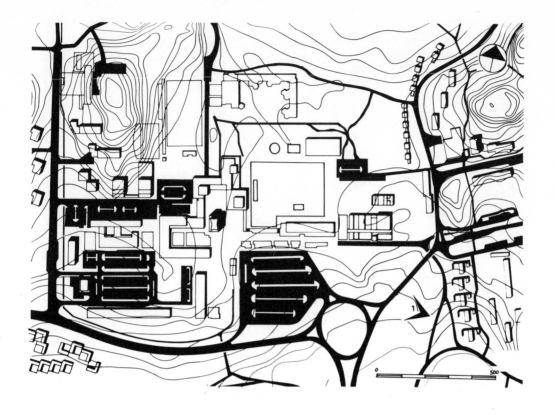

Fig. 26 Finland: Tapiola. Town centre.

tall buildings built on high ground, accentuating the existing relief and giving variety to the urban landscape. Individual houses are better sheltered from the winters in the valleys and the different types of building succeed one another according to the topography, as in Hässelby Strand. The arrangement of the buildings also allows for the most pleasant outlooks, as on to the lake shore at Hässelby Strand.

Albertslund is an exception in this respect, as the residential zones consist of prefabricated houses, which are extremely monotonous in appearance, superimposing a uniform pattern of housing on a naturally flat landscape. Its advantage lies in the combination of a fairly high density with a majority of individual houses, most of them with their own garden (in the case of the houses with a patio, this is completely enclosed), which provides their only 'country' outlook.

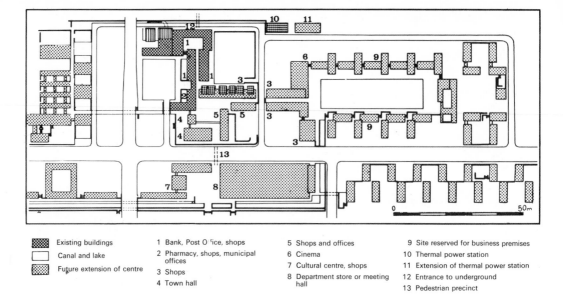

Fig. 27   Denmark : Albertslund. Town centre.

<table>
<tr><td>Existing buildings</td><td>1 Bank, Post Office, shops</td><td>5 Shops and offices</td><td>9 Site reserved for business premises</td></tr>
<tr><td>Canal and lake</td><td>2 Pharmacy, shops, municipal offices</td><td>6 Cinema</td><td>10 Thermal power station</td></tr>
<tr><td>Future extension of centre</td><td>3 Shops</td><td>7 Cultural centre, shops</td><td>11 Extension of thermal power station</td></tr>
<tr><td></td><td>4 Town hall</td><td>8 Department store or meeting hall</td><td>12 Entrance to underground</td></tr>
<tr><td></td><td></td><td></td><td>13 Pedestrian precinct</td></tr>
</table>

In most of the Scandinavian new towns, the size of the dwellings (see below) is of less importance than the quality of the construction. This is particularly true in Tapiola, where the different styles of building, with their varied arrangement and methods of construction, all combine in making a general pleasing impression formed by buildings of admirable and often exceptional quality, which do credit to the reputation of Finnish architecture. The tastefully exploited natural beauty of the site and its systematic preservation during the phase of construction form a background especially pleasing to inhabitant and visitor alike.

These natural advantages of woodland and water are also to be found in most of the new districts of Stockholm. But, with some notable exceptions, such as Hässelby Strand and Farsta Strand, which are built on a lake shore and obviously acted as test pieces for Swedish architecture, the quality of the actual constructions is unremarkable.

The mastery by Scandinavian architects of the art of composing masses and in the use of different materials for buildings and façades does not rule out research into methods of mass production. Whether concerned, as in Tapiola and the Swedish towns, with single elements such as doors, windows, heating systems and balconies, or with complete constructions, as in Albertslund, the Scandinavian new towns are in the vanguard of architectural research.

There is no escaping the fact, however, that Albertslund, with its individual prefabricated housing, of whichever type, does not give a very pleasing impression. One disadvantage of this type of construction is the need to build a long line of identical housing to make the best use of the machines used in their construction, the cost of which is reckoned to be slightly lower than that of housing of similar size and quality built by conventional methods. It is hoped that this cost will be further lowered as experience of prefabrication increases.

Modification of existing plans, especially for expansion, only becomes a problem in the town centres, because it is always an easy matter to build new residential units. The expansion of the centre may be necessitated by a change from the part assigned to it in the original project (as in Albertslund and perhaps later in Tapiola) or by the creation of new residential units dependent on it. Both in Albertslund and Tapiola large areas have been set aside for expansion, though not always well situated (the largest section of Albertslund will be separated from the centre by the railway), and these meanwhile remain unused, leaving a gap in the urban landscape. In the Stockholm region expansion of the centres is more difficult: by 1966 Vällingby had used up its last free spaces and could not develop further except by building above the railway or by demolishing neighbouring buildings.

Administration

The Scandinavian new towns, unlike their British counterparts (see Chapter 1), have no need of special legislation.

In Denmark, where a plan of nationwide zoning (1962) served as a framework for town planning, the different communities drew up master plans independent of a third party (in the built-up areas a development plan was drawn up by a special committee), outlining their main plans, which were then translated into detailed town plans opposable by a third party. These plans had to be approved by the government.

In Sweden the local authority is responsible for planning. A government representative attends the local council's debates and the government's approval must be obtained for the council's plans, but, at least where Stockholm is concerned, these amount to mere formalities. There is no legal obstacle to be overcome when a city like Stockholm wishes to create new towns in areas where suburban authorities are responsible for planning, so long as a friendly agreement can be reached.

In Finland the town council is responsible for drawing up master plans, which, after ministerial approval, become opposable by a third party. In the main urban areas groups of councils draw up regional plans. Where, as in many places, these plans do not exist, considerable initiative is left to the builders themselves.

In practice, systems of control vary from one country to another. In Sweden, the city of Stockholm acquired land, often several decades in advance, in its own region and in that of neighbouring authorities and is itself responsible for development. Albertslund is the responsibility of Hestederne, on whose territory it is situated, while Tapiola has grown up thanks to the initiative of a co-operative association, the Housing Foundation, and especially to that of its president, Heikki Van Hertzen.

There is no general rule for the controlling authority. In Albertslund, the town council of Hestederne retained this role for the development of the centre but rented housing land to non-profit-making building societies on a ninety-nine year lease, at a rent payable in full at the signing of the lease, for the construction of housing according to a master plan and detailed plans drawn up by planning consultants.

In Tapiola the Housing Foundation is in charge both of planning and of construction and has created the famous garden city on land belonging to a suburban rural community – Espoo – without help, financial or otherwise, from the state. As a result, they have had to sell about 90 per cent of the housing to make the most of the capital invested and to recover the costs of construction. The housing is run by residents' associations, who are shareholders in various public services (electricity, heating, hot water supply, open spaces, cleansing, drainage, roads, social and cultural facilities and so on). In this way the Housing Foundation gradually hands over the running of the town to its inhabitants and can concentrate its efforts on further building. Its planning department carries out some of the work of architecture and town planning and oversees the majority, which is subcontracted. Such is the prestige of Tapiola that most of the well-known Finnish architects (such as Aarne Ervi) have been bent on winning renown there, so that the garden city has become a world-famed architectural workshop.

A different system prevails in the Stockholm region. When the city develops its own territory it usually draws up the plans and designates other authorities to carry out the different parts of the plan (town centre, blocks of housing, industrial zone, etc.) and to work them out in detail. These authorities are usually non-profit-making co-operative municipal associations (such as Svenska Bostäder, Familjebostäder, Stockholmshem), sometimes a private association (such as Farsta Centrum) and sometimes a private association financially controlled by the city (such as Hyreshusi Stockholm). These may build amenities that are usually the responsibility of the state or the local authority, subsequently selling or renting them to the authority normally responsible for them (usually the town council), which then runs them with the assistance of local specialist societies: this is so with the majority of cultural and medico-social units. Schools, on the other hand, are built directly by the local authority concerned and infrastructures of transport by the town (in the case of roads) or by a local society (in the case of the rail system).

Housing is allotted through a system of waiting lists, often with a wait of several years, without any link between the allocation of housing and the place of employment, unlike the system in Britain's new towns. In Albertslund the local authority is responsible in principle for the choice of tenants, but in practice, being so limited in size, it leaves this task to the co-operative building societies. Stockholm has a waiting list and in 1966 families with three children had an average wait of six years and those with only one child a wait of eight years. In Tapiola, potential tenants have to rely on announcements in the press and are chosen by a special committee, on social grounds.

Relationships between the organizers of the new towns and the local authorities vary considerably, therefore, from one country to another. No problem arises in Albertslund, because the local authority, Hestederne, is itself in charge, acquiring land, preparing it and handing it over to construction companies. It builds schools, sports grounds and social and cultural facilities with financial aid from the state, or puts their construction into the hands of building societies and then assumes responsibility for running them, with the aid of local rates. In Tapiola no problem arises either, but for different reasons: the garden city is sited on the territory of a rural authority (Espoo) whose headquarters are some distance away. The Housing Foundation has taken charge of the work of infrastructure, which would normally be the responsibility of the local authority, the limited resources of the latter entailing greater expense but also giving more freedom of action to the new town itself. The cost of preparing the land is reckoned at 7 per cent of the total cost of construction. The amenities have been financed as usual by the local authority: an indoor swimming pool costing £250 000, a medical centre, primary schools, libraries and children's home. Other amenities, such as youth clubs and churches, have been financed by private societies or groups and a sports centre by the state. The total cost of the buildings equals £400 per person from the local authority and about £100 from the Housing Foundation.

Espoo itself levies local rates at a high level (12 per cent of total income) and retains a purely administrative function, despite the distance involved, for the time being, until an administrative reform is instituted.

Stockholm, which is both city and county authority, is in charge of plans, rents land to builders on a sixty-year lease, remains responsible for social and cultural facilities, exercises administrative powers and levies local rates. When, as is becoming more and more common, the city has to develop land belonging to another authority, it draws up plans, which then have to be approved by the authority concerned, who is officially responsible for them. The two usually form a joint association, such as the Salem-Stockholm Housing Construction Company, formed for the building of housing on land in Salem owned by the city of Stockholm (the Söderby area) and administered by the local building society, Svenska Bostäder. In practice, the administrative problems arising from Stockholm's expansion beyond its own administrative boundaries will only be solved by the proposed formation of a new regional authority.

So far, things have gone smoothly, either because the local authority is in charge of development (Albertslund, Stockholm) or because the infrastructures were dealt with by the constructing body (Tapiola).

Finance

The question of finance, of primary concern to the creators of a new town, has not presented very great difficulties in the Scandinavian countries. The far-seeing financial policy carried out by the city of Stockholm since the beginning of the century enabled it to establish new towns on land that it had acquired long before, either on its own territory or on that of neighbouring authorities. The city council decides the function of the land and after drawing up an outline plan rents the land to building societies on a sixty-year lease. Tapiola is a special case, as here the Housing Foundation acquired 270 ha of land in 1951 from a single owner for £20 million, or £6·50 per m².

Similarly, Albertslund is a special case in Denmark, as here the authority of Hestederne bought the land by agreement at varying prices, at an average of 25p per m². It prepared the land and then resold it to building societies at a price that allowed for the cost of infrastructures, usually carried out by the constructors, and of general facilities such as open spaces, but not for tasks usually carried out by the local authority, the average selling price amounting to £1·25 per m².

The financial problems have been solved by normal means, under the aegis of the new town authority, without recourse to special mechanisms, as in Great Britain.

In Albertslund the building societies take out long-term loans of thirty to sixty years from public credit companies, at a high rate of interest for public loans (more than 8 per cent with costs). In Tapiola the Housing Foundation has been faced with permanent problems of finance, first to raise the capital necessary for acquiring land and then for its development. It has had to have recourse to short-term loans, often at a high interest (7·5 per cent), before recovering the money by the sale of the prepared land to building societies. Access to public funds was only possible when the majority of housing intended for sale (70 per cent) came within the framework of the 'Arava' programme of social housing: about a third of the cost of these houses is covered by a long-term public loan (thirty-five years) at a low rate of interest (varying between 1 and 5 per cent according to the duration of the loan), another third by private loans over ten years at 7·5 per cent, and another third through private shares, which might be partly covered by equivalent loans. About 10 per cent of the houses are built within the same Arava programme but intended for letting, public loans supplying 60 per cent of the cost of construction. The remaining 20 per cent of the housing has no access to public loans.

Commercial premises (shops and offices) are usually built by the Housing Foundation and then sold to their owners, who have no access to public funds for this purchase. Present costs are as follows: offices – about £90 per m²; central shops – about £180 per m²; local shops – about £60 per m², including a share in the costs of general fittings.

In the new areas of Stockholm, on the other hand, renting is the norm. The building societies themselves have to raise the necessary capital: the centre of Vällingby cost the Svenska Bostäder 40 million kroner (£3 250 000) and almost as much again for its later extension in 1966. The building societies have to raise capital through public loans, at about 4 per cent, and private loans at about 7 per cent. Where private houses or commercial premises are sold, the loans are transferred to the buyers. The government fixes a ceiling price for housing (at present £55 per m²), lends 30 per cent of this sum at 4 per cent for thirty years and can grant an interest rebate to bring complementary private loans to the same rate, these commencing at 7 per cent and lasting thirty years. This system of interest rebate is now being dispensed with but has to be replaced by a system of perequation of rents to avoid a resultant sharp rise in rents. For building other than housing there are no public loans and the building societies have to use their own capital. Public loans are occasionally available, however, for shops in the main centres, and the city of Stockholm also guarantees loans contracted by private building societies. Factories are usually built by the firms themselves, but building societies may build standard factories for renting, as the Svenska Bostäder has done at Botkyrka.

The lack of a special system of finance as advantageous as that instituted in Great Britain for the new towns (see Chapter 1) has led to fairly high costs for their occupants, whether they are tenants, as is usual in Stockholm or Albertslund, or buyers, as is most often the case in Tapiola.

In Albertslund, the building of private houses (either in terraces or with patios) in prefabricated sections has been economically successful, a house of 95 m² costing £2800. Services and other costs brings the price to £4400, but rents, calculated at 3 per cent, are about £34 a month, of which about a tenth is covered, for most households, by government aid.

Rents are slightly higher in Stockholm, their average rate in 1966 being 42p per m² per year in the new sectors. The cost of housing is in fact appreciably higher: £5800 for each of the 10 000 houses in the five-year plan undertaken by the main municipal building society, Svenska Bostäder, at an average of 80 m², or £70 per m². The average size rises constantly, from about 60 m² in 1950 to 70 m² in 1960 and 80 m² at the present time. Rents are fixed to cover the cost of loans (interest plus 9 per cent of redemptions per year), repairs, maintenance, administration and general expenses.

Commercial rents are higher: about £7·50 per m² per year on the average in the centre of Vällingby, varying in accordance with the position and type of premises and especially with different floors of the building (ground floor rents being more or less double that of higher floors and three times that of the basements), and also according to their usage, preferential rents being paid for some facilities such as assembly halls and cinemas and higher than average rents for banks. As a result, ground floor shop rents exceed £15 per m², rents for offices on higher floors vary from £9 to £11 per m² and those for basement stores only £4·50 to £6 per m². In the secondary centres, however, commercial rents barely exceed housing rents.

In Tapiola, on the contrary, 91 per cent of new housing is sold to its occupants, prices being about £70 per m². In practice this involves a deposit of about 25 per cent of the total price (except for luxury houses) and monthly payments at the level of rents (at present about £35 for a four-roomed flat of 80 m²).

These rents or monthly payments seem comparatively high, especially compared with those in the new towns in Britain (see Chapter 1), illustrating only too well the result of a lack of special financial planning for the new towns. They do, however, allow the body responsible to ensure the financial equilibrium of the operation (without profits when local authorities or non-profit-making societies are in charge, but also without a loss that the local authority would refuse to make good). In theory this overall system of finance could use the profits from some premises (especially shops, offices and factories) to cover the cost of major facilities for the town, but their small scale (see below) limits these possibilities, while housing rents only ensure a partial balance between actual housing costs and the facilities directly linked with them. Here again, a single authority can treat the question of finance as a whole.

Employment

Unlike the new towns in Britain, town planning schemes carried out in connection with the large cities of Scandinavia are not based on the need for a balance between employment and the working population. This fact, which can make the financial equilibrium of the operation difficult (whereas in Great Britain the provision of employment would cover the chief cost of the main facilities of the new town), accounts for the lack of exact and complete data on employment; though a number and variety of types of employment are considered desirable, nothing is actually done to attract them, so that only shops and services are really up to full strength.

Industrial employment is nearly always planned independently of housing construction. One industrial zone, Johannelund, in the new town of Vällingby, with its own underground railway station, has more than half of its 26 ha occupied and by 1966 provided 3000 jobs, which, however, were nothing like enough for a population of 60 000. Many of the workers also live outside Vällingby, which was almost completed before the factories were built. In Tapiola 522 jobs (a quarter of the proposed 2000) were provided by 1966, when the garden city was 80 per cent completed. Service industries only were planned in concert with housing, 15 ha, nearly all now in use, being set aside for them in the Vällingby area.

Office employment is not likely to help in restoring the balance, for there has been no encouragement for dispersal to aid its installation in the new towns. There are, however, some rare exceptions: in the Vällingby area, three large office blocks of 60 000 m^2, providing 2500 jobs, house the national Ministry of Power and there are several small firms at Råcksta, 1 km from the main centre and near an underground railway station. Other office premises, including those of the municipal building society Svenska Bostäder, which constructed them, are installed in the actual centre of Vällingby, providing about 3000 office jobs altogether. This equals the number of jobs in industry, which themselves are notoriously insufficient. In the Farsta area there are just over 2000 office jobs, including those of the national Telephone and Telegraph Company and of an insurance company, which chose this position to be convenient for its head office at Skanstull, on the outskirts of the old city (the 'city of stone'), on the same underground line. Tapiola houses architectural and town planning firms and hopes to attract dispersed government departments and the head offices of the Finnish branch of Esso, amounting to the still low total of 1000

Vällingby area, distribution of employment in local services

Type of employment	Number of jobs	Part-time jobs	Percentage of part-time jobs	Floor area (m²)	Floor area per job (m²)*	Ground area (m²)	Ground area per job (m²)
Shops	2619	782	29·9	95 803	43·0	79 912	35·8
Teaching	1040	358	34·4	83 542	92·1	269 328	313
Leisure activities	232	184	79·3	158 402	113·1	4 747 534	33 900
Child care	162	77	47·5	6 639	53·7	18 248	89
Social services	95	26	27·4	2 590	31·6		
Medical services	320	115	35·9	7 466	28·4	2 553	9·7
Funerary services	20	3	15·0	2 660	143·8	169 010	9 140
Police	50	0	0	1 507	27·9	347	6·4
Building maintenance	109	3	2·8	7 942	73·9	10 432	97
Communications	229	24	10·5	46 129	212·4	1 180 645	5 440
Domestic service	1360	725	53·3	0	0	0	0
Government service	413	33	8·0	44 349	111·8	176 915	447
Total	6653	2330	35·0	314 469	57·3	6 655 104	1000·3

*Part-time jobs count as a half.

Source: Gunner Åsvärn, *PM angående prognosstudier om servicestandarden*, 10 February 1966.

jobs. Albertslund contains the head office of a co-operative supply store, providing 500 jobs, and a college of advanced education.

Office employment is, of course, added to by services of a general (primary schools, postal services and transport) or central nature (health and hygiene, secondary education, etc.).

The centre of Vällingby contains a post office, two travel agencies, the railway station, newspaper offices, an employment agency, a medical centre, a dental service, a maternity hospital, a child clinic, a police station, a library with rooms for study, a youth centre, churches with their own youth clubs and offices, schools, a hotel, etc. Although there are no official figures, the brochure recently published for Vällingby refers to 7000 jobs in the central area, 2200 of them in the town centre proper. These totals must include jobs in the shopping centre. In Tapiola the actual services account for a little under 400 jobs, the schools for 200, banks and post offices about 100, local government a little over 300, municipal services and transport about 150 each, making a total of 1300-1400. This total, representing 60 per cent of all employment, is nevertheless fairly low when compared with the size of the working population – about 20 per cent. However, part of the proposed increase in employment proposed for Tapiola is concerned with services:

> The administrative centre.
> Social and cultural facilities (medical centre, sports centre, youth centres,
>   library, theatre, swimming pool, etc.).
> Special and secondary schools.
> Municipal services.

All these give a total of about 725 jobs, representing about 20 per cent of all expected employment.

A study of the pattern of employment in the new towns of Scandinavia, therefore, shows a serious deficit. This is not surprising in the case of office employment: it has already been noted in the new towns in Britain (see Chapter 1) and on the outskirts of most large cities. The low rate of industrial employment is more abnormal.

Town centres

In practice, the main economic activities, particularly the commercial activities, of the Scandinavian new towns are to be found in the centres. Although it is difficult to lay down general rules, there seem to be three stages officially recognized in Sweden:

New town centre, catering directly for the new town population of 60 000 and indirectly for a much larger area: Vällingby, Farsta, Högdalen, Skärholmen. The centre of Albertslund, if its population reaches the expected 40 000, will be of this type.

Local centres catering for 5000 to 20 000 inhabitants. The present centres of Albertslund and Tapiola belong to this category, though the latter includes the amenities of the first category centre, in the absence of one of this size.

Groups of a few shops in residential areas.

The centre of Albertslund, the first section of which was opened in October 1965 for a population of only 8000, contains a department store, a small supermarket, a baker, a shoe shop, a dyer, a pharmacy, a draper, a shop for baby clothes, a hairdresser, a photographer, a bookshop, a shop selling clocks, watches and optical instruments, a florist, a furniture shop and an ironmonger, amounting to fifteen different shops. Added to these at this first stage were a number of services – post office, banks, restaurant, dentist – and some leisure facilities – a bowling alley and library. By 1966 the second stage was completed, adding more shops (fishmonger, butcher, greengrocer, etc.) and another pharmacy. The third stage, planned for 1967, added more shops and offices and further extensions will be added if they prove necessary. Important sites have been reserved for these, in particular 1 ha for a large store or other shops, a cinema and a cultural centre. A further eight sites comprising 33 000 m^2 of floor space have also been reserved: the town intends to sell them to firms providing the maximum number of jobs, especially offices.

The centre of Vällingby was the first large new commercial centre to be built in Sweden. It seemed a hazardous undertaking at the time (around 1950) and for this reason it was a municipal society, Svenska Bostäder, that was entrusted with it. When it was opened on 14 November 1954 it contained forty shops and two large stores. In 1955 thirty new shops and various services and facilities were put into service. At this time, the commercial centre consisted of 24 000 m^2 of floor area, of which about half was sales area. Later on, special facilities were opened: in 1956 a meeting hall, a cinema, a medical centre and a church; in 1962 a hotel, temporarily in use since then as a nurses' home; in 1963 a large store and some shops and offices; in 1964 a large car park (for 600 cars), a service station and some shops; finally, on 1 April 1966, the final stage of the centre was reached, with the opening of twenty shops, some offices, some services (a bank, an insurance agency, assembly rooms and a ballet school). Altogether the sales area of its hundred shops has now reached 19 000 m^2, the total area being 37 000 m². That of the offices, services and various facilities in the centre amounts to about 33 000 m². These extensions of the centre have made use of land to the north reserved for this purpose, much of it being taken up by the car park, leaving only enough space for an office block, some services and workshops, already under construction. Any further extensions would mean building above the railway line or demolishing some of the large blocks of flats around the centre: this possibility has been considered. All the shops are on ground level, with unloading below ground, surface approaches being for pedestrians only except for the roads surrounding the centre.

It may be noted that the number of shops has not increased at the same rate as the sales area, each phase of extension having meant the enlargement of many stores by absorbing neighbouring premises in the newly constructed blocks.

The centre of Farsta is similar in size and position – south of the capital – to Vällingby. The neighbourhood unit in whose centre it is built, for which it caters primarily, has a population of about 25 000. Other customers come from the neighbouring units of Gubbängen, Hökarängen, Sköndal, Fagersjö and Farsta Strand, making a total of about 80 000. A further 200 000 may come by car journeys of less than a quarter of an hour. The town plan was drawn up in 1957, seven years later than that of Vällingby, and it was opened in 1960, with office blocks added in 1965. Unlike the centre of Vällingby, its construction was undertaken by private building firms encouraged by the success of Vällingby; an *ad hoc* company was formed, with the financial support of six others. The original sales area covered 21 000 m² and was subsequently extended to 28 000 m². Half this total is taken up by three large stores, and the other half by about sixty shops with accompanying storage space and offices taking up about 25 000 m², about half of it for the large stores. Various facilities, services and offices added 27 000 m² before the 1965 extension and there is also parking for 2000 cars.

There are other centres of this size, such as Högdalen, either at the planning stage or under construction. The Täby centre, which is to be built by a private company to the north-east of Stockholm, will cater for a primary population of 18 000 and a secondary population of 120 000. The planned sales area is 22 500 m² out of a total floor area of 33 000 m², with parking for 2500 cars. Situated between two railway lines, with two railway stations, it will consist of a huge main building (100 by 30 m) housing the two large stores and about forty shops. On the north-west will be a large semicircular office block twenty-two floors high, with services and social facilities bordering a long pedestrian way linking one of the stations with the two main stores, so that pedestrians and motor traffic is completely separated.

The Skärholmen centre, built by the municipal society Svenska Bostäder, will be the largest commercial centre of all the new towns around Stockholm. Apart from Skärholmen itself, it should cater for the places along the south-west axis (Sätra, Vårberg, Bredäng, Vårby, Solgården, Alby) and to some extent for the whole south-west section of the built-up area, or for some 300 000 people in all. Two large stores are planned, sixty-five shops and twenty-five services of various kinds (banks, post offices, workshops, etc.), giving a total 40 000 m^2 of sales area and as much again for other shop premises, not counting services and general facilities. Planned with a motorized population in mind, it will include a huge three-storey car park with room for 4000 cars. Built on a 16 ha site in a valley, near the motorway linking Stockholm to the continent of Europe, it allows for a total separation of traffic, with underground deliveries and pedestrian ways on ground level. Numerous facilities include an 180-room hotel, a secondary school and a technical college. Building began in 1964 and the centre was opened in 1968. In 1966 an extension of the underground railway was begun.

The commercial pattern of the Swedish new towns is completed by the centres in neighbourhood units, which play the part of secondary centres. That of Hässelby Strand, a neighbourhood unit built near Vällingby at the end of the underground railway and on the shores of Lake Mälar, has a population of 10 000 and an area of 1 ha. It contains about twenty shops with a sales area of 1980 m^2 out of a total floor area of 4000 m^2. It also contains a youth centre, a day nursery and a café, and a church is to be built in the centre. Motor traffic is barred. The secondary centre of Hässelby Gård (a nearby neighbourhood unit with a population of 15 000) is slightly larger, with twenty-five shops and about 3400 m^2 of sales area. The centre of Blackeberg, one of the earliest units with a population of 10 000, has thirty shops with a sales area of 2900 m^2. That of the Råcksta unit, near Vällingby, is smaller. The same pattern can be seen in the Farsta group, with units at Hökarängen, Gubbängen and Sköndal. Some more isolated centres, like Fruängen and Hagsätra, have about thirty shops.

There is not the same gradation of shopping centres in Tapiola, which is the only new town near Helsinki and whose population is still below 15 000. A main centre and three secondary centres – one in each neighbourhood unit – provide for shoppers. The main centre was entrusted to the well-known architect Aarne Ervi in 1954; it is built round a 1 ha lake made in a natural hollow and is separated from the neighbourhood units by green belts and barred to motor traffic. The main centre is distinguishable from the secondary centres by the quality of its architecture and also by its possession of numerous facilities – a high-level office block, a restaurant, church, swimming pool and administrative and cultural centres. The whole centre has a total floor area of 12 000 m². At present it contains about thirty-five shops grouped in a square round a pool, open on one side towards the lake but not on the same level. The secondary centres each have about twenty smaller shops with about 2000 m² of sales area each. There are only a very few scattered shops.

Plans for these shopping centres are usually preceded by market research. For Skärholmen, in fact, two surveys were carried out: one by the Stockholm Chamber of Commerce, with estimates of the population to be catered for, and the other by the building society Svenska Bostäder, with estimates of spending power. Next came frequentation studies (the results of those carried out for Vällingby, from a sample enquiry, were used in the market research for later centres).

The new towns of Scandinavia seem to have been modelled round their centres. These are far from being wholly commercial, however, with offices, services and other facilities bringing variety to their role and often occupying as much or more space than the shops themselves. These centres have been as great a success aesthetically – with people everywhere flocking to see Tapiola – as economically, the success of Vällingby, Farsta and the other centres being reflected in the number of their present activities.

But the importance of the centres and particularly of the main ones cannot disguise their weaknesses, especially their lack of industry and offices. Although the Scandinavian new towns have never attempted an automatic link between housing and place of work, they did hope to achieve the best possible balance between employment and the resident working population – a hope that has not been realized in the new towns so far created.

Though it may be too soon to judge the situation with regard to Albertslund, a balance is far from being attained in Tapiola, with 3000 jobs for a population of 15 000. Even with future improvement, it is doubtful whether the number of commuters (at present about 5000) will be much altered.

In Sweden it is more difficult to judge the situation because of the absence of a single organizing body. In Vällingby, however, a census showed 9000 jobs in 1960 and 13 000 in 1966, with a population rising to about 60 000, with over 25 000 of working age, giving about one job to every two workers. Added to this, a third of the jobs in the Vällingby area are occupied by workers from outside, so that two-thirds of the working population have jobs outside their own area. This would also seem to be the pattern in the other Swedish new towns.

Population structure

Like all newly created centres of population, the Scandinavian new towns have an unbalanced population structure. The populations are youthful: in the Vällingby area, in 1964, 40 per cent of the population was under 21 (compared with 15 per cent in the centre of Stockholm), 38 per cent aged 21-45 (compared with 28 per cent in the centre of Stockholm) and only 18 per cent aged 45-65 and 4 per cent over 65 (compared with 22 per cent in the centre of Stockholm). But this structure changes rapidly, for ten years earlier (in 1954) Vällingby had 58 per cent of its population in the age group 21-45. The length of the waiting list for housing in the new towns (seven to eight years in Albertslund) tends to counteract the very youthful structure of the population.

Mobility of the population is fairly high: about 10 per cent in Vällingby, including internal moves, but much less in Tapiola with its majority of owner-occupiers who benefit from a standard of living unequalled throughout Finland.

The average size of dwellings – and of households – tends to increase, as we have seen in the Stockholm area (see section on Finance above). The number of people per dwelling is nevertheless fairly low: 3·13 on the average in 1964 in the 13 000 dwellings built in the Stockholm area by Svenska Bostäder. This fact is linked to the low birth rate in Sweden, where 48·6 per cent of all families are childless and only 2·2 per cent have four or more children. Although there are no exact figures, it seems that the type of dwelling and size of rents in the Scandinavian new towns attracts the middle or upper middle classes (the average income in the Vällingby area being higher than the Stockholm average).

Commuting and transport

The insuffiency of jobs (see section on Employment above) makes commuting a necessity, so that in the Vällingby area in 1960, of the 25 000 workers only 5000 worked in the district (with its total of 9000 jobs), or 20 per cent, half (12 000) working in the centre of Stockholm and 30 per cent elsewhere. Local jobs had risen to 13 000 by 1966, so that these differences were less but still considerable. Similarly in Tapiola, there are less than 3000 jobs among 7000 workers, with half the jobs occupied by workers from outside, so that four out of every five workers living in the garden city are commuters.

This makes it important to ensure good relations between the new town and its parent city. We have seen (Sections I and II above) that, with the exception of Tapiola, these new developments were part of regional planning in which public rail transport played an important part, so that their sites were chosen to fit in with the new rail systems and operations could even be slowed down

Construction of the Stockholm underground railway

Section	Date of opening	No. of intermediate stations	Date of opening of shopping centre
Farsta line (18 south)			
Slussen Hökarängen	1950	10	
Kungsgatan–Slussen	1957	3	
Hökarängen–Farsta	1958	1	Farsta, 1960
Farsta–Farsta Strand	1967	1	
Vällingby (11 north) and			
Hässelby Strand (18 north) lines			
Kungsgatan–Vällingby	1952	16	Vällingby, 1952
Vällingby–Hässelby Gård	1956	2	Hässelby Gård, 1955
Hässelby Gård–Hässelby Strand	1958	1	Hässelby Strand, 1958
Hägsätra line (19 south)			
Slussen–Stureby	1951	8	
Stureby–Högdalen	1954	2	Högdalen, 1959; Bandhagen, 1958
Högdalen–Rågsved	1959	1	Rågsved, 1959
Rågsved–Hagsätra	1960	1	Hägsätra, 1960
Fruängen line (14 west)			
T. Centralen–Fruängen	1964	11	Fruängen, 1964
Bagarmossen line (11 south)			
Skärmarbrunk–Hammarbyhöjden	1958	1	Bjäklagen, 1955
Hammarbyhöjden–Bagarmossen	1958	3	Kärrtorp, 1961
Sätra line (13 west)			
Liljeholmen–Örnsberg	1964	2	
Örnsberg–Sätra	1965	4	
Sätra–Skärholmen	1966	1	Skärholmen, 1968
Skärholmen–Vårberg	1967	1	
Östermalstorg line (13 and 14 east)			
T. Centralen–Östermalstorg	1965	1	
Östermalstorg–Ropsten	1967	3	

when new fast lines failed to be installed, as in the outskirts of Copenhagen. The building of Albertslund was not started until a good rail service was installed, with three trains an hour linking the new town to Copenhagen's central station in a twenty minute journey. The Stockholm underground railway, with six trains an hour during the day, provides all the new districts built round the railway stations with a journey of less than half an hour to the city centre. In 1966 the line was continued to Skärholmen before building of the new centre was started. Only Tapiola, relying on private enterprise, is limited to a bus service, which covers the 10 km separating it from the centre of Helsinki in about three-quarters of an hour.

On the local scale, internal transport services are secondary in type and are usually provided by branch lines or loop lines.

Even though public transport plays a predominant part, especially for commuters, that of the motor car has greatly increased and with it the need for increased parking space. In the Stockholm area, one parking place per household is allowed for, plus common parking for visitors at the rate of 0·2 to 0·5 spaces per household. In Albertslund space has been set aside for 1·5 parking spaces per household, though for reasons of economy not all of these have yet been constructed. In Tapiola the rate has increased from less than one parking space per household in the beginning to one for each flat and two for each house. Similarly, car parks in the centres have had to be enlarged (from 650 to 1250 places in Vällingby, with a probable necessary increase to 2500; from 1500 to 2000 at Farsta; from 800 to 1500 in Tapiola). 5000 places are planned for Skärholmen (originally 4000) and 2000 for Täby (originally 1500), or four and two-and-a-half times the sales area respectively (or roughly the norm in the USA).

Amenities and social life

Although they are essentially commercial by nature, the centres of the Scandinavian new towns possess many other amenities. Their creators have succeeded in their aim of affording the population a desirable number of amenities and it is notable that non-profit-making social and cultural amenities have found a place. Secondary schools have been opened at Vällingby and Skärholmen and colleges of advanced education at Albertslund and Tapiola. Medical and social centres, churches and libraries have sprung up in all the main centres. Swimming pools, sports centres and bowling alleys cater for non-cultural activities. Hotels are planned, but clients have been lacking (the hotel at Vällingby having had to be turned into a nurses' home). Essential cultural and social life has been provided by cinemas in all the main centres, theatres at Vällingby and Farsta, cultural centres like the one planned for Tapiola, youth clubs and meeting halls – a life all the more difficult to create where the population is youthful, often works outside the new town and has only lived there for a short time. Nevertheless, clubs and societies of many different kinds are on the increase (seventy at Vällingby and about thirty in Tapiola). The pleasant architecture of the meeting places and their central position assist the formation of these groups, though it would be an exaggeration to claim a very lively social life in the Scandinavian new towns: as elsewhere, the motor car and television are the enemies of social intercourse and its establishment can be no easy task.

Conclusion

Whether the developments in town planning connected with the large built-up areas of Scandinavia can be correctly termed new towns or not is debatable. Their small size, their position in direct contact with their parent cities, their low rate of employment and their lack of a genuine social life of their own make them more like new sectors, differing as much from the new towns of Great Britain, planned on the principle of autonomy (see Chapter 1) as from the new towns planned for the Paris region on a much larger scale (see Chapter 4). They are closer in type to possible developments round the large cities of the French provinces and may here serve as useful examples.

The administrative situation in Sweden in particular should afford an example to be copied and it seems that on the whole, as in Great Britain, a single authority for planning and construction produces happy results. On the other hand, the lack of special financial planning leads to comparatively high rents, with a resultant narrowing of social classes. The low rate of employment shows one of the weaknesses of such small-scale developments: as we have seen, present plans in Scandinavia are altogether larger, in terms of populations of 100 000 – 300 000 (see Sections I and II above).

However, the main lesson to be learnt from the new districts of Stockholm and the garden city of Tapiola is that their chief success lies in the quality of their architecture and landscaping, at a relatively low cost.

3 : New Towns and land use in the Netherlands

Introduction

The Netherlands are an interesting example of land improvement and town planning in several respects. For one thing, the shortage of space in a country that, to quote M. Pierre George, is the only one to be literally overpopulated[1] makes an overall policy of land use essential. For another, the Netherlands afford a unique example of reclaiming land from the sea[2] and its use in many different ways after reclamation. Also, the built-up area of western Holland, Randstad Holland, is an equally unique example of ring development (which would otherwise have remained in the realm of theory), which poses difficult problems of expansion if the centre is to be maintained for agricultural or leisure interests.

The urban expansion of the large built-up areas (Amsterdam, The Hague and Rotterdam) has so far been carried out by the creation of new sectors added to the existing cities, with their own facilities but with a lack of employment, not unlike the new sectors of the Stockholm suburbs (see Chapter 2). At present the tendency is towards the creation of new towns, large in size by Dutch standards (with populations of 100 000) in the development areas (such as Lelystad, future capital of the polderlands) or along the axes of development of the large built-up areas of the Randstad but unconnected with the areas already urbanized. The quality of town planning in the Netherlands and the difficult conditions under which it is carried out make its study particularly valuable.

I The main principles of land use

The local authorities (consisting of twelve provinces and about a thousand towns) play an important part in the Netherlands. The central government controls the provincial governments, which in turn control the town councils.

---

[1] A population of 12·5 million, giving a density of 375 per km², four times that of France, with a rapid rate of increase due to a high birth rate (21·3 per cent) and an exceptionally low death rate (7·6 per cent).

[2] It has been said jokingly that God made the world, except for Holland, which the Dutch made themselves. Certainly, if the dikes were to be breached, more than half the nation's territory would be flooded.

Responsibility for land use and town planning is shared between these three: the government, by reports on land use, decides the general scheme, followed by provincial plans (which have to have government approval) and local plans, opposable by a third party, which must be approved by the province. State influence is further exercised through Treasury grants and the provision of services.

Two successive reports, made by the government Department of Land Use and published in 1960 and 1966, show the outlines of the advocated policy. Accompanying the second report was a map on the scale 1:500 000 suggesting possible land use and distinguishing four types of housing, industrial and dock areas and five types of park and leisure area. In addition, it gave a road and rail plan.

The general proposals were in line with the policy of the Ministry of Economic Affairs, which in 1958, in agreement with the government Council for Land Development, inaugurated special development areas where priority would be given to employment. These development areas would comprise the northern provinces of Friesland, Drenthe and Groningen, Zeeland in the south-west, some eastern sectors (in Overijssel), some southern sectors (North Brabant, the north of Limburg and the area round Eindhoven) and some western sectors (the extreme north of North Holland).

Theories and basic decisions

The first theory is that of population growth, with an expected two-thirds increase before the end of the century (from 12·5 million in 1967 to 20 million). To this has to be added the theory of regional growth. Present population movements entail a huge movement away from the north, the east and the south-west and a concentration in the west (particularly in the Randstad Holland). Shortage of space in the west and the wish to create employment in the development areas led to a proposal to reverse this tendency completely. While, according to present tendencies, more than half the population growth would take place in the west, the policy aims at reducing this proportion to about 40 per cent before 1980, according to the 1960 report, and even to about 20 per cent by 2000, according to the 1966 report. The population of the west would increase by only 25 per cent by the year 2000. Such a complete reversal of present tendencies indicates merely wishful thinking and is probably unrealistic. Population growth in the south would be slightly checked (with a 50 per cent increase by the end of the century) but that of the east and especially of the north and south-west would be greatly increased (by about 130 per cent by the end of the century). By this time, the polders would support a population of about 500 000. Details of this population policy tend to vary: for instance, the checking of growth in the west does not apply to North Holland.

A fundamental question concerns the way of life of the next generation. Experts in the Netherlands realize that caution is necessary here, because a study of the subject raises more questions than it can answer. One certainty is that the number of motor vehicles (at present 1·5 million, or less than one to every eight people) will be almost trebled (to about one to every three people, or nearly 7 million by the year 2000). A result of this will be a much greater general mobility and a greater opportunity to benefit from any existing social and cultural facilities. The 1966 report stated that one characteristic of the future way of life would be the demand for a wider choice of activities and concluded from this that, in the realm of planning, great importance must be given to the preservation, wherever possible, of the variety of natural and man-made qualities in the country and to the creation of a new and varied environment for living.

It can also be forseen that the future population will be largely urban and will require more space than at present, trebling the housing area (for a population increase of about 70 per cent). New types of urban housing will appear, but a variety of urban landscaping must be kept, with a majority of detached houses but without excessive use of space. Variety and the accent on detached houses are necessary in order to provide the population with a high level of public services, a choice of means of transport (private or public) and a pleasant environment. To achieve all this in the Randstad necessitates a dispersal of population into other parts of the country.

Resulting plans

These theories and general principles can be translated into various plans of action:

> The inevitable but as far as possible limited expansion of the Randstad Holland.
>
> The limitation of this expansion inland in particular directions north of Kennermerland, south of the polders, in the urban area of Gelderland and in the north of Zeeland.
>
> The preservation of an undeveloped area for agriculture and leisure activities in the centre of the Randstad.
>
> The creation of a second conurbation in North Brabant based on existing towns.

The extension of this conurbation towards the delta, where new harbour facilities would be built round the Scheldt basin.

Large-scale expansion of the urban areas of central and southern Limburg.

The development of a series of medium-sized towns in the north and east, especially in Twente and the central part of the province of Groningen.

The national master plan of 1966 was not in itself a plan of action but rather a general outline and a basis for further discussion, capable of alteration. Its authors stressed that, with a target as far ahead as the year 2000, it was impossible to make completely reliable forecasts, but that such a target was necessary in the planning of land use and for allowing the time required for studying, financing and completing tasks such as underground railways, afforestation and the rebuilding of town centres. The plan could also serve as a basis for a programme of investments in relation to regional planning.

As well as looking ahead, the master plan also suggested some necessary short-term measures:

The creation of a complex of urban centres in the north and in Overijssel (Groningen, Twente, Leeuwarden, Zwolle, Emmen, the dock area of Delfzijl-Eemshaven, Assen, Hoogeveen, Drachten, etc.).

New development at the tip of North Holland (especially Den Helder and Hoorn).

New development in the Scheldt basin to form a centre for new harbour development in Zeeland.

The development of Alkmaar and Purmerend in the urban area south-west of the Ijsselmeerpolder and of Lelystad (a new town in the polders) as overspill areas for the north of the Randstad.

The development of Zoetermeer, Hellevoetsluis, Dordrecht and Breda as overspill towns for the south of the Randstad, in connection with the replanned urban development round The Hague.

The acceleration of the programme of main road construction.

Apart from these immediate questions, the authors stress the particular problems of the Randstad (Fig. 28). The master plan shows the possibility of a successful development of the conurbation but the region of The Hague and Rotterdam has very little scope for expansion. However, the fact that The Hague, in its role of administrative capital, has undergone particularly vigorous expansion, as well as the creation of an almost completely new town at

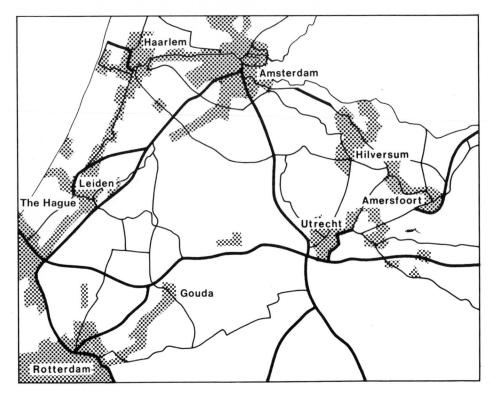

Fig. 28 The Randstad Holland.

Zoetermeer to the east of the city, shows that compromise with general principles has to be made. The report proposes immediate action (already embarked upon) in the siting of administration, research bodies and industry in particular, but also tertiary employment, though it is sometimes unrealistic in its suggestions. In area planning, the national programme provides for the outward expansion of the Randstad (into North Holland, Ijsselmeerpolder and Zeeland) in order to keep an ample rural area in the centre for agriculture and leisure activities. Also, the character of the historic city centres must be retained, requiring the preservation of non-built-up areas between the cities of the Randstad. It is obvious that careful co-ordination is needed between the plans for the Randstad and those for Zeeland and the polders.

The implementation of the policy

The 1966 report did not limit itself to outlining a policy of total planning but also dealt with the means of achieving it, first of all by two general measures. First, the success of a policy of national planning demands close co-operation between the various government departments responsible (housing, transport, public works and water supply, finance and economic affairs, industry, agriculture, social and cultural activities, etc.). This co-operation was ensured by the Government Planning Council. Secondly, this co-operation demands the active participation of the people of the country, expecially the local authorities and the representatives of the country's economic and social forces. The creation of a consultative Planning Council has gone part of the way towards achieving this, but there is still a need for a nationwide sense of purpose and for research in economic and social fields and the training of experts in these fields to carry out the schemes.

Then there are the financial and administrative measures necessary to implement the policy, which could not be achieved without considerable expense. During the last decade, costs of services (state education, transport, public works, water supply, housing, etc.) have played an increasing part in the national budget. Forecasts and comparisons with other countries (the USA, Great Britain and France) make it likely that this tendency will continue and be extended to other fields (provisions for outdoor leisure activities, urban rebuilding and the battle against atmospheric and water pollution). All these expenses will increase faster than the national income, so that new methods of finance will be necessary. Some of the facilities (roads, town parking, urban rebuilding, water supply and leisure areas) will largely be paid for by their users, but this cannot cover all costs and it will be necessary to resort to loans if the savings to firms and individuals from these facilities increase faster than investments – or, otherwise, to taxation.

On the administrative level, while not altering the existing three-tier administrative system of state, province and town, it is possible to adapt it to the needs of national planning without having recourse to a special law or to the creation of a fourth tier. The co-operation of the towns has to be sought both for particular undertakings, such as the water supply, and for general undertakings, two in particular. One is the case of small country areas facing problems that are too big for them (such as those areas in the rural zone in the centre of the Randstad that become responsible for leisure areas for the inhabitants of neighbouring towns) and the other is that of built-up areas formed from a number of towns (such as the Gooi region, The Hague, the North Sea Canal or the Limburg mining area). In this last instance, it seemed desirable to go beyond mere co-operation and provide for an inter-town council elected by universal suffrage. Provincial and municipal boundaries will sometimes need to be modified to accord with developments in town planning. The polder zone, contrary to earlier expectations, does not seem to require the creation of a new province, since the different polders all have links with existing neighbouring provinces: Wieringermeer with North Holland, the North East polder with Overijssel, etc. These two polders already have their own local councils. The Ijsselmeer polders (East Flevoland, South Flevoland and Markerwaard) are at present administered by a national council. The creation of new communities in the rural areas and a special council for the new town of Lelystad, eventually to become a new community, now need to be planned.

Administrative measures for reversing the present population movements between the regions must also be decided on, especially measures to attract industry to the development areas. But those responsible for national planning in the Netherlands, unlike their British or French counterparts, consider that the desired results can be obtained without undue government pressure and with the avoidance of government action, such as the need for official approval or development grants. Apart from financial encouragement, the measures to be taken are political and psychological, outlining the general development desired, including in the provincial and town plans concrete suggestions in line with this development and encouraging employment by the provision of services and by the dispersal of government jobs into the development areas.

These are the chief points in a policy of national planning, which also has close connections with other problems, such as the financial policy, housing policy and the policy of industrialization.

II Planning policy in Amsterdam: the new sectors

Amsterdam, nowadays one of the three main built-up areas of the Randstad Holland (the others being Rotterdam and The Hague), was a fortified town from the fifteenth century onwards. This gave it a unity and an individual character, respected by planners until the nineteenth century, when the abandonment of former road patterns and height and style of buildings led to the creation of ugly, crowded sectors outside the old city. Thanks to regulations in the Housing Act of 1901 and to the Berlage plan for the south of the city (1917), Amsterdam was restored to its tradition of high quality development.

The 1935 plan

In 1928 a plan for town expansion was started, under the auspices of the new department for development and town extension in the Ministry of Works; it was published in 1935[1] and became law in 1939. This plan, like others through-

[1]*Grondslagen voor de Stedebouwkundige ont wikkeling van Amsterdam algemeinen vitbreidingsplan* (Amsterdam, 1935).

out Europe at that time, provided for a moderate increase in population (to 960 000 by the end of the century) and proposed new planned sectors to the west and south, together with the creation of parks (especially Amsterdam Woods, which were planted before the war to give work to the unemployed), squares and sports grounds, the enlarging of the docks and the industrial areas, the cutting of new canals, tunnels, railway lines and motorways. After inevitable delays, these plans were carried out after the war, the 1935 plan transforming an overcrowded city (with 0·8 m² of open public spaces per person in 1850 and 2·2 m² in 1930) into a spacious built-up area, with 28 m² of open spaces per person by 1965. The 1935 plan had to undergo many revisions, subject to regulations, and plans for the northern sectors were included in a revision published in 1955.

The 1962 plan

But the need to revise the 1935 plan had more general causes:

> An underestimate of the population increase in the built-up area (despite the stability or even slight decrease of the population of the city proper), the post-war rise in birth rate and increased movement into the Randstad not having been expected.
>
> The need to lower the population density of the nineteenth-century ring of development as well as that of the old city.
>
> The drop in the average number of people per dwelling, due to the ageing population.
>
> The rise in the general needs of space per person, as much in floor area as in ground area (general facilities, green spaces, etc.).

Also, planning questions can no longer be confined to the city of Amsterdam or even to the whole built-up area, but must be extended to the urban areas of North Holland and even the whole of the Randstad. The polderization of the Zuider Zee has also hastened this process.

It therefore became necessary to draw up another plan in co-operation with neighbouring areas that might house future citizens of Amsterdam. The preparation of this regional plan was begun in 1958 and was concerned not only with Amsterdam itself but also with Dorn, Amstelveen, Ouder Amster, Weesp and Amsterdam Bijlmermeer (a new community between Weesperkarspel and Weesp, administered for twelve years by the city of Amsterdam, which will probably absorb it in the future).

This plan, prepared by the city of Amsterdam, in co-operation with the town planners of its adjoining communities under the auspices of the provincial authorities, was completed in 1962 and approved by the province, the government and the local councils concerned, but did not have the force of law. It was seen as susceptible to continual revision. Its main aim was to plan possible developments of Amsterdam to the south-east (the west and south being already developed, the south-west occupied by the Amsterdam Woods, the north – the left bank of the Amstel – in process of development laid down in the 1955 plan). So the southern community of Amstelveen, a dormitory suburb whose inhabitants work in the centre of Amsterdam or at Schipol international airport, is due for major expansion. Neighbouring towns and the city of Amsterdam are working out detailed plans (that of Amstelveen itself having been published already) based on the master plan of 1962. Plans for rebuilding the older quarters are also being prepared.

In essence, the plan proposes:[1]

> The residential development of north Amsterdam (100 000 population).
> The creation of a new residential sector, with factories and offices, to the south-east (100 000 - 120 000 population).
> The expansion of the southern town of Nieuweramstel for a population of 100 000.
> The rebuilding of the historic centre without altering its character.
> The creation of secondary centres of employment in the new sectors on axes of fast and varied transport systems (factories, offices and shops), 200 ha having been reserved for the provision of 100 000 - 150 000 jobs altogether, the original centre remaining the main centre of employment, with almost 200 000 jobs. New zones of heavy industry are planned beside the North Sea Canal and the dispersal of textile industries is encouraged (Fig. 29).

The 1962 plan also provides for a city railway especially catering for commuters, underground in the centre and on a viaduct to serve the new south-east extension. This railway is planned on the Swedish pattern (see Chapter 2): that is, the shopping centres will be built near the stations, the height of the blocks of flats will decrease with their distance from the station in each sector, the distance between houses and station will only rarely exceed 500 m (or up to 800 m for detached houses), so that it can easily be covered on foot. Green spaces will be preserved between the residential units, which will be free from motor traffic; car parks will be beside a separate road network, at a maximum

[1]City of Amsterdam Department of Public Works, *Urban Development and Area Planning in Amsterdam* (Amsterdam, May 1967).

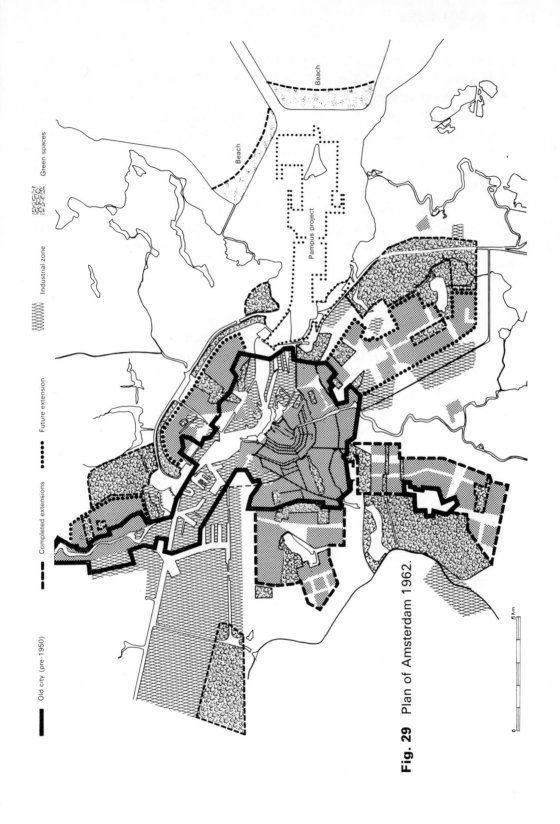

Old city (pre-1950)   Completed extensions   Future extension   Industrial zone   Green spaces

Beach

Beach

Pampus project

5 km

0

Fig. 29 Plan of Amsterdam 1962.

of 250 m from the housing blocks, which will be reached on foot or by bicycle. Dates of construction are from 1965 to 1980, work having already begun.

It is expected that after 1980 the urban area of Amsterdam will have reached the edge of the Randstad, that is, towards North Holland and the Zuider Zee polders, with the creation of new towns with populations of 100 000 or 150 000 (Purmerend, Volendam, Edam, Ijdrecht). Also, the great success of the Amsterdam Woods, despite problems of terracing and planting, has led to schemes for three similar city parks, making a total of four parks at intervals round the city (the present one to the south-west and others to the south-east, north-east and north-west). As well as this, the demolition of the walls will leave a strip of green between the old city and the partly rebuilt nineteenth-century sectors.

This plan for the whole built-up area has been drawn up in co-operation with the province of North Holland, which has itself drawn up various plans and studies concerned with the province as a whole or in part.[1] A provincial Planning Department has proposed the creation of large industrial zones along-side the North Sea Canal, the umbilical cord linking Amsterdam with the sea, an extension of the city to the north-east (towards the new towns of Ijdrecht and Lelystad in the polders), to the north-west (towards Womerveer and Alkmaar) and to the north (the creation of towns with populations of 100 000 - 200 000 based on small towns with populations of 10 000 - 20 000). A radial pattern with interrupted development along the radii has been preferred to a concentric pattern or to a radial pattern with continuous development along the radii, the chosen pattern being thought to give the best means of preserving green spaces between the built-up areas.

New sectors

The 1935 plan proposed the creation of a residential area to the west of Amsterdam, to be built round an artificial lake used for recreation and to be divided into neighbourhood units with populations of 30 000 - 50 000. The area would be self-supporting, except for regional services, for which it would still rely on Amsterdam, and would be linked to an industrial zone planned for the south-west of the city. This residential area would also contain extensive sports grounds and some horticultural land. Its creation was decided on in 1948, when planning began, and work on it began in 1951. The first housing blocks were completed by the end of 1952 and by now about 40 000 dwellings are

[1]North Holland Provinciale Planologische Dienst, *Drie Miljonen Noord Hollanders* (Haarlem, SI, 1967).

Fig. 30   Amsterdam West.

completed as planned and are occupied by about 135 000 people (Fig. 30).

The 1935 plan also proposed an extension of Amsterdam to the south, separated from the western development by the industrial zone, the 900 ha of Amsterdam Woods and Schipol international airport. The Buitenveldert sector, resulting from this project, contains over 8000 dwellings and a population of about 30 000. Building began in April 1958 (after the start of planning in 1955) and the first housing was finished in 1959. Added to it are the new sectors of Amstelveen immediately to the south, with a population of 18 000 in 1945, 60 000 in 1967 and 100 000 expected before 1980.

To the north, in accord with the 1955 plan, preparations were begun in 1956 for a new sector (Nieuwendam-Noord) of about 5000 dwellings and 20 000 inhabitants. Building began in August 1962, the first housing being completed in 1963. Two other new sectors are either planned or under construction and the total population of this northern extension will reach about 50 000, with almost 15 000 dwellings.

Finally, in accord with the 1962 plan, which also proposed the development of supplementary sectors to the north, the city development now and up to 1980 is concentrated in the south-east with the development of the community of Nieuweramstel and the creation of a large residential zone of 900 ha able to house a population of about 114 000. In addition, there will be a 250 ha industrial zone, 200 ha for main services and 450 ha of green spaces and sports grounds serving both the new residential area and the present town, which is lacking in these facilities. Preparation of the land began some years ago and the first housing was being built by the end of 1966 and occupied by 1968 (Fig. 31).

There are considerable differences in the composition of these various sectors. For one thing, the proportion of individual housing is very variable: more than 30 per cent in about 1955 in the earliest western sectors (Slotermeer, Geuzenveld and Slotervaart); only 20 per cent at Osdorp and even less at Overtoomseveld and Westlandgracht, built about 1960; barely 15 per cent in the south of Buitenveldert (1960 - 7) and 10 per cent at Nieuwendam-Noord (about 1965). A similar proportion is planned for the south-east, while the new sectors of the outermost communities (Amstelveen in particular) contain a far higher proportion of individual housing.

Inversely, the proportion of high-level housing blocks of five storeys and over is barely 10 per cent at Slotermeer and Hotewaart, 20 per cent at Osdorp and Overtoomseveld, 10 - 15 per cent in south Buitenveldert and Nieuwendam and probably higher still in Amsterdam itself.

The composition of these new sectors has also changed. From 1945 until recently their populations were thought of in terms of tens of thousands (in practice, 5000 - 40 000) with the sectors separated by main transport systems and broken up into units by secondary transport systems, almost rectilinear in pattern. Buildings of varying heights, high- and low-level blocks of flats and individual houses had their part in a definite plan: for instance, the Sloterpass, the lake in the centre of the western sector, is surrounded by high buildings to reinforce its central character. Each sector, and even each smaller unit, has a

Residential area	Green space	Industrial zone	Railway, railway station	Main road	Canals
Urban centre	Tertiary employment zone	Boundary of sports and leisure area	Underground, underground station	Secondary road	

Fig. 31 Amsterdam South-East (under construction).

day nursery and nursery and primary schools. Other amenities – junior schools, training colleges, social centres, indoor swimming pools, local offices, etc. – are to be found in the main sectors, while the three main churches of the Netherlands – Lutheran, Calvinist and Roman Catholic – are scattered more irregularly, as are the service industries. Whatever the buildings may be, the planting of green spaces, provision of recreation areas and the tree-lined roads achieve pleasant surroundings, which justify their appellation of garden cities by the Dutch authorities, although they have been built on very different plans and principles from those of Ebenezer Howard.[1]

The new sector of Nieuwendam-Noord is built on the same principles but in a style at once more regular and more monotonous, with a predominance of low-level blocks of flats and with individual houses, detached or terraced, on the outer edges. In the Buitenveldert sector, to the south, the layout is equally regular, with high-level flats lining the central main thoroughfare and individual houses grouped on the south side (in the direction of Amstelveen) and on the west (in the direction of Amsterdam Woods, with sports grounds, schools and free university ensuring an easy transition from the pre-war sectors to the south of Amsterdam).

Densities are relatively high: 36 dwellings (housing about 120 people) per hectare for the new western sectors as a whole (varying in practice from 100 to 150 per hectare according to the number of public buildings in each sector); 41 dwellings (145 people) per hectare in Nieuwendam-Noord; but only 27 dwellings (85 people) per hectare in Buitenveldert to the south, not so much due to lower density in each unit as to the larger area taken up by regional amenities (sports grounds and the university). The expected density in the residential south-eastern sector is similar: about 110 000 people to 900 ha, or 120 - 125 people per hectare. But the composition of the sector is to be completely different. We have seen that these new sectors were to be built on the Swedish pattern around the stations of the planned city railway with the height of the buildings decreasing from the centre to the outer edge of the sector. Also, motor cars will be restricted to special roads leading to car parks, leaving extensive residential areas to pedestrians and cyclists. The arterial road network will have a spacing of about 800 m, with elevated carriageways and with pedestrian ways and cycle tracks underneath (though the reverse would have seemed better planning). Minor roads will practically disappear, because of the part played by the car parks. Two other systems – cycle tracks with a spacing

[1] Van Walraven (Albertus), 'La Revisione e l'attuazione del piano di Amsterdam', *Urbanistica*, No. 38, March 1963.

of about 60 m and pedestrian ways with a spacing of about 200 m – will be added to the road system.

The city railway, three lines of which will serve the south-east extension, will have stations at intervals of 700 - 1000 m. More than 80 per cent of the housing is planned within a radius of 500 m of the stations and individual houses from 500 to 800 m. These stations will have car parks, bus stops and cycle sheds. The shopping centres will be sited in the immediate vicinity of the stations, which will be surrounded by the tallest blocks of buildings. The bus system, offering an alternative service, will have a spacing of 800 m, the same as the arterial roads, so that no house will be more than 400 m from a bus stop. The bus and rail systems will connect with the main line stations. Green spaces will be preserved between the sectors and along the fast traffic routes. The siting and construction of the buildings are planned to give the maximum privacy within the dwellings while facilitating outside contacts. Sheltered walks will give access to flats, shopping centres, general amenities and car parks. There will be various types of green space:

> Lawns and play spaces between the blocks of flats and the private gardens of individual houses.
> Public gardens, not more than 800 m from any housing in the sector.
> Large central parks, sports grounds, lakes, etc.

The different-sized centres will not only be shopping centres but will include socio-cultural facilities, public services, offices, service industries and places of worship. Sited near the stations of the city railway, they will be well served by the railway, the bus service and the roads (with car parks). The schools will usually be near the centres and will be used in the evenings for social and educational activities. The principal centre of the south-east extension, situated at its geographical centre, will be served by the main line railway, the city railway and all the bus routes and will have huge car parks. It is destined to play the role of regional centre to a whole section of the built-up area of Amsterdam, rather as Skärholmen in relation to that of Stockholm.

As the plan for one section of this extension (that of Bijlmermeer) shows, there will be a great demand for very long buildings enclosing micro-sectors. Industrial methods of construction will also be largely in use, so that Amsterdam, while keeping the same outlines of development, is preparing a set of new sectors on modern lines.

Amsterdam's neighbouring communities find themselves confronted by similar problems. A characteristic example is that of Amstelveen, south of the capital and east of the Amsterdam Woods, with its new sectors in direct line with the southern extension of Buitenveldert. It has recently published a detailed plan, drawn up in conformity with the official regional plan. This town has a dynamic quality, one example of which is the regular publication of statistics on the state of the town and its population.

This exercise in town planning has achieved as varied a combination as possible of high-level flats (ten to sixteen storeys) and individual houses, with a small proportion of low-level flats (three storeys), and with ample green spaces in all the sectors, the greenery succeeding remarkably in enlarging the spaces between the buildings and softening their lines. 85 per cent of the housing is of very standardized construction, despite a number of architects and styles. Statues, canals and bridges of many varied types complete the charm of residential areas served since 1961 by a new shopping centre planned by three well-known private firms of architects. Its shops, offices, socio-cultural amenities and huge car parks make it a centre of attraction for all the southern suburbs of Amsterdam and for the city itself. So far, offices, cultural centre and a number of shops have not been completed.

III Town planning in Rotterdam: the new sectors

Rebuilding

Rotterdam, second city of the Netherlands but chief international port, has a longer commercial and industrial history than has Amsterdam. Damage from the bombardment of 14 May 1940 and the destruction of the port in September 1944 by German troops necessitated a huge task of rebuilding, which was not completed until about 1960. Complete replanning was needed, both for the use of available space and for the life of the city, whose resurrection is symbolized, both for its citizens and for the world, by the famous statue by the French sculptor Ossip Zadkine at Leuvenhaven, overlooking the Maas.

Many of the basic ideas behind this tremendous task cannot fail to interest us. For one thing, because of the total destruction of the centre and of one eastern section of the city, it was decided that the former boundaries would be dispensed with. About 250 ha of land in the centre and 628 ha on the outskirts were bought up *en bloc*. The former owners were indemnified by the right to other land of equivalent value at the time of the bombardment, with the obligation to build on this land, under pain of losing their right to it, to a value at least equal to the demolished buildings, repayable when building was completed. This system avoided financial speculation and at the same time gave freedom to rebuild to a new plan.

It was decided in the 1946 plan to exclude former industrial activities from the centre and to reserve it for administrative, cultural and commercial activities, while the land appropriated on the city's outskirts could be used for the construction of modern factories and new residential areas (10 000 dwellings were rebuilt in the centre in place of the 25 000 that had been destroyed). This marked the beginning of the policy for the new sectors.

As for the new centre itself, it presented an aspect at once lively and spacious: motor traffic was successfully routed and pedestrian ways developed, such as the famous and elegant Lijnbaan galleries opened in 1954, despite their proximity to the gloomy Coolsingel, a street lined by offices and administrative buildings of often massive proportions.

Regional planning

The city's Department of Town Planning and Construction (with a staff of over 300) is responsible for the preparation of town plans. In practice, there is no official plan but only a master plan, accepted by the city council, drawn up ten years ago and acting as a basis for operations. Next come detailed plans for each sector, especially for those on the edges of the built-up area. If the new sectors extend beyond the city limits, co-operation must be reached between the city and the local district council concerned. Rotterdam's Town Planning Department draws up plans that have to be approved by the local council and when the new sector is built a new district may be created (Hoogvliet having sprung from Rotterdam and Portugaal). The suburban district can also procure planning advice or refuse all new development, in which case the provincial authorities must decide between the wishes of the district and the needs of urban growth. A consultative body in the Rijnmond district, run by an elected council, was created in 1965 to study and co-ordinate questions of regional planning: this body may eventually have powers of decision.

At a higher level, as part of the national plan, the provincial plan provides for the extension of Rotterdam towards the edge of the Randstad, with new towns with populations of 70 000 - 80 000 in the south (Spijkenisse) and southwest (Hellevoetsluis) based on existing small towns, and also for the preservation of green spaces separating the built-up area from those of Delft and The Hague. As well as being the official plans, these have met with general approval (Fig. 32).

As in Amsterdam, this regional planning policy relies on a planned financial policy similar to that practised in Stockholm:[1] the purchase of agricultural

[1]P. Merlin with P. Guertin, 'Urbanisme à Copenhague, Stockholm, Helsinki', *Cahiers de l'IAURP*, vol. 9, October, 1967.

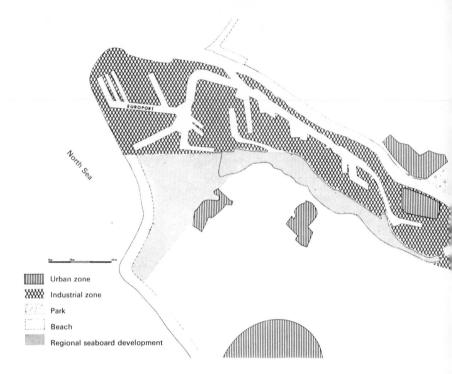

Fig. 32 The Rotterdam area : zoning pattern.

land, which is then prepared for building by the city. In Rotterdam, however, the land is resold and only rented for industrial buildings.

Transport policy rests in the improvement of communications across the Maas (bridges and tunnels) and the creation of a city rail network whose first section was opened in 1968, intended to serve the new southern and north-eastern sectors and later the new towns themselves.

The new sectors

Over the last twenty years the population of the city of Rotterdam increased by about 220 000 before becoming stabilized: the whole built-up area increased by more than twice that amount. Extension has therefore been essential and the city annexed a good deal of land over the years. Thanks to its own and the province's planning policy, development has been mainly concentrated on completely new sectors. At present, the new sectors of Hoogvliet in the south-west, Pendrecht in the south and Capelle in the north-east, and then the new towns of Spijkenisse and Hellevoetsluis, will be absorbing Rotterdam's overspill until at least 1980.

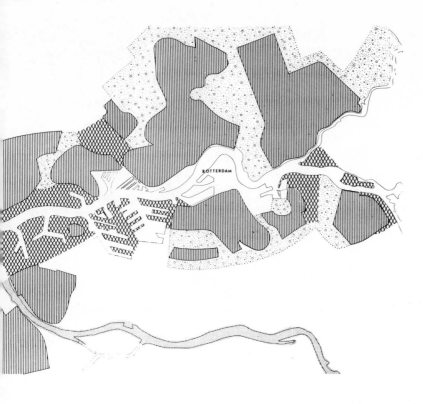

These sectors are planned as direct continuations of the built-up area, except for the new town of Hellevoetsluis and, in a lesser sense, that of Spijkenisse, which is separated from the built-up area by the Old Maas. They have their own amenities and shopping centres and some employment, although there is no official balance between employment and the working population. Hoogvliet, for instance, has only a little light industry and service industry, otherwise being dependent on the nearby port. In Capelle there are plans for service industries and for an industrial estate of 100 ha providing 10 000 jobs: a small number in comparison with its expected population of 200 000.

The new sectors are often very uniform in appearance, that of Pendrecht (with 6000 dwellings, housing 22 000 people) consisting of the repetition of a residential unit covering a little over 1 ha. The sector covers 135 ha in all, 99 ha of these devoted to housing (Fig. 33). Each unit consists of three- or four-storey blocks of flats with communal gardens and play spaces, making up 68 per cent of the housing. 24 per cent consists of individual houses with their own gardens and the remaining 8 per cent consists of old people's flats. The following table shows the constitution of one of these units:

Single storey housing
2 storey housing
3 storey housing
4 storey housing and blocks of flats
Individual houses
Schools
Public buildings

Fig. 33   Rotterdam : Pendrecht sector.

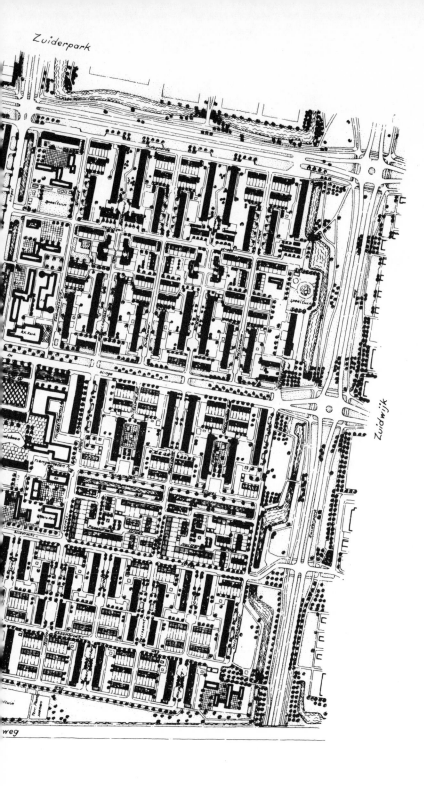

Zuiderpark

Zuidwijk

	m^2	per cent
Area of construction	2 776	24·8
Roads	1 850	16·5
Green spaces	1 240	11·1
Public gardens	3 970	35·4
Private gardens	1 364	12·2
	11 200	100·0

The housing density is about sixty per hectare in the residential areas (forty-five per hectare for the sector as a whole). The sector contains the following amenities:

A shopping centre (whose influence extends beyond the Pendrecht sector itself) with 128 shops.

154 shops in other parts throughout the sector.

51 commercial agencies of various kinds.

4 churches.

6 schools with playing fields.

30 ha of green spaces (within and outside the residential areas), or 13·5 m² per person and 47·5 m² per dwelling.

The population of these new sectors is very youthful. At Pendrecht, in the 1960 census, nearly twice as many young children were counted as in Rotterdam. Young adults (25 - 39) were also over-represented, making up a third of the population, while there were less adolescents of 15 - 25 (less than 9 per cent) and especially less old people (over three times less aged 50 - 65 and four times less over the age of 65).

Membership of the different churches – an important question in the Netherlands – does not show any particular pattern except perhaps a larger proportion of the population without any religious affiliation. There also seems a slightly higher number of electors voting for the Socialist Party. The social picture shows a large proportion of middle-class workers with relatively high incomes: 32·2 per cent compared with 15·9 per cent in Rotterdam. There are also slightly more working-class but less upper-class elements in the population.

These proportions are characteristic of all the new sectors and it will be interesting to watch their future development.

IV   A new town in the polders: Lelystad

The most original element of land use planning in the Netherlands is undoubtedly its ceaseless, centuries-old battle against the sea, which, especially in this century, has led to large-scale land reclamation made especially necessary by the demands of a growing population. The vastest of these undertakings has been in the Zuider Zee area and, more recently, in the Delta region.

Planning in the polder zone

The plan worked out by the engineer Lely (to close the Zuider Zee with a dike and to create four polders with a total area of 225 000 ha in the resulting artificial lake) was put into force after 1918, when Lely became Minister of Works. The dike was completed in 1932 and the first polder, the Wierngermeer, was reclaimed before the war and ready to house 8000 people on its 20 000 ha. The North East polder (48 000 ha) was reclaimed during the war and today houses 30 000 people. The plan for the three southern polders (East Flevoland, South Flevoland and Markerwaard) proposed linking the affairs of the polders to those of neighbouring provinces, particularly the north of the Randstad Holland (Gooi and the Amsterdam conurbation). The latter was scheduled to extend outwards radially, with one axis of growth towards the north-west in the direction of Lelystad, the proposed capital of the polder region (Fig. 34).

The essentials of the plan were for a rural nucleus in each of the polders, with concentrated urban development along the Amsterdam-Lelystad axis. Two large new towns, with populations of about 100 000, would be built along this axis: one at the south-west tip of South Flevoland, separated only by an arm of the lake from the Randstad, the other Lelystad itself, the capital and geographical heart of the polders.

Future extension of these two new towns has been allowed for and an area sufficient for 500 000 people in the polder region has been set aside, both for building and recreation space, mainly in these two built-up areas, which will be separated by a transition region chiefly devoted to leisure pursuits and by an industrial zone along the canal that separates the South Flevoland and Markerwaard polders.

Besides Lelystad, which provides industrial and service employment as well as administrative, cultural, social and commercial facilities for the whole polder region, secondary centres, one to each polder, will have an extensive part to play. This is so already in the case of Emmeloord in the North East polder and is becoming so in the case of Dronton, in East Flevoland. Eventually the villages in each polder will become large enough to provide a certain number of services (though this was not so in the North East polder) without being far from the land to be worked. About 3000 inhabitants apiece has finally been proposed as the ideal size, corresponding to an area of 90 km^2, making an average distance of 10 km between the village and its most distant farmland.

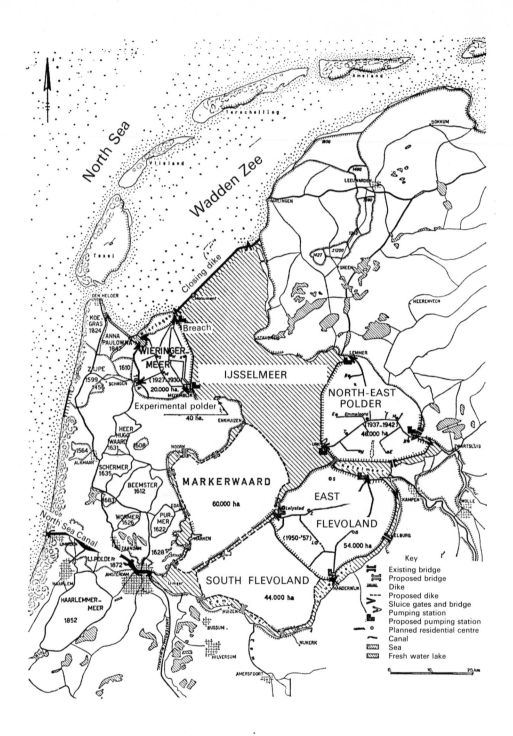

Fig. 34 The Zuider Zee polders and surrounding areas.

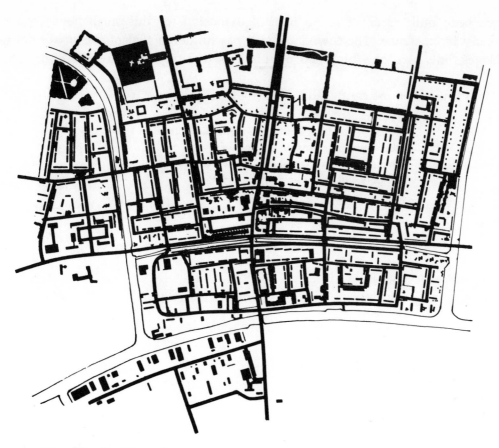

Fig. 35 Emmeloord.

A small new town: Emmeloord

The town of Emmeloord, capital of the North East polder, was founded in 1943 and now has about 8000 inhabitants (1800 dwellings), about sixty shops, some banks, an agricultural exchange, various commercial undertakings, a hotel, a theatre and a number of churches. It serves as a secondary shopping centre (for daily purchases) and a meeting place for the inhabitants of the polder. The central square, bordered by the inner canal, is the seat of administrative buildings (the offices of agricultural organizations, the labour exchange, tax collector and custom house) as well as the hotel, restaurant and theatre combined, banks, shops and flats, the new town hall and, above all, the great water tower, 64 m high and visible from all over the polder. The shops are mainly concentrated along one very busy curving street, with about fifty shops, which, however, do not provide enough competition. A second restaurant and a 120 bed hospital have been built recently and a plan of extension for this small new town is already in existence. The town's growth has hindered that of the surrounding villages, only two of which had populations reaching 1000 by 1960 (Fig. 35).

Statistics for the North East Polder (1965)

Dwellings built on farmland	1792
Dwellings for farm workers outside the villages	1008
Other dwellings outside the villages	771
Government-built dwellings in the villages	2866
Privately built dwellings in the villages	360
Total number of dwellings	6097
Restaurants	10
Offices and commercial premises	115
Shops	128
Schools	53
Churches	36
Hospitals	1

Amenities in Emmeloord (1965)

Type	Existing			Planned		Total		
	No.	Area (ha)	%	No.	Area (ha)	No.	Area (ha)	%
Dwellings and private gardens	1756	38·2	15·5	113	5·3	1689	43·5	14·5
Business premises	51	15·9	6·4		13·8		29·7	9·9
Commercial premises	166	23·4	9·5		31·0		54·4	18·1
Sports		32·6	13·2				32·6	11·0
Green spaces		6·9	2·8				6·9	2·3
Woods		71·2	29·0				71·2	23·8
Public roads		39·9	16·2				39·9	13·3
Public waterways		11·2	4·5				11·2	3·7
Miscellaneous		6·7	2·9		3·0		9·7	3·4
Total		246·0	100·0		53·1		299·1	100·0

A large new town: Lelystad

The Lelystad plan is by no means a new one but it did not begin to take shape until 1958 when Professor Van Eesteren was entrusted with the preparation of the town plan by the Ministry of Waterworks. For this task he brought together an engineer, an architect and several draughtsmen and also received help from

Amsterdam's Planning Department (on economic questions, for example) and from the Technological Institute of the province of South Holland, a semi-public body. Work leading to the plan's publication[1] lasted for the five years 1959 - 64.

The construction of the town is now under way, with 300 out of the first batch of 500 houses occupied by the end of 1967. The Rijksdienst voor de Ijsselmeerpolders is in charge of operations, there being nothing comparable to the development corporations of the British new towns in charge, although many think this desirable, since the body actually in charge is really intended for organizing rural development. Problems will also arise if, in ten years or so, the East Flevoland polder becomes an independent district like the North East polder.

At the moment the Rijksdienst voor Ijsselmeerpolders is in direct control of construction but later, as elsewhere in the Netherlands, it will probably call on co-operative and private building societies. The same body is responsible for the technical work of preparing the land and main services, handing over to a body nominated by the government (Openbaar lichaam) once the town is occupied. This body gives way in turn to an elected town council when the new town comes into being.

There is no very clear government policy about the role of this particular new town. For a long time a town with a population of 20 000 was considered, hardly larger than Emmeloord. When Van Eesteren took charge a population of 50 000 was suggested, with the possibility of a later increase to 100 000, on 4000 ha. The Ijsselmeerpolders' plan allows for an extra reserved area but in the course of the plan's preparation this body became rather worried by the size of the operation and the money needed for its completion, which partly explains why the study of the plan lasted five years. The author of the plan also received very few instructions and, because of his double reputation as academic and former director of the Town Planning Department in Amsterdam, no one saw fit to suggest a programme to him. He was therefore able to make his own plan for a town with a population of 100 000 and to outline plans for a future extension to 200 000. For this he had to ensure that the plan would allow for outward growth (westwards across the great canal on to the Marker-waard polder by a road bridge and tunnel and a railway branch line, and eastwards across the motorway leading from Amsterdam to the northern provinces).

[1]C. Van Eesteren, *Stedebouwkundigplan voor Lelystad* (The Hague, Ministry of Transport and Public Works, 1964).

The Lelystad plan is integrated in the general plan for the southern polders of the Ijsselmeer, studied above, and adheres to its proposals about main communications: the motorway link with Amsterdam along the axis of the polder zone and the rail link. The government will have to subsidize the railway company if this rail link is to be formed within the next decade, but no decision on this has yet been taken. The Lelystad plan also takes account of the detailed studies that have been made to decide the nature of the embankments of the great canal in the neighbourhood of Lelystad (especially in connection with its influence on the local micro-climate, winds, etc.).

The town plan itself is based on the idea of creating a large urban centre, rectangular in pattern, on an east-west axis, at a higher level than the town itself, which is on the same level as the dikes enclosing the polders, so that the town looks towards its centre and not towards the waterfront, as might be expected. The town's internal structure is not made up of varied neighbourhood units. This was deliberately avoided by its creator, although green spaces exist right through to the centre and about ten secondary centres, varying in size but unimportant in comparison with the main centre, have been planned for the new town. The internal pattern depends largely on the road network: main roads, spaced at 1·5 km (at a 6·5 m level), and secondary roads (at a 3·5 m level) (Fig. 36). The drainage system separates the roads and keeps children away from them. The plan allows for one parking space per dwelling, with the possibility of later increase, and for 10 000 parking spaces in the main centre, a total which may also need to be increased, according to the author of the plan. The Van Eesteren plan concludes with the detailed plan for the first stage of the operation (for 17 000 inhabitants) considered as a single unit, with an initial phase for 7000 inhabitants and a complete plan for the first housing groups, to house the polder's agricultural workers and those connected with the building of the new town.

Internal transport is planned in the form of a city bus service. The town is surrounded by an enormous green belt only broken by two large industrial zones to the south-west and north-east. The housing density decreases from the centre to the outskirts and 75 per cent of the housing is in the form of individual, mainly terraced, houses. Whatever the type, very low densities are planned, with a little over 30 000 dwellings on more than 6000 ha, a point that has received adverse criticism.

As the construction of the town is scheduled to last thirty years, it has been impossible to make a detailed study of the employment to be provided and space has had to be reserved according to current trends. So far, no firms have shown much interest in Lelystad, especially as there are no official incentives,

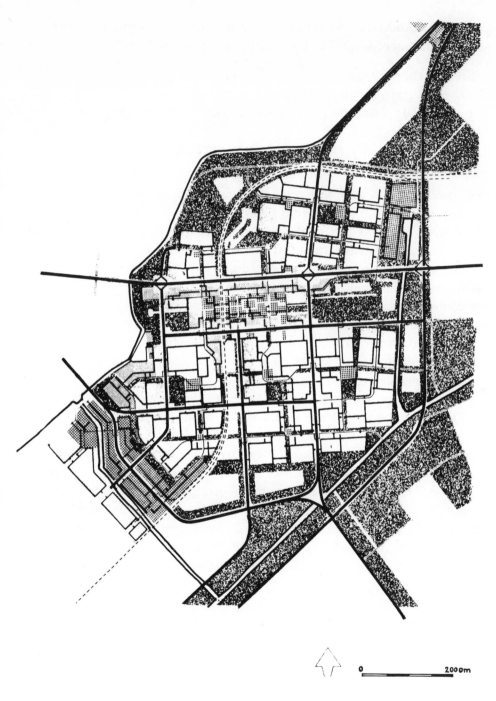

Fig. 36 Plan of Lelystad.

0   2000m

financial, fiscal or otherwise. As it is not even in a development area, the town receives little assistance. Some fairly certain developments include:

> Offices of the Rijksdienst voor de Ijsselmeerpolders, with an expected 900 employees by about 1975.
> The National Veterinary Institute (under construction), with 450 employees by 1975.
> The central electricity station of the province (250 employees by 1975).
> About 200 agricultural workers by 1975.

It is hoped that there will also be a certain amount of industry.

As for commerce, the first shopping centre will be only one of the town's secondary centres, planned to contain thirty shops. The first phase, started at the beginning of 1967, consists of seventeen shops, which were opened when the first 300 houses were occupied, at the end of 1967. The second phase (1968) consists of four new shops and a supermarket, to be followed by the third phase with eight more shops. The shops opened in the first phase are food and day-to-day purchases, other goods being provided for in the other two phases. The centre will also contain a restaurant, banks and offices, with services and service industries nearby (garages, petrol stations). However, this is not to be a pattern for later centres, particularly the main centre.

As in all the new towns of the Netherlands, all the necessary amenities are planned, so that the opening of the first housing groups and of the first phase of the main shopping centre coincide with that of a primary school, day nursery, meeting hall, sports ground and park. Next to this centre is also planned a sports centre to cater for a population of 10 000, including playing fields and athletics grounds, tennis courts, swimming pool and skating rink. A second primary school and day nursery and a secondary school are planned at the same time as the second batch of housing. Parks are already being planted out in the first sector and also to the north of the town, on the shores of the Ijsselmeer, for recreational purposes. A community centre is planned for the main centre of Lelystad.

We have seen that the first group of 539 dwellings was begun towards the end of 1966. It was not, however, carried out according to the Van Eesteren plan, which was virtually abandoned by the official department in charge without being replaced by any other plan. For reasons of prudence, it is still referred to as the Van Eesteren plan. Building of the second batch of housing began in 1968.

The first batch of housing, occupied at the end of 1967, was sited at the eastern edge of the area planned by Van Eesteren as the main town centre. It consisted of 256 houses (205 of them terraced) and 45 flats in three-storey blocks. The cost of construction was very reasonable (about £4550 for a house of 100 m², not including the land), allowing moderate rents, with government aid: £15 - 35 a month, including central heating and hot water. State aid with rents diminishes proportionately yearly, ending in the eighth year.

The present target is 3600 dwellings (housing 13 000 people) for 1975, 11 250 dwellings (for over 40 000 people) by 1985 and 30 000 dwellings (for 100 000 or more) by the year 2000.

It would be fruitless to try to study the professional structure and the size of future households in the new town, especially as there is no detailed plan for employment or for the size of the houses. What is certain is that the earliest inhabitants will be workers employed in building the town or draining the polder or at the electricity station.

On the other hand, the age structure of the new town has been forecast by comparing the state of Lelystad in 1975, 1985 and 2000 respectively with the known state of Dronten (East Flevoland) on 1 January 1966, of Emmeloord on the same date and of Vlaardingen, a suburb of Rotterdam, in 1959, with the following results:

Predicted age structure in Lelystad

Age	Date		
	1975	1985	2000
0-14	44·7	40·0	34·5
15-24	12·8	14·8	12·9
25-39	25·4	23·8	25·3
40-54	14·0	16·0	14·8
55-64	2·5	13·9	5·8
65+	0·6	1·5	6·7
Total	100·0	100·0	100·0

Absence of any long-term planning is obvious from these observations. Starting from a perhaps somewhat unrealistic plan, work was begun without much regard to this plan and without ensuring a coherent scheme. It would seem that this inadequacy is due to the lack of any official body responsible for the creation of the new town.

Conclusion

The Netherlands afford a remarkable example of planned development, whether for the country as a whole, the large built-up areas or the newly reclaimed zones. Some aspects of the policy may be questioned (for example, the wish to check the growth of the Randstad Holland) and its realism doubted, and it can be seen that some decisions are in opposition to the policy previously affirmed, as with the construction of the new town of Zoetermeer, east of The Hague, in the interior of the Randstad; or a rare empiricism may be noted, as with the building of Lelystad. Nevertheless, on the whole, the Netherlands have worked out a policy, succeeded in getting it accepted by the public and provided the means of carrying it out (by an efficient financial policy, important investments in urban transport and in city railways in particular, generous public financing for housing and a simple and effective legislation for planning), without any administrative organizing body for the new towns, a fairly new element in the town planning policies of the Netherlands.

One reason for the growth of new towns in the Netherlands was the wish to extend the Randstad outwards while preserving open leisure areas between the towns. Another was to find a modern solution to the question of human settlement in the polders.

The present tendency is towards the creation of large new towns (large on the Dutch scale, that is, with 200 000 inhabitants) along the preferential axes of development of the large built-up areas, preferably based on existing small or medium-sized towns (except, of course, in the polder zone).

These new towns are still at the planning stage, except for the small towns of Emmeloord and Dronten in the polder zone and for Lelystad, now under construction. But there is bound to be a break with the Dutch tradition of fairly dense residential areas containing a majority of collective housing in immediate contact with existing built-up areas. Keeping in mind the past quality of Dutch town planning, it will be interesting to observe the experiments and to see whether they are as successful as is hoped.

4 : New towns policy in France

After giving examples of new towns in Britain, Scandinavia and the Netherlands, one turns with some diffidence to those in France, where the ambiguity of the term 'new town' is particularly evident. It may imply large-scale housing estates on the edge of large towns or, more rarely, the creation of a new industrial complex like that of Mourenx in a rural area. It may imply towns created around new urban areas as part of the planning scheme for the Paris region, or urban developments of a different kind aimed at solving the problems of growth in large built-up areas in the provinces.

We will see first France's limited achievements in this field, particularly housing estates and new urban areas, and then touch on current plans for the Paris region and the provinces, so that the reader can form his own judgement.

I First post-war achievements in town planning: the
grands ensembles

A great deal of study, reports and articles have been devoted to the *grands ensembles*, so that it is unnecessary to examine them in detail here: instead, their main characteristics will be noted.

Suburban grand ensembles

The policy of rent control, the economic crisis and the war created an almost complete gap in building for several decades. This, with the rise in birth rate and the movement of the population away from the countryside, created a housing crisis after the Liberation, the effects of which can still be felt. The reaction of the public authorities was to aim at building the largest number of houses as quickly as possible, without equal regard to choice of location, improvement in quality or the financing of necessary amenities.

There is no exact definition of a *grand ensemble* (housing estate), but it generally signifies a large-scale building operation of at least 500 dwellings. There are various promoters of the schemes, mainly public or semi-public bodies, such as the *Société centrale immobilière de la Caisse des Dépôts* (SCIC), *l'Office* central interprofessionel de Logement (OCIL), the offices publics d'HLM and l'association Baticoop, and some private bodies such as the sociétés d'HLM or promotion societies such as the SAGI and SACI.

There are different methods of financing the schemes, varying according to legislation and regulations. State aid usually plays a considerable part: the Lopofas, logécos and HLM account for the majority of housing, which is largely rented (95 per cent according to the 1962 census).

For a long time there was no special legislation to deal with these new developments, which therefore came under existing regulations, mainly embodied in the 1943 Act. It was not until 1958 that priority development areas (ZUP) were designated, having fixed limits and aimed at avoiding dispersal of effort involved in building on land badly equipped with infrastructures and ensuring the parallel development of housing and amenities. They were to consist of at least 500 dwellings with corresponding amenities and scope for future employment. The Fonds national d'Aménagement Foncier et d'Urbanisme (FNAFU) could advance money and grant interest-free loans to the public body or private organization entrusted with the development of the priority area; state grants were also made available. A right of pre-emption of four years, extendable by two years, was given to those public authorities acting for the government in this respect. This legislation had considerable effect and within three years about a hundred ZUPs were designated, twelve of them in the Paris region, the largest of which – Aulnay-Sevran, Créteil, Vitry and Massy-Antony – were planned to house populations of between 30 000 and 60 000.

In November 1964 the Institut national d'Études démographiques (INED) estimated[1] a total of 200 grands ensembles of over 1000 dwellings (95 in the Paris region and 105 in the provinces), making a total of 365 000 dwellings (197 200 in the Paris region and 168 300 in the provinces). Their growth was rapid: over 60 000 dwellings a year. The present number of dwellings in the grands ensembles is therefore almost 500 000, housing 2 million people, more than half of them in the Paris region, where about one person in six lives in a grand ensemble.

The dwellings making up the grands ensembles are larger than average for France (with an average of 3·3 rooms compared with 3·09) and a fortiori larger than rented accommodation (2·67 rooms), though the rooms themselves are often small. The relatively high average number of rooms is due not so much to a high number of large dwellings as to the low proportion of small dwellings.

[1]Paul Clerc, Grands ensembles, Banlieues nouvelles, INED, Travaux et documents, Cahiers No. 49 (Paris, PUF, 1967).

Despite their relatively large size, these dwellings are often overcrowded: in 1964 they were reckoned to house an average of 4·10 people (1·25 per room) compared with 3·12 for France as a whole (1·01 people per room). Living conditions are usually satisfactory: each dwelling contains a bathroom and WC and 82 per cent have central heating; there is always a lift for buildings of five or more floors.

The populations of the *grands ensembles* are youthful, mainly made up of young families with several children. Three-quarters of the heads of households are between 25 and 45 (compared with 37 per cent for France as a whole). Age for age, they have 0·5 more children on the average. As for the social pattern, the most striking characteristic is the lack of non-workers and of non-salaried workers (9 per cent of the heads of households compared with 50 per cent for the country as a whole). The socio-professional composition of the salaried workers is about average for urban populations. Their income would be 40 per cent above the national average but, allowing for the size of the households, this difference is reduced to barely 20 per cent, particularly reflecting the lack of non-working households: their standard of living seems in fact very similar to that of other households of the same size and age group. Contrary to a theory often expressed, the mobility of these households (7 per cent per year) is the same as for other urban populations. In fact, the population of the *grands ensembles* is very similar to that of new housing in general, though income is 20 - 25 per cent lower and rents half way between those of older housing and of new housing in the private sector.

The *grands ensembles* have often been criticized for their monotony, the banality of their architecture, lack of amenities, shops and employment, blaming these for the obvious lack of community spirit and even for such things as prostitution, young adolescents forming gangs and committing various misdeeds, etc. The term 'sarcellite' has been coined to describe this phenomenon, from the name of the best-known *grand ensemble* of the Paris region. If much of this censure is deserved, even though the authorities concerned are endeavouring to remedy the situation by providing amenities and employment (an industrial zone and offices have been built at Sarcelles), many forget the inescapable imbalance of the situation. A youthful population, mainly consisting of large families and working away from its home surroundings, is not best qualified to produce a desirable type of night-life.

Whatever criticisms have been heaped on the *grands ensembles*, those who live in them judge them less severely than do outside observers. According to the INED enquiry[1] more than three-quarters of the households interviewed

[1]Paul Clerc, op. cit.

thought that the advantages of living in the *grand ensemble* outweighed the disadvantages. 37 per cent of those expressing an opinion condemned the principle of the *grand ensemble* but 63 per cent approved of it. A large majority (nine out of ten) were satisfied with their housing and were enjoying better conditions than previously. The *grands ensembles* have at least achieved their aim of helping to cope with the housing crisis. Their weakness does not lie in their standard of housing but in the chief problem of town planning for the last two decades: the need to deal with large areas, density of building near the stations, the closeness of the outer boundaries of the built-up area – especially in the Paris region, where the PADOG, sanctioned in 1960, has enclosed the built-up area in a veritable '*carcan*', opening the way to unofficial development – have led the bodies in charge of the *grands ensembles* to site them on plateaux poorly served by rail transport and also to swallow up the last few remaining open spaces on the city's outskirts. A map of the *grands ensembles* on the outskirts of Paris is very significant in this respect, showing them at an average distance of 10 km from the gates of Paris, especially on the northern and south-western outskirts, avoiding the suburban areas of the east and the Orge valley, where available land is rare, and the western residential suburbs, where it is expensive. These sitings have largely compromised the policy undertaken since 1960 of repairing the lack of amenities in the suburbs. Most of the *grands ensembles* are not big enough to justify a large expenditure on amenities and the developers will avoid the expense of them if possible. It is unfortunate that space has not been reserved for their later construction, especially as the suburbs are sorely deficient in them.

The disadvantages arising from this concentration on simple building rather than town planning have been well shown in an enquiry made by CINAM[1] in four *ensembles* built by SCIC in the Paris region (Sarcelles, 'Les Sorbiers' at Chevilly-Larue, 'Les Planètes' at Maisons-Alfort and the 'Vaux-Germains' at Chatenay-Malabry). The authors of the enquiry related the needs and aspirations of the inhabitants, as far as they could discover them, to theories of planning:

> The necessity of a link with Paris for commuting as well as for shopping and leisure pursuits, the part played by intermediate centres in the suburbs seeming very limited.
> The necessity of inclusion within the surrounding urban area, in order to make use of the amenities.

[1]Compagnie d'Études industrielles et d'Aménagement du Territoire (CINAM), *La vie des ménages de quatre nouveaux ensembles de la région parisienne (1962-1963)*, 3 vols.

The possibility of arousing a sense of citizenship in the population by
breaking the architectural monotony, re-aligning roads and pathways,
improving the appearance and size of public buildings (for example,
enlarging shop window space as well as selling space), making the
functions of different parts of the town more interdependent and
forming small residential units where people could feel more at home.

The lack of amenities is particularly felt by flat dwellers (shortage of
playing fields, the rigid assignment of open spaces and limitations
attached to their use).

The wish for some unplanned space to themselves, either within or
outside the dwelling.

The wish of the inhabitants to have some share in the running of their
neighbourhood, shown by residents' organizations, and their claims
to obtain from the developers of the *grands ensembles* some share in
the running of them.

After nearly two decades of building, the *grands ensembles* have helped to
spotlight the problems of town planning in areas of rapid urban development.
They cannot develop into new towns because they only fulfil one function of a
town: housing. For the creation of a genuine town life, employment – providing
a variety as well as a quantity of jobs – and the provision of commercial,
administrative, socio-cultural and leisure amenities are essential.

The creation of new towns: Mourenx, Hérouville-Saint-Clair, Le Mirail

Some *grands ensembles* are not situated on the outskirts of large towns and so
may correctly be termed new towns: for example, Behrens-les-Forbach,
Guenange and Farebeswiller in Moselle, and especially Mourenx in the Basses-
Pyrénées. The latter, with a population of about 12 000, was created for the
benefit of the industries set up after the discovery of natural gas at Lacq
(electricity station of the EDF, the factories of Pechiney and Aquitaine-Chimie,
etc.). Despite being at a distance from any large built-up area, Mourenx exhibits
the faults of the *grands ensembles*: monotony of architecture and of the position-
ing of buildings, lack of amenities and of community spirit, separation between
housing and work areas. The shopping habits of the population, as observed in
1960, illustrate well the lack of urban character: over 50 per cent of daily
requirements and clothing were purchased outside Mourenx, mainly at Pau;
this proportion rose to 93 per cent (77 per cent of this from Pau) for larger
purchases. But, as M. Cornière points out, this lack of shopping facilities results

from the size of the development: 'It must be realized that what the people of Mourenx lack is only to be found in large towns.'[1]

This need for a larger development was realized by the authors of certain projects for ZUPs in the provinces: that of Hérouville-Saint-Clair at Caen will have a population of over 30 000; that of Le Mirail at Toulouse 100 000 and Saint-Dizier-les-Neuf 30 000. They also hope to avoid some of the other faults of the *grands ensembles*. In Hérouville the aim is to seek variety in housing and landscaping and to create a multi-functional centre, containing secondary schools, sports stadium, indoor swimming pool, children's homes, administrative centre, cinema, recreational centre, etc. In Le Mirail, M. Candilis aims above all to break with the architectural forms and layout of buildings that have justly earned the *grands ensembles* criticism of lack of inspiration and to create surroundings favouring meetings and exchanges. Large zones of employment are also planned (Fig. 37).

So, little by little, past experience helps to decide what conditions may lead to the building of genuine new towns in France. To achieve this, a planning strategy for each region will have to be formulated.

II A landmark in French town planning: the master plan for the Paris region

The master plan for development and town planning in the Paris region, made public on 22 June 1965 by M. Paul Delouvrier, general delegate to the District of the Paris region, marked the achievement of the first phase of the operation undertaken by the District, whose function, defined by law on 2 August 1960, is to study the questions arising from planning for all or part of the region. Town planning studies were in fact entrusted to the *Institut d'Aménagement et d'Urbanisme de la Région parisienne* (IAURP), a body whose function is the long-term study of planning in the Paris region, which is at the disposal of the general delegate to the District (formerly to the prefect of the Paris region), who is its president. Before publication, the master plan was submitted to the ministries concerned and studied on 26 November 1964 by a special council presided over by the head of state. Local authorities and regional assemblies (the administrative council of the District, the consultative economic and social committee and the planning committee for the Paris region) were then consulted and published their opinions. After this, complementary studies were under-

[1]Paul Cornière, *Réflexions sociologiques sur Mourenx*, paper delivered to the IIe Colloque national de Démographie, 12-14 November 1964.

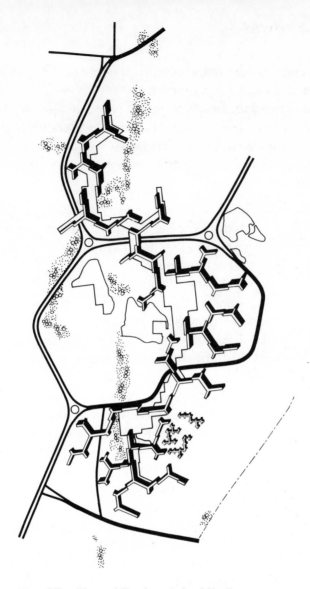

Fig. 37 Plan of Toulouse-Le Mirail.

taken, leading to a report replying to these opinions and giving the present situation of the master plan. This report was submitted by the prefect of the Paris region to the administrative council of the District in January 1969.

The main outlines of the master plan

The main outlines of the master plan cater for future development. On the national scale the work of the 1985 section of the general commission on the plan and of other experts on future affairs led to the following predictions:

That purchasing power would be doubled by 1985 and more than trebled by the end of the century.

That office jobs would increase twice as fast as jobs in industry.

That leisure time would increase considerably and the need for leisure activities would be quadrupled by the year 2000.

That the demand for urban transport per person would increase by 30 per cent.

One fact was therefore established: for a static population, the needs of each region of France, including the Paris region, would be far greater in the future than at present, with existing facilities (whether of housing, transport or leisure activities) unable to meet the demand.

But would the population remain static? Without becoming too involved in detailed figures, some indications may be given. From 1850 to 1950 the population of France remained constant. However, during this time the urban population doubled and that of the Paris region trebled, because of migration from the provinces and abroad. Since 1945 or a little earlier France has seen births exceed deaths by about 60 per cent. With immigration aiding economic growth, the average population increase has reached 500 000 a year. Movement away from the countryside has increased, less towards Paris than towards the other built-up areas. The growth of the Paris region has, however, also been accelerated by the excess of births over deaths (70 000 per year) added to the number of new arrivals (90 000 per year). The growing youthfulness of the Paris population will increase this excess of births, which should reach 100 000 per year by the end of the century.

During this time, what will be the pattern of population movements? The population of France is expected to increase from 50 to 75 million in the course of the last third of this century. The urban population – according to the INSEE – will double from 30 million to about 60 million, while the rural population will decrease from 20 to 15 million. Will the Paris region continue, as at present, to increase at a rate similar to that of the other French towns, doubling its population from 9 to 18 million? Everyone is agreed that this would be undesirable. But the excess of births over deaths alone will represent almost 3 million extra inhabitants. Even if emigration should balance immigration, Greater Paris would still have a population of 12 million by the year 2000, between 12 and 18 and perhaps even more if Paris should exert an increasing attraction. The plan presupposed a total of 14 million inhabitants: what does this total imply?

That immigration into the Paris region would decrease from 70 000 to
30 000 people a year between 1965 and 2000.

That the average rate of increase in the Paris region would decrease to
1 per cent a year by 2000 (at present almost 2 per cent) despite a
continuing excess of births over deaths.

That Paris's share in the French urban population would drop from
30 per cent to 23 per cent.

That while the population of Paris would increase by a little over half,
that of the other French cities would be multiplied by 2·2, implying
a rate of growth twice as fast.

That the towns best able to help in checking the growth of Paris, that
is the 'balancing' regional capitals and the towns of the Paris Basin,
would almost treble their populations, implying a rate three times as
high as that of Paris.

The hypothesis of a population of 14 million seems in fact highly optimistic.[1]
The needs of even a constant population would increase and the population
itself may increase willy-nilly. It must also be noted that the rate of growth
recommended for Paris is lower than that predicted for the world's largest
cities (Tokyo, New York, Washington, Rome, Copenhagen) and barely higher
than that predicted for London, where the excess of births is slight and which
is part of a country where, unlike France, there is no longer a movement away
from the countryside.

How will the needs of the population increase? Relying on the figures given,
one may predict:

That the overall spending power of the population will increase by 5·5.

That the number of private vehicles will increase by 2·5: 4 million cars
by 2000.

That commuting will more than double.

That jobs in public services will almost double, while jobs in industry
will only increase by 30 per cent.

That the number of dwellings will almost double and their total area
almost quadruple.

[1]The findings of the 1968 census nevertheless seem to confirm this hypothesis: the
Paris region has increased at the rate of 140,000 people a year but this shows a relative
slowing down in the immigration rate of about 70 000 a year between 1962 and 1968
and 90 000 between 1954 and 1962, while the excess of births over deaths (50 000
between 1954 and 1962 and later 70 000) continues to increase. In the same period,
the large provincial conurbations and the large towns of the Paris Basin have increased
at a higher rate of growth than that of the Paris region.

That space for leisure activities will need to be increased five to ten times.

All this has to be catered for in planning for the Paris region of the future and these estimates are, if anything, conservative.

Decisions to be made

Five million new inhabitants, 2 million extra jobs, 20 million more journeys every day to be catered for. The aim of town planning is to ensure a distribution of population, employment and facilities that, even if not creating an Utopia, will allow the Parisians of the twenty-first century a better life than at present.

The growth of the built-up area in the past has been influenced by its single main centre, with hardly any secondary centres and with an outdated transport system, the metro going back fifty years and the suburban railway a hundred years. There has been an almost total lack of public amenities, and especially of open spaces, all available space having been gradually absorbed by town development, producing an increasing density (Paris is the most densely built-up city of the developed countries of the world).

In the case of the *grands ensembles* of the post-war years – which did at least succeed in housing the homeless – and of the suburban developments of the Loucheur Act, the result is the same: people are housed where land is available without regard to social and educational facilities such as hospitals and schools, shops, transport services or recreational opportunities. This state of affairs must be avoided as far as possible in the future. The Paris of the year 2000 must be given a new pattern, breaking the monopoly of the single centre by creating new urban centres in the present suburbs as well as in newly developed areas. The expansion of the city must take place along main axes of development, safeguarding amenities and especially recreational areas. In short, Paris must be transformed from a built-up area into an urban region.

Practical planning decisions

How were the axes of development chosen? Where should the new urban centres be, which would transform the suburbs and form the nuclei of genuine new towns?

Several requirements governed the choice of these axes. One was the preservation of the forests of Saint-Germain, Rambouillet, Sénart, Fontainebleau, Montmorency, etc. Another was the fitting of the development of the Paris region into that of the country as a whole, and particularly that of the Paris

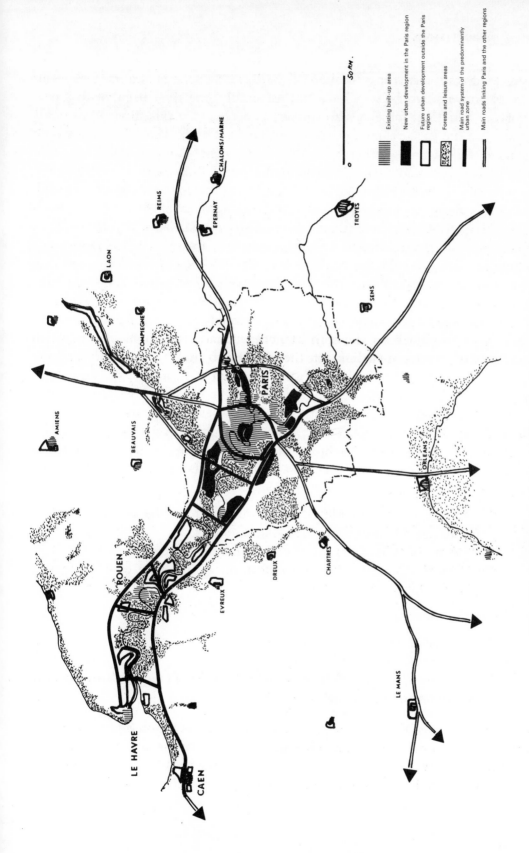

Fig. 38 Development of the Paris region in relation to the Paris Basin.

Existing built-up area

New urban development in the Paris region

Future urban development outside the Paris region

Forests and leisure areas

Main road system of the predominantly urban zone

Main roads linking Paris and the other regions

50 KM.

0

AMIENS

LAON

BEAUVAIS

COMPIEGNE

REIMS

EPERNAY

CHALONS/MARNE

LE HAVRE

ROUEN

PARIS

TROYES

CAEN

EVREUX

DREUX

CHARTRES

SENS

ORLÉANS

LE MANS

basin. In this respect, the attraction of the Basse-Seine area is a main element, with its port, its two railway lines and, especially, the river itself, with a new motorway and three pipelines to follow: altogether an axis directed towards and serving the Paris region and not to be ignored by it. There is also a strong argument for planning other axes of development along valleys that form already equipped and easily incorporated natural links with the rest of the country: of these, the Haute-Seine and the Marne are the two chosen (Fig. 38). Would this mean the building of huge cities within these narrow valleys? Even if this were wished, existing (especially industrial) installations would make it impossible. The character of the valleys as leisure areas, especially with their stretches of water, would also be destroyed. The plan is, therefore, to build new urban centres on the plateaux overlooking these valleys, where they will have scope to develop into genuine towns, while the view over the valleys, themselves preserved as leisure areas, will be preserved. The main Basse-Seine axis will be split into northern and southern branches, continuations of which will form areas of development linking with the Haute-Seine to the south and the Marne to the north. These axes, with their tangential structure, should help to break the concentric, single-centred pattern of the built-up area of Paris.

The siting of urban centres, centres of future new towns, along these axes cannot be dealt with in detail here, but the decision was guided by availability of sites and transport facilities and by their ability to help in the transformation of the existing suburbs (Fig. 39). As a result, the following were chosen on the northern axis:

> The centre of Bry-sur-Marne, Noisy-le-Grand, at the head of a linear urban development along the Marne.
> The centre of Beauchamp, in the Montmorency valley.
> The centre of Cergy, a future prefecture, at the head of development planned to the west of Pontoise.

And on the southern axis:

> The centre of Tigery-Lieusaint.
> The centre of Évry, a new prefecture.
> The centres of Trappes-Guyancourt and Trappes-Étang de Saint Quentin.
> A centre on the plateau south of Mantes.

If only one part of the predicted increase in population is housed in extensions of the present suburbs (current movements of population cannot be checked and, anyway, the new towns are not yet ready to receive their new inhabitants), then it can be hoped that in the further development axes 3 million people can

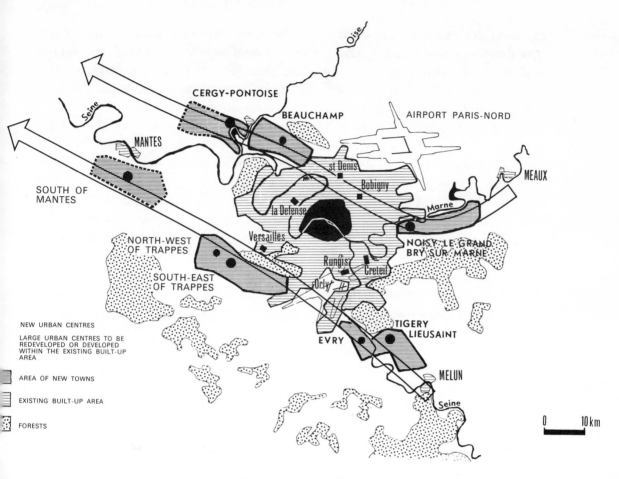

Fig. 39 Master plan for the Paris region: simplified sketch.

be housed in new towns by the year 2000, the largest towns housing 500 000 (the population of Lyon). A large population seems a necessity to attract office jobs, large stores, out-of-the-ordinary shops, theatres and recreational facilities of all kinds: in fact, all that distinguishes a large town from a huge *grand ensemble*.

Apart from these centres of future new towns, new centres will be created in the suburbs to revitalize areas that have too often been left in leper-like isolation. This role will be assumed by the centres of Saint-Denis, Rosny-sous-Bois, Créteil (a prefecture), Bobigny (a prefecture), Rungis, Choisy-le-Roi, Versailles and La Défense.

These axes of development and new towns within a 50 km radius of Paris are not the only possibilities. Others have been considered and even studied. There has been, for example, the theory of a 'Paris bis'. But how much of the 12 000 new dwellings to be built each year in the Paris region could this new capital absorb? The remainder would only increase the growth of the present city. And how could this 'Paris bis' achieve in one generation the prestige obtaining to Paris itself after more than twenty centuries of crowded history?

Another suggestion has been for about ten satellite towns on the British pattern, with populations of about 60 000 each. But, apart from the fact that these towns would be too small to possess certain fundamental town functions (businesses, landscaping, a university), they would only solve the problem of the growth of the built-up area for five years, or ten at the most. This is a problem the British have had to face at the end of ten years (see Chapter 1).

Yet another suggestion has been the enlargement of existing secondary built-up areas (Meaux, Melun, Corbeil, Mantes, etc.), but for a long-term solution they would need populations of 500 000 and their centres and facilities are not on a large enough scale to cope with such numbers.

The master plan does not confine itself to physical problems of planning only but examines in particular three of the main aspects of town life: employment, leisure activities and transport. After analysing the present demand and that which can be predicted a generation ahead, it deals with the respective parts played by public transport and private motoring. The former will be needed in particular for commuting between the centre of Paris and the suburbs and between the suburbs and the new towns. It must also cater for the not inconsiderable minority (over 25 per cent in Los Angeles at present) who do not possess their own car, so that they are not cut off from the life of the town. Cars will be mainly used for leisure, shopping and business and for commuting within the new towns and between sectors of the suburbs. A large network of fast roads (about 1600 km) and a fast rail network (a regional express) will serve the new towns and airports in particular and cross Paris from one side to another, with many stops linking with those of the metro. These two systems form the pillars of a solution to the transport problem.

The development of employment, according to the national planning policy, will lead to a far greater increase of jobs in offices and public services, and even in commerce, rather than in production industries. In Paris itself, industry will decrease and the workers will be replaced by clerks or managerial staff. In the new towns the master plan aimed at a freedom of choice that avoided any link between work and housing like that of the new towns in Britain (see Chapter 1). But for this freedom of choice not to be a drawback it means that as many and varied types of employment as possible must be installed in the new towns. Transport facilities will, however, make it possible for everyone to choose his place of work, such a choice being one of the main features of a large urban region that it would be unwise not to retain. This reinforces the present decision to site the new towns near the existing conurbation.

Though it is difficult to gauge the future demand for leisure facilities, it is certain that this will increase very rapidly, with a corresponding need for more space. The conservation of woodland, both public and private, and the use of the rare stretches of water for water sports have therefore become some of the town planners' major objectives.

III Studies for new towns in the Paris region

A master plan for development and town planning is not an end in itself. Though it may show the main directions of policy to follow and the main outlines of the 'map of the future', determination and concrete proposals are needed for carrying it out.

The new towns and particularly their centres will form the visible results of the policy put forward in 1965. To this end, studies were carried out, first under the auspices of the IAURP, in the form of structural plans (town plans on the scale 1:10 000 accompanied by an explanatory report, comprising a detailed programme of housing, employment, amenities, etc.) and general studies of amenities, transport and population, etc. Gradually, conforming to the (unpublished) directives of the Prime Minister dated 18 July 1966, plans for the new towns were brought out, using for administrative support (finance and recruitment of personnel) l'Agence foncière et technique de la Région parisienne (AFTRP) and the IAURP. Those of Évry and Cergy-Pontoise appeared on 18 July 1966, that of Trappes on 13 December 1967 and those of Noisy-le-Grand (Marne valley) and Tigery-Lieusaint on 12 June 1969. Work is at present being carried out by these planning commissions, which should later be transformed into development organizations of a public character. The studies for Évry and Cergy-Pontoise are farthest advanced and public bodies were established in April 1969, taking over from planning commissions. We will therefore deal with these two cases before attempting to discuss the problems that they present – or will present – to the developers of the new towns as well as to the regional and national authorities.

Studies for Évry[1]

The suggestions put forward by the planning commission for the new town of Évry rest on certain main principles:

[1]'Évry – Centre urbain nouveau et ville nouvelle', *Cahiers de l'IAURP*, vol. 15, May 1969.

The predominance of the centre in the work of town planners must be reflected in the structure of the town. This principle, implicit in the regional plan, seems artificial in the case of a new town on the outskirts of the built-up area, at the heart of an area already urbanized (Sainte-Geneviève-des-Bois, Corbeil-Essonnes) or in process of urbanization (Ris-Orangis). The main task is to restructure a sector that already has a population of nearly 200 000 (having increased rapidly from 103 000 in the 1962 census) in the probable direct zone of influence of the future urban centre, which will eventually house between 400 000 and 500 000, creating an urban nucleus including residential sectors and an urban centre on a regional scale, exerting a wide attraction and giving character to the town. This supposes a voluntary principle seemingly at variance with present tendencies (particularly on the other side of the Atlantic) towards the dwindling role of urban centres due to motorized transport. Such an urban centre, if it is to play its part fully, has to concentrate various activities – commercial, administrative, university, cultural, employment and leisure – which will be capable of creating a place frequented for more than functional reasons, which would be the surest sign of its success. The balance between resident working population and local employment was examined, to avoid the conditions likely to create a super *grand ensemble*, rather than to ensure the link between the two that formed a basic principle of the new towns in Britain (see Chapter 1). It may indeed be feared that commuting by too large a proportion of the working population will have an impoverishing effect on the life of the town as a whole, prejudicing the success of its commercial and leisure facilities. A partial balance is planned: the new town would have about eight jobs – as varied as possible – to every ten resident workers. Of these, six would work in the town and four commute (to Paris or to other parts of the suburbs), so that one job in four would be occupied by a non-resident. Such a provision, allowing for possible commuting, is in line with the principle of freedom of choice already stated in the regional plan and demands for its success a large increase in transport facilities. As for the type of job, if one aims at a blance (about 75 000 secondary jobs are planned to a little over 80 000 tertiary jobs), the importance of the employment of women must be stressed and a decision made on the economic character of the new town. For instance, the paper-making and publishing concern mainly working at Corbeil-Essonnes could be extended considerably.

The mobility of the population is a *sine qua non* condition of its use of the facilities available – work, general amenities and the town life of the centre. The provision of transport services with their necessary infrastructures within the town itself is essential for this purpose. The needs of private motoring cannot be ignored and require a good road system and public and private parking space (1·5 - 2 spaces per dwelling). But an efficient public transport system is necessary both for the considerable number of people without cars and for journeys where private motoring is either impossible or undesirable. For instance, if private cars alone were used in the town centre, so much parking space would be required that the character of the centre would be ruined.

The creation of an urban landscape with a continuity, which is lacking in the suburbs, is aimed at. For this, it is important for the road network not to cut through the sections of the town, and to avoid this it is planned to keep a central area free from such interruption where social amenities will be sited, and this will be served by public transport.

The proposed town plan is a direct outcome of these principles (Fig. 40). Its essential characteristics are:

Development along special axes allowing for the creation of the centre and the organization of transport systems while keeping a desired continuity. These axes consist of one main north-west to south-east axis between the motorway and the Seine and others towards the new urban centre of Tigery-Lieusaint, Sainte-Geneviève-des-Bois and along the Essone valley.

A road system with a network of fast roads leading into the town and ending in large car parks (5600 spaces) and another, internal system linking the residential areas with the centre and with each other. However, in this central sector (with a population of 120 000) it is hoped to encourage the use of public transport, though whether by bus or rail has yet to be decided. As well as this, the regional express services will provide for long-distance travelling.

The centre is of primary importance, its character resulting from the concentration of many functions, amenities and services in one spot. Though it is impossible to list all these in advance, the plans are for out-of-the-ordinary shops, large stores, leisure facilities and entertainments making up the life of the town; immediately beyond these,

‖‖‖	Existing built-up area	▭	Amenities	▬▬	Fast road
■	Urban centre	⬚	Existing green spaces	──	Access road
‖	New residential areas	⠿	Proposed green spaces	┽┽┽┽	Main railway line
⬡	Industrial zone			·········	Local railway line

0   2 km

Fig. 40 Évry : proposed pattern.

administration and public services and business houses; then offices and public services not used by the public at large – schools, universities and cultural and technological institutions and workshops. The centre consists of several main sections: the 'forum', transport terminus and meeting place; the *place representative*; the *boulevard urbain*; the *parc urbain*, etc.

Many of the details have yet to be settled. Studies for overall plans, many already under way, have a large part to play, as have the results of the earliest developments and the opinions of the first occupants (workers in firms, public services and building).

Studies for Cergy-Pontoise

Just as we have seen that various key principles guided the commission working on the study for Évry, so four basic aims can be picked out from the work on its counterpart, Cergy-Pontoise:

> The desire to master the time factor is the most original of these. The creation of a new town of the size of those proposed for the Paris region is bound to take several decades, let us say a generation. It is only when it is nearly finished that it can offer its inhabitants the variety of choice that forms a main object of the regional master plans. So, although Cergy-Pontoise is to be served eventually by three motorways and one or more lines of express rail, the present picture is far less rosy. To avoid a 'deprived generation', each sector has been planned independently and once the first is built, as part of the prefecture of Val-d'Oise, a first urban centre will be established. The commission did not conceal its wish to practise a short-term policy, considering that the fate of the town would be decided in the course of the first five years.
>
> The wish to develop the possibilities of the new town as a centre for open-air leisure activities, because of the nature of its site. The town is to take the form of a horse-shoe enclosing a meander of the Oise, within which parks and a centre for water sports will be created (Fig. 41). The siting of this leisure area in a small space within the surrounding residential sectors will give the town its special character and attraction, giving it a life of its own and distinguishing it not only from the rest of the built-up area but from the other new towns.
>
> The search for a balance between the possibilities of local employment

and the resident working population is seen as of great importance. As at Évry, the balance cannot be perfect and only 150 000 new jobs are planned for a new population of 380 000 (about 165 000 workers). It is also realized that this apparent balance conceals commuting in both directions between the new town and the remainder of the region (studies have shown that about 50 per cent of the workers would be employed locally, allowing for the 150 000 jobs planned). Jobs in the centre (60 000) would be mainly in two groups: first that of the prefecture and then the main centre at the head of the horse-shoe. More than 40 000 jobs (especially in production) would be sited in special zones.

Importance is given to the town's external contacts. The commission demanded the addition of two fast roads to the three motorways planned and another fast rail link (monorail or otherwise) between the new town and La Défense on one side and Normandy on the other, as well as the two existing rail services and the planned regional express. But above all they stressed the importance of the first stage of the plans being carried out.

The structural plan published in October 1968 is largely a result of these studies. It deals with the preparation of the site and aims at a balanced growth at each stage of the town's development. The leisure area within the meander of the Oise is to occupy a central position. Up to five sectors will be established initially (the sector of the prefecture between Cergy and Pontoise, Éragny, Puiseux-Courdimanche (which is to contain the main centre), Boisement-Vauréal and Jouy-le-Maurecourt) in a horse-shoe shape round the meander of the Oise. The development of existing communities will form another series of sectors with their own centres and varied amenities. The development of the leisure area within the meander of the Oise, consisting of a centre for water sports and a 250 ha park will give priority to the recreation of the population at the expense of other building. It will not be crossed by any motorways but most of it will be accessible by car, except for the lake and beaches, which will be served by public transport, or even by ferry boats.

One of the present most difficult problems for the commission of enquiry is the existence of two large urban centres to be created successively: first, that of the prefecture (where 12 000 jobs are provided for) at the centre of the first sector, and then the main centre of Puiseux-Courdimanche (with jobs for 40 000), which will not be built until later. The distance between them (40 km), their relative positions and the present use of the land between makes any future

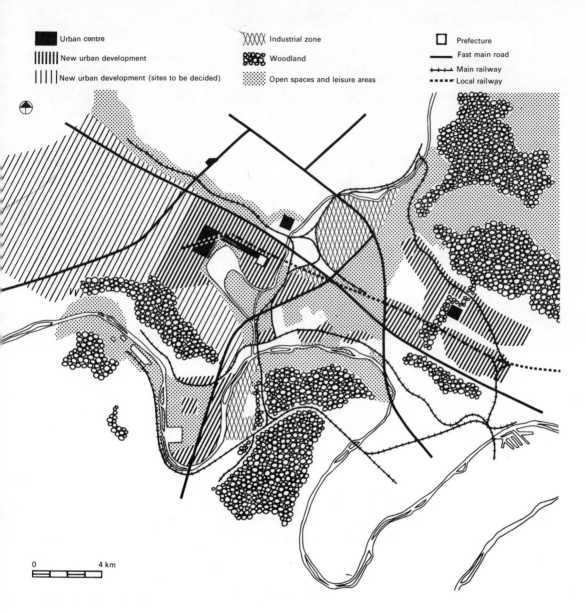

0   4 km

Fig. 41 Cergy-Pontoise : its natural setting.

amalgamation out of the question. There is surely a danger that the success of the first centre will cripple the development of the main centre, or, on the other hand, that amenities and firms will be reluctant to establish themselves in the first centre, preferring to await a site in the main centre. But the necessity of giving the population of the earlier sector a centre of employment, services and amenities demands the creation of a first centre that at this stage of the new town's development will not only consist of offices. The commercial activity of the town may eventually be concentrated in the prefecture, while the centre of Puiseux-Courdimanche will mainly consist of business concerns. Such a slight risk must be accepted for the sake of the original population.

General characteristics of the plans for new towns in the Paris region

Studies are well under way for the new town of Trappes as well as for that in the Marne valley (whose urban centre will be established at Noisy-le-Grand) and have also been undertaken for the new town of Tigery-Lieusaint. From the two examples of Évry and Cergy-Pontoise that we have studied in detail, and from the plans for the other new towns, the following general characteristics of these studies in town planning may be recognized:

The first is undoubtedly the major role accorded to the urban centre. This was enshrined in the master plan for the whole region and is particularly clear at Évry and in the Marne valley. The aim of these powerful centres is twofold: the creation of a centre of work and amenities for the population of the new town and aid in the restructuring of the life of the existing suburbs. This second aim is especially important in the case of Évry, where the new town will be at the centre of a ring of existing urban developments (the built-up area of Corbeil, Viry-Chatillon, Sainte-Geneviève-des-Bois, etc.) and sectors being rapidly developed (Grigny, Ris-Orangis), which already nearly enclose it. It is also of great importance in the Marne valley, where the urban centre of Noisy-le-Grand will be linked to suburban development and at the head of a line of new urban developments established on the plateaux above the left bank of the river. And at Trappes, without competing with Versailles, the urban centre will serve a large suburban area at present poorly equipped (the valleys of the Chevreuse and the Bièvre, Rambouillet, etc.). This role is of less importance at Cergy-Pontoise and Tigery-Lieusaint, which are established in more or less virgin areas.

The part played by leisure areas, especially stretches of water, is also notable. The rapid development of this type of leisure activity – in which France seems to be following the American example – makes it necessary to develop suitable sites, which prove a great asset when they are in or near the new towns. Both at Cergy-Pontoise, where the town is planned around the leisure area to be created in the meander of the Oise, and at Mantes, where a meander of the Moisson, though not so central to the town, will play a similar role, leisure facilities seem predominant in plans for the new towns. Stretches of water at Jablines and Viry-Châtillon-Grigny will contribute considerably to the character of the new towns of the Marne valley and Évry. At Trappes also, a great deal of trouble has been taken to develop the lake of Saint-Quentin and the valley of the Mérantaise; the same with the forest of Sénart, the woods of Rougeau and the Seine valley at Tigery-Lieusaint.

A balance is definitely sought between employment in the new town and the resident population. According to the master plan for the region, this balance need not be as constricting as in the new towns in Britain, where one cannot obtain housing without a job in the town, but it will leave the inhabitants free to choose a local job if they so wish. It is realized that a complete balance cannot be reached and present studies rely on hypotheses varying between 75 jobs (in the Marne valley) and 90 (at Cergy-Pontoise) for every 100 workers resident in the new towns. Apart from this, commuting will reduce the proportion of those working in the new town to probably between a half and two-thirds. But the main thing is that the choice should exist. The question of types of employment is rather more complicated and the lack of present knowledge of the evolution of patterns of employment and the restrictions of localized employment make detailed predictions difficult. But it seems that a compromise will be necessary between the present tendency for production industries only to be established on the outskirts of the urban region and the expected rapid growth of offices and public services in the course of the next generation. The main uncertainty concerns the possibility of attracting office jobs to the centre, as well as work requiring frequent contacts and exchanges of information.

The importance of infrastructures for transport is stressed in each case, with variations between one town and another but in accordance with a common policy. The new towns have to accept the fact that they are living in the age of the motor car but limits have to be set to its use, even in a new urban area, for reasons of cost, space (roads and parking facilities) and hygiene (pollution). The usual criterion is a distinction between motives of travel, with freedom of access where this is necessary and parking permits for private vehicles. These restrictions should never lead to the conditions existing in the old centres. Most travelling for pleasure, shopping and business, as well as to work within the new town or commuting between the new town and the suburb, will be done by car. On the other hand, commuting between the new town and Paris will be mainly by public transport. Separation of motor and pedestrian traffic – and sometimes of long- and short-distance motor traffic – is common, with variations between one town and another. In Évry, the motor car is confined to long-distance travel. In Noisy-le-Grand, car parks are banned from the centre. In Trappes, preference is given to motoring by parallel routes on an east-west axis. But, though the new towns are planned with the motor car in mind, public transport is not neglected and the provision of good services is regarded as essential. In the first phase an adaptation of existing railway lines by constructing new branches if necessary (Évry, Cergy, Tigery-Lieusaint) is planned until the regional express service is in action. Internal public transport has so far not been studied in detail but it is expected to vary from one town to another. Évry plans a form of transport with its own track, in the shape of a figure of eight, serving the central area. Noisy-le-Grand plans a method of transport linking the centre to the car parks, so that these can be some distance away. In each case, it is thought necessary to ensure the possibility of choice between the different solutions later on, as well as the development of the original methods.

The wish to retain flexibility of planning does not apply to the actual transport infrastructure. The planning of the urban centre or centres, residential areas and employment zones has a similar aim. At Cergy-Pontoise in particular there is an insistence on the necessity of ensuring a balanced community from the start, which demands careful long-term planning. This has also been given detailed study at Trappes.

A search for the interdependence of the various elements making up the new town (residential areas, employment zones, the centre and leisure areas) as well as between the new town, the existing suburbs and the surrounding areas is also a common characteristic of studies in planning for the new towns.

Some problems in the new towns

Planning is one but not the only main aspect of the policy for the new towns established in the Paris region. The new towns in Britain (see Chapter 1) have shown the importance of administration and finance as well.

In the case of administration, though the regional master plan has been considered by the government and adopted by the elected regional councils and the representatives of professional economic and social organizations, it has still not been formally approved. As for the decision to create the new towns, though this was made in accordance with the master plan, the developers were chosen and land was acquired, it did not mean the creation of any special administrative body comparable to the British development corporations. Commissions are formed to carry out studies in town planning, land development and facilities, to instigate and co-ordinate the first purchases of land and consider in detail the programme and target of the work to be undertaken. Their role is an essentially temporary one and they may then come into the employment of whatever body is developing the new town in the form of public bodies, as is already the case at Évry and Cergy-Pontoise. Relationships with the local authorities, which are on too small a scale to carry out new town developments themselves, will then be clearer, whether new communes are created or a new type of intercommunal authority established.

Some important action has already been taken. For one thing, the *zones d'aménagement différé* (ZAD) have a policy that solves the problem of finance by giving the state (represented by the financial and technical department of the Paris region) the right of pre-emption where owners have signified their intention to sell and the possibility of acquiring land at its price before the institution of the ZAD (allowing for revaluation in the meantime). The ZAD include the central areas of the new towns and their surrounding sectors, especially those with short- or medium-term plans. For instance, acquisition of land has begun for the future prefecture of Val-d'Oise at Cergy and the compensation settled on this occasion has every chance of legal acceptance. Also, grants from the government and the FNAFU are used to build housing in the new towns. In the 1966, 1967 and 1968 programmes, acquisitions of land were planned as well as the preparation of the sites for 39 200, 52 000 and 46 000 dwellings respectively, not counting private developments (especially at Évry and Trappes). As well as this, the financing of land acquisition for the urban centres was undertaken between 1966 and 1968.

Despite these two lines of action, the new towns will feel the lack of any individual financial mechanism. The long-term loans at low rates of interest and differing dates of repayment granted to the British development corporations have enabled them to balance their books after an average of fifteen years and to charge very moderate rents for their housing. A similar measure for the benefit of the new towns in France would be the best means of enhancing their value for their future inhabitants.

IV A new set of studies: master plans for the metropolitan areas

Administration

The master plan for the development of the Paris region could not remain as an isolated factor without destroying the necessary balance between the capital and the provinces. In fact, the new set of studies that originated in the Paris region in 1962 was extended to include the main provincial urban regions some years later when in 1966 the interministerial Planning Commission created the *Organisations d'Études d'Aménagement des Aires metropolitaines* (OREAM).[1] Their first task was to formulate a master plan for the development of the following metropolitan areas:

Lyon-Saint-Étienne
Nancy-Metz-Thionville
Nantes-Saint-Nazaire
The valley of the Basse-Seine (Rouen-Le Havre)

Eventually, they will have to deal in detail with the main outlines of the various studies for the development of urban centres and decide on the means and methods to be used in implementing the policy of the master plan.

The various studies in town planning were incorporated by the work of local offices and by the *Groupes d'Études et de Programmation* (GEP) created by the departmental directors of the Ministry of Supply. Also, for studying the particular problems of the Paris Basin, an interministerial group for the development of the Paris Basin was created in 1966, its general secretary heading a commission of enquiry formed by personnel of the IAURP. This commission of enquiry was entrusted with the preparation of a master plan for the development of the Paris Basin and more detailed directives to pass on to local commissions of enquiry (especially to those of the valleys of the lower Seine, the Oise, the Aisne and the middle Loire).

Finally, at the national level, the *Service technique central d'Aménagement et d'Urbanisme* (STCAU) was created in 1967 to undertake general studies as a guide to the regional and local planning bodies and to co-ordinate their work in a methodical scheme. An *Institut de Recherches urbaines* (IRU) was created in 1968 to carry out town planning research on the national level.

---

[1]The commission to study the development of the Basse-Seine valley was set up in 1965; those for the Oise and Aisne valleys not until 1967 and that of the middle Loire valley in September 1968.

It is still too soon to show the result of the work of OREAM. By the end of 1967, only the commission of enquiry for the development of the Basse-Seine valley had published its findings: the others were expected in 1968. They can only be shown as far as they have gone, although many of the measures are still under discussion and have not been finally accepted. Their main outlines will be shown, and their different plans studied and an attempt will be made at a synthesized picture, especially of the plans for new towns.

The present situation of the OREAM studies

OREAM LYON-SAINT-ÉTIENNE : The OREAM Lyon-Saint-Étienne undoubtedly forms the chief potential rival throughout France to the power of the Paris conurbation. Working from recent figures, the likeliest theory has been retained (exponential growth in the ZPIU): an increase from 2·1 million (1962) to 3·7 million by the end of the century. The level of employment would diminish but would remain higher than the national average. The overcrowding of the valleys of the Saône and Rhône, the wish to preserve the Dombes area and avoid unregulated development and to create a discontinuous urban area in order to preserve leisure areas without overcrowding available sites, and the needs of industrial zones and of the future international airport, all combined to decide on a triangular pattern, its apex the city of Lyon and its other angles two new towns based on Bourgoin and Ambérieu (Fig. 42). Unusual tertiary employment would be restricted to Lyon itself, with the site of Bron acting as a link during the first phase (before the building of the new towns) and then as secondary centre (tertiary sector, university and research). The new towns would need to be large enough (with populations of 15 000 - 300 000) to justify the possession of their own amenities, near enough to Lyon, despite the 30 - 40 km break for leisure areas, and with satisfactory links to ensure the unity of the urban region. This plan, with its eastward extension of development in the Saône and Rhône valleys (the Sainte-Étienne region is declining and any co-ordinated scheme of development would be difficult) necessitates the creation of premises for a concentration of tertiary employment in Lyon itself and of industries in the new towns.

OREAM MARSEILLE-AIX-FOS: Rather than becoming a rival to the Paris region, the urban region built around Marseille seems likely to become the capital of the Mediterranean sector of the French Midi, orientated towards the other lands bordering the Mediterranean. Its population should almost treble between 1962 (1 150 000) and the end of the century (3 200 000) and double by 1985 (2 300 000). It was estimated at about 1 350 000 in 1966. A very low level

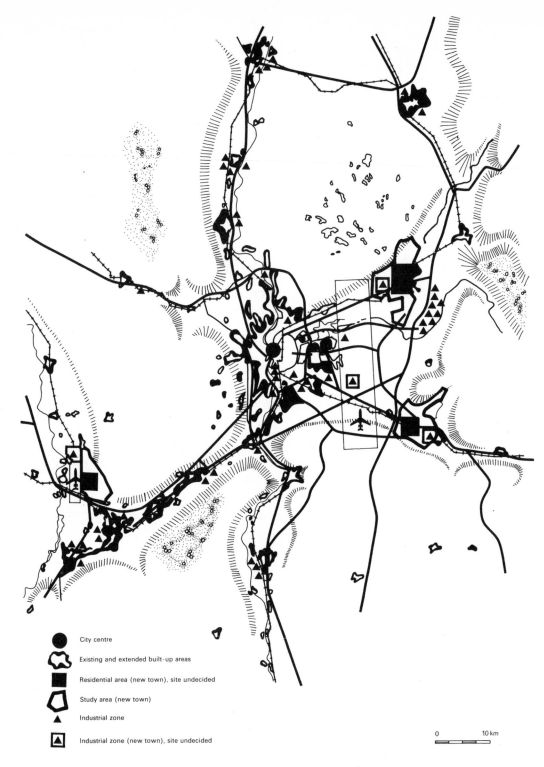

City centre

Existing and extended built-up areas

Residential area (new town), site undecided

Study area (new town)

Industrial zone

Industrial zone (new town), site undecided

0   10 km

Fig. 42   Proposed development of the Lyon-Saint-Étienne urban region.

of employment (0·36) was expected (the region of Marseille already having the lowest level of all the French urban regions, at 0·37); the OREAM has since predicted a slightly higher level (0·40 in the year 2000). The establishment of large firms requiring skilled labour seems desirable in an area that attracts plenty of unskilled foreign labour.

The plans are not yet final but the following factors may be listed:

Varied land use to the west forbidding any large-scale development other than that at Fos.

The necessity of avoiding the destruction of the natural surroundings by unregulated residential development.

The aim of a fairly high urban density (eighty people per hectare, not counting industrial and leisure areas) on the Mediterranean pattern.

Stress laid on motorways rather than railways and plans for public road transport.

The need for improved links with Paris as well as with Turin and Nîmes-Montpellier.

OREAM NORD: The fundamental problem for northern France is the restructuring of an economy that grew up around the coalfield, and therefore the formation of a new coherent system of urban organization in a national and, even more, international framework. Such a plan should ensure the maximum freedom of choice for firms and individuals alike. Although the present difficulties of the regional economy result in a negative population movement, it has been assumed that this area's share of the French population will remain constant: from the present 3 million to 5 million by about 2010 (with about 3·3 million in the central area compared with the present 1·9 million). An average rate of employment of 38 per cent is planned for 2010, with considerable regional variations (46 per cent at Lille and 36 per cent in the coalfield).

Three courses have been considered, each demanding the intensive growth of the coastal region and the more moderate development of the Valenciennes area. The course most likely to be chosen is based on a Lille-Arras axis (with two motorways). This plan shatters the 'defensive solidarity' that surrounds the mining region at the moment and replaces it with a 'solidarity of interest' round the new development area. It also helps to solve the financial problem. This axis of development would rely on a frequent transport service after the style of the Paris regional express, while a Paris-style metro would serve the dense central area. A small new town – Lille-est – is already being planned.

OREAM LORRAINE: The fundamental choice for planners in a highly

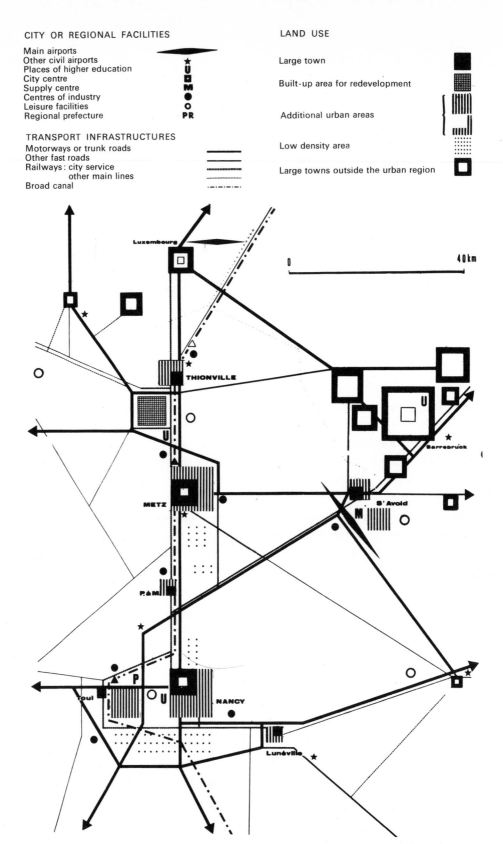

CITY OR REGIONAL FACILITIES

Main airports
Other civil airports
Places of higher education   ★ U
City centre   □ M
Supply centre   ● O
Centres of industry
Leisure facilities   O
Regional prefecture   PR

TRANSPORT INFRASTRUCTURES

Motorways or trunk roads
Other fast roads
Railways: city service
          other main lines
Broad canal

LAND USE

Large town

Built-up area for redevelopment

Additional urban areas

Low density area

Large towns outside the urban region

Fig. 43 One of the schemes studied for the development of the urban region of Lorraine.

industrialized region on the threshold of vast changes is in the field of regional economic development. Two possibilities have been established: the population of the area studied (1 million in 1962) would increase either to 1 700 000 or to 2 100 000 (or even to 2 200 000). The plan chosen will be nearer the higher figure, or even higher because of the demands of land development. The standard of living (with an expected rise of 2·5 per cent per year) will be two and a half times higher.

Four plans have been considered and widely discussed:

> The natural and separate developments of Metz and Nancy.
> A study of the whole Moselle valley, with the siting of established industries between Metz and Nancy and an outward extension towards Toul and Thionville. The coalfield is not included in this plan.
> A study of the Nancy-Sarre-Luxembourg triangle, based on the Moselle valley, with proposed specialization in administrative machinery at Nancy-Toul and economic activities at Metz (Fig. 43).
> The overall development of the Nancy-Sarre-Luxembourg triangle, with the creation of a diagonal axis through Toul-Nancy-Saarbrücken.

The concept of new towns created *ex nihilo* is rejected because, on the scale of Lorraine, they would be necessarily small in size and would detract too much from the large towns in Lorraine. All the plans therefore prefer new urban developments, which are extensions of Nancy (east of Toul) and of Metz (to the south). Linear development between Nancy and Metz has been rejected through lack of space.

OREAM NANTES-SAINT-NAZAIRE: The Nantes-Saint-Nazaire region is not yet a regional capital, nor even a pole of attraction for the people of western France, and could only become so as the result of deliberate policy, especially in the creation of new centres of employment. Present theories allow for a tendency for movement of population into the city, with the population increasing from 560 000 in 1962 to about 1 100 000 by the end of the century, by which time an employment rate of 37 per cent is predicted (37·5 in 1962). Employment in agriculture would decrease but employment in industry would keep pace with the growth of the population, while tertiary employment would increase considerably (+140 per cent).

The sites themselves would act as limiting factors. The three solutions studied entail a large industrial settlement (between Donges and Saint-Nazaire), the creation of a large tertiary centre linked with the extensive growth of Nantes and the smaller-scale development of Saint-Nazaire. One proposal is for a new town between Nantes and Saint-Nazaire, another for the development of Nantes towards the north-west and a third for a ring of about fifteen small residential units built round four new centres and linked to neighbouring industrial zones.

OREAM BASSE-SEINE: Here the main decision to be taken was concerned with the balance between the upstream and downstream parts of the valley: for reasons of planning on a national scale the downstream section was chosen. The 1962 population of 1 050 000 will be multiplied by 2·4 to 2 500 000 before the end of the century. A figure as high as 3 million was rejected, because it did not seem desirable to develop the region to such an extent, as a natural extension of the Paris region. In the field of employment, fewer workers are predicted in agriculture, but a growth is predicted in the number in industry and particularly in tertiary employment.

In keeping with these decisions, which meant the siting downstream of Rouen of some industries that would otherwise have tended to be sited upstream, the plan proposes concentrated development between Rouen and Le Havre on both sides of the Seine and stretching above Rouen as far as Évreux; the development of Le Havre towards the north-east and of the districts of Pavilly-Barentin and Bolbec-Lillebonne on the right bank; new towns first at Bourg-Achard and then near Pont-Audemer on the left bank; the growth of the conurbation of Rouen to a population of 500 000 by the end of the century and the creation of a new town (Le Vaudreuil) in the south, in the loop of the Seine near its junction with the Eure; the expansion of Vernon, Gaillon and Évreux upstream. This plan relies on the new Normandy motorway and a future overhead railway.

The master plan for Basse-Normandie was published at the end of 1967.[1] The creation of the first new town, Le Vaudreuil, was decided on in the same year and a commission to work on the plan was formed at the beginning of 1968, in close co-operation with the work of OREAM.

The main characteristics of current studies in regional planning

Of the many points that have to be considered when drawing up a master plan of town planning and development on a regional scale, three seem of particular importance throughout the studies for the regional capitals and the master plans for the Paris region and the Basse-Seine alike:

The main purpose of the development.

[1]Mission d'études de la basse vallée de la Seine, *Projet de schema d'aménagement de la Basse-Seine* (Rouen, March 1968).

Quantitative predictions (especially of population).

The particular form of urban development with regard to the first two points.

A fourth point of consideration also seems of importance: the picture formed by the members of the studying commission of the future way of life of the citizens for whom they are planning. Unfortunately, the difficult studies of the future, which might answer such a question, have not been undertaken.

The main aim of development

This fundamental question, affecting the types of development planned, elicits answers that vary from one place to another. The master plan for the planning and development of the Paris region put forward the aim of allowing individuals and businesses alike as much freedom of choice as possible in place of residence, place of work, place and type of shopping, place and type of leisure, friends, etc. This choice, depending on the unity of the urban region, has not been ruled out anywhere but it has been given paramount importance only in the Nord. It is, however, implicit in the plans for Lyon-Saint-Étienne, Lorraine, Nantes-Saint-Nazaire and elsewhere.

Another fundamental element in many of the OREAM, strengthened by unfavourable economic conditions, is the need for an almost complete switch-over of occupations (in Lorraine, the Nord and even Marseille, Nantes and Basse-Seine). One result of this may be a disregard of present urban patterns.

The idea of the regional capital is in the forefront of the plans of the organizers of OREAM but often in differing and even opposing forms. The Lyon-Saint-Étienne region is the only one really fitted to rival (if not balance) the Paris region. Lyon's economic strength and its position seem to justify an ambition in which the Alpine areas (especially Grenoble) could share, given sufficient co-operation. The Marseille region is too conscious of its own weaknesses and its dependence on Paris to attempt a similar role: it sees itself rather in its traditional role as capital of the *Midi méditerranéen*, a link with the Mediterranean countries and the gateway to a large part of France and even Italy and Switzerland.

In some of the other urban regions, near the frontiers (Lorraine and the Nord) the idea of balancing the metropolis on a national scale seems somewhat outdated: Metz needs to be linked with Luxembourg and Saarbrücken as much as with Nancy, and the Nord could only be artificially detached from its extensions in Belgium. Then, in some cases, there is no true metropolis, either because of the geographical separation underlined by historical rivalry (Nancy and Metz) or because the urban region is too small to swallow up other regional centres (Nantes-Saint-Nazaire with Rennes and Angers).

These factors stress the difficulties that lie ahead in achieving the aims set for the *métropoles régionales* within the framework of the national policy of development.

Predictions of population and employment

The first master plan of development to be published, that of the Paris region (1965), stressed the fact that, in order to limit the growth of the Paris region (9 million in 1965) to less than 14 million by the end of the century, a progressive slackening of population movement must be achieved.

This aim of a considerably slower rate of growth than that of the general urban population throughout France (estimated to be doubled between 1962 and 2000) could only be achieved if some provincial cities increased at a higher than average rate: a role destined to be played by the *métropoles régionales* and the major towns of the Paris basin.

Population statistics established by the OREAM show the essentially voluntary nature of this proposal. Working in an unfavourable economic period, the directors of the OREAM were horrified by the original hypothesis of a trebling of the population of the *métropoles* between 1962 and the end of the century. The OREAM for the Basse-Seine was the only one to be receptive to this idea, but it has been instructed to aim at a lower target. At Marseille-Aix-Fos, a 180 per cent increase is predicted between 1962 and the end of the century. Elsewhere, predictions are considerably lower:

> An increase of between 50 and 80 per cent for Lyon-Saint-Étienne.
> A 50 per cent increase in the urban region of the Nord.
> A lower prediction of 70 per cent and a higher prediction of 110 or 120 per cent for Lorraine.
> 100 per cent at Nantes-Saint-Nazaire.

Even if the higher hypothesis is retained in each case and even if allowance is made for the fact that the zones studied include some rural areas, it is clear that, at the most, a doubling of the population of the metropolitan areas will result. Equal attention must be paid to medium-sized towns if the limits set to the Paris region are to be maintained. In this respect, the effect of unfavourable economic conditions on plans for the future based mainly on past tendencies may be questioned. The same could be asked about predictions in the field of employment. If a more rapid development in tertiary employment than in industry is accepted, it is still not certain whether this fits the national picture of a rapid growth of services and offices that are to have priority in the large conurbations. A study in depth of the development of different types of employment and the needs of siting them has yet to be made.

The chief aspects of planning: the role of the new towns

The aims of planning are reflected spatially: the wish to maintain the unity of the urban region leads to the planning of the main centres not too far apart, to ensure links between them and to dispense with any automatic local balance between population and employment (as in Lyon and the new towns planned at Bourgoin and Ambérieu); the wish to separate the northern development from the coalfield leads to the planning of development along the Lille-Arras axis, etc.

Other characteristics may be recognized in the decisions taken: for instance, the slow rate of population increase, once seen as normal for existing built-up areas, limits the extent of new developments.

At Lyon, the two new towns planned will only absorb 30 per cent of the population increase. Yet another factor contributes to the limitation of the size of new developments: the realization of the low power of attraction of the main provincial towns makes those entrusted with their development reluctant to create centres of growth that would rival the original centre in facilities and opportunities of employment.

The rate of growth of the provincial urban regions limits the possibilities of creating large new towns, especially where, as in the Basse-Seine, new developments are fairly widely dispersed. The inevitable result is that the new towns are reduced to the status of satellite towns round the parent city on which they depend. The term 'new town' is also not used everywhere. It is used for the two developments planned to the north-east and south-east of Lyon and for some of those in the Basse-Seine, but in Lorraine the term 'urbanisation additionelle' is used, seen as a natural extension to Metz or Nancy or to the zone of linear development in the Nord.

Even if the variety of terms used and needing definition is equivocal, there does exist a great variety of urban planning according to the equal variety of aims for development. But the exact role to be played in an urban region of 1 - 5 million inhabitants by, for instance, a large new town (the Lyon region), a smaller town (Basse-Seine), a satellite town or an urbanisation additionelle has not yet been defined. The distribution of functions and facilities and the rebuilding of the original centres need to be studied in each particular context and can only be decided after more detailed study.

5: Town planning and new towns in the USA

The United States, as well as the countries of Eastern Europe, form an interesting point of comparison. Planning mechanisms, in the economic field as well as in actual development, are fundamentally different from those of western Europe. The federal system and the doctrine of free enterprise are the two main causes of a dearth of planning on a national scale.

What planning there is is confronted by many problems: unregulated urban expansion, problems of transport in towns where the motor car reigns supreme, and racial segregation of residential areas and facilities. All this, added to the limited powers of any bodies entrusted with regional planning, gives prime importance to the smallest local authorities, the counties and towns. For these reasons, the new towns of the United States reflect local problems rather than any policy of regional development.

I Planning policy in the large cities of the USA

In this land of free enterprise, the very term 'planning' is suspect, so that it is hardly surprising if the creation of regional planning bodies is belated and their role limited.

Administrative organization

As a rule, each city has its city planning commission, which issues instructions to a large firm of experts entrusted with planning studies, especially of re-development, but not with carrying out these plans, except at Boston, with the Boston Redevelopment Authority. The regional organizations have, on the contrary, no official status: established by the local authorities, they have only a (very slight) power of persuasion. A recent bill, however, gave them certain prerogatives: the federal government now asks their advice about programmes demanding federal funds but this advice does not necessarily carry any weight. So the regional planning bodies have functions but no power, and in the case of powerful local authorities their functions count for very little. Under these conditions, it is impossible for them to put forward any plans for sweeping regional development.

There do exist regional bodies assigned to particular fields, such as transport, atmospheric pollution, green spaces, water supply and drainage, some of them with wide powers, including grants from the rates. The role of the regional planning bodies is in particular to achieve co-ordination between the local authorities and these specialist bodies. Sometimes the regional planning body is itself a specialist regional organization with this extra co-ordinating role. This is so in Philadelphia, where the Penn Jersey Transportation Study became the Delaware Valley Regional Planning Commission in 1965, and in New York, where the Tristate Transportation Study was entrusted with this role.

There are also in places official associations with the task of formulating a policy of regional development. New York and Los Angeles each have their Regional Plan Association, which can be at odds with the regional bodies that give advice on programmes requiring federal funds. These private associations, mainly financed by private foundations, often have more freedom than the official regional bodies to propose clear and original plans. For instance, in New York, the Regional Plan Association published a regional plan in 1929 and is shortly to publish another, proposing the creation of ten new employment zones.

The role of federal aid

As in many other fields, the role of the federal government lies mainly in financing studies and undertakings without necessarily prescribing their forms. The National Housing Act of 1954, which came into force in 1955 under the title 'Programme 701', sought to encourage studies in planning by allowing the states, regions, counties or towns to have two-thirds of their studies financed by the federal government. Over thirteen years, more than $150 million have been expended under this scheme on 5000 different projects. Similarly, large-scale studies of regional transport are mainly financed by the federal government via the Bureau of Public Roads. Dating from 1962, the Highway Act ensured that in the conurbations the transport system would be linked to other aspects of planning: the federal government no longer subsidizes any road plan that has not been examined by the authority responsible for regional planning.

The role of federal subsidies is especially important in the case of redevelopment schemes. Federal aid can be obtained once approval is given by the federal redevelopment office. The local redevelopment agency borrows money for its operations and the federal government makes up two-thirds of the deficit on these (three-quarters in some exceptional cases) once the land has been acquired, prepared and resold to private promoters, without any obligation on their part to rehouse the former occupants.

Regional plans

Each great conurbation enjoys the services of a regional planning body and sometimes of more than one (one official and one unofficial, as in New York and Los Angeles). These bodies are all working on regional town planning schemes, some of which, like the plan for Washington (1961), have already been published.[1] In other places, provisional plans have appeared, as in San Francisco Bay.[2] The plan for Washington is the only one to make a clear proposal for the creation of a series of new towns.

Policies also vary considerably. In Washington, the now famous plan consists of a star-shaped pattern with six main bands of development. This seemed the best pattern for a very rapidly increasing built-up area (with a population of 2 million around 1960 and one of 5 million predicted by the end of the century) to provide an efficient system of public transport and preserve intervening green spaces. The siting of the corridors of development was decided by the position of existing small towns capable of acting as nuclei to new towns with populations of about 80 000 - 100 000 planned along these axes. Later, in September 1966, a guide to regional development was published, setting out the regional plan in detail.

In San Francisco, the firms working on the regional plan examined first of all the unconnected plans of various local authorities before studying three possible patterns: linear (or corridor), polycentric and dispersed. After consultation with the various local authorities, the Association of Bay Area Governments published their final regional plan in 1969.

II   Administration

Compared with the limited powers of official planning bodies, private enterprise plays an important part: in fact, the new towns of the USA are for the most part private and profitable undertakings (see Section IV below).

New towns created by private enterprise

In the USA, new towns seem a natural product of the activities of private promoters. These, having satisfied the demand for individual houses in the suburbs of the great cities, turned their attention to the wider market of upper-

[1]National Capital Planning Commission, National Capital Regional Planning Council, *A Plan for the Year 2000. The Nation's Capital.*
[2]Association of Bay Area Governments, *Preliminary Regional Plan for the San Francisco Bay Region* (Berkeley, November 1966).

middle-income families. This wider market, with its demands for greater facilities than those of the suburbs, led to the planning of large-scale operations – consisting of over 10 000 dwellings – for which the term 'new town' seemed the most appropriate and generally acceptable.

The success of such operations demands the acquisition of huge areas of land, ideally sold or developed by a single owner, or by him through a subsidiary company. This happened, with some local differences, at Reston, Foster City, Redwood Shores and Valencia. It is equally important for the promoter to have sufficient funds available to acquire the land, if necessary, and to prepare it, etc. We shall find (see Section IV below) that the difficulties encountered in the course of these operations often spring from the financial incapacity of the promoters: Reston Virginia Incorporated became bankrupt in 1967 and was taken over by the Gulf Oil Company, which formed a subsidiary, Gulf Reston Incorporated.

Relationships with official planning services

The regional authorities – not to mention the federal authorities – possess so little power that the promoters of the new towns carry on negotiations with the lowest-level authority: the county, if the new town is not linked with an existing town, or otherwise the existing town itself. These negotiations are relatively simple where the interests of the promoters coincide with those of the local authorities, with whom they are usually on excellent personal terms. The siting of new towns on the territory of a town or county can in fact bring in revenue if the housing is accompanied by industries paying local rates (based on the value of land and buildings) without bringing expenses as great as housing (schools, social facilities, etc.). With bitter rivalry between one town and another and one county and another to attract firms for the sake of revenue, it can readily be seen that the creation of a new town is to be prized, even if the housing costs the town or county more in the long run than it brings in. In theory, the county possesses four main means of controlling the promoter's activities: the basis of local taxation, the role of interlocutor played by the county's planning committee, the extension of water supply and drainage systems and the regulation of sites. In practice, however (as observed in Foster City, Redwood Shores, Valencia and Columbia), it seems that the counties are not always in a position or wishful to make full use of these opportunities for control.

Reston is the exception to this rule: its site was chosen in agreement with the regional authorities and the new town seems a partial realization of the 1961 regional plan, while the promoter's assistant is a former member of the body that drew up the plan. The concern with quality and with the creation of a true urban environment, rare in the USA, which guided the first promoter, has helped to make this operation, approved by Fairfax County, a model development.

Internal administration of the new towns

An important administrative problem will arise in the new towns after some years: that of the eventual creation of a new authority, at least in those cases – and they form the majority – where the new town is built on land directly controlled by the county. In theory, the inhabitants of the new town can demand the creation of their own local authority once a total of some hundreds is reached and a 75 per cent poll has been recorded. The promoters are usually strongly opposed to this eventuality, since they prefer to deal with an established authority, which, because they constitute an important source of revenue, is therefore well disposed towards them, rather than with a new authority representative of the population. As for the population concerned, it is not in its interest, at least at first, to demand an independent authority, because this might only cover the residential areas and very high local taxation would be necessary to meet the cost of essential facilities, particularly schools. Nevertheless, the future creation of a new authority is taken for granted by most of the new towns. The promoter prepares for this by instigating residents' associations to organize certain collective amenities, as in Valencia. In Columbia the promoter has created an association with his own representatives in the majority but in which the residents will play an increasing part until they are in the majority by the time the town is completed and then able to take control. This association is entrusted with the maintenance of communications, parks, leisure facilities, communal activities, etc. It can grant loans and levy a property rate (about 0·75 per cent of the value of the property per year).

The search for new administrative patterns

It is uncertain whether the convergent interests of the promoter and the local authority concerned correspond with those of the region as a whole on the one hand and the population of the new town on the other. This population chooses a mode of living that fits in with the changing pattern of the American Way of Life (see Section III below) and is attracted by the prospect, unusual in residential areas of the USA, of many and varied amenities. But it seems doubtful whether the promises of the advertising brochures can be fully implemented, whether or not the size of the new towns allows for such a high level of amenities, and whether the promoters have the resources to finance or even to attract such facilities. In some of the new towns financial difficulties have been so great (see Section IV below) that no attempt is made to conceal the necessity of cutting down the programme of amenities (a notable example of this is at Reston, where the promoter became bankrupt and the development was taken over by a large oil company).

From the point of view of the local authority, on the other hand, the new towns are not part of any general policy except, as at Reston, by chance. Resulting from this are a poor deployment of regional facilities, unregulated growth, the risk of open spaces being swallowed up, etc. Also, the methods of financing the new towns of the USA limit them – and their promoters do not disguise this fact – to the comparatively well-to-do, so that they do nothing towards solving the housing problems of the underprivileged.

There are those who deplore this state of affairs: those in charge of regional planning, who are aware that their only power lies in persuasion, and the federal authorities alike. The new Ministry of Housing and Urban Development, created at the beginning of 1967, has found it necessary to favour legislation allowing for the creation of public bodies similar to the development corporations of the new towns in Britain. But it would be difficult to get such a measure passed by Congress, which is traditionally in favour of free enterprise, and public opinion would first have to be won over, since the federal government is mainly seen as an extortioner. It would also be necessary to overcome the hostility of the great cities who are not anxious to see federal resources diverted to urban redevelopment or the creation of new towns: a problem that arises in other countries as well. However, such legislation seems necessary if genuine new towns are to be created in the USA. Meanwhile, the regional authorities, such as that of Washington, can only propose developments (such as the plan for the expansion of Germantown as an official undertaking) without any powers except those of persuasion over the local authorities and promoters and control of plans for amenities carried out with federal aid.

III   Town planning

The new towns are private undertakings whose overall role is slight compared with new developments as a whole. They only comprise one aspect, and a relatively small one, of the country's planning problems, however much may be claimed for them by their promoters.

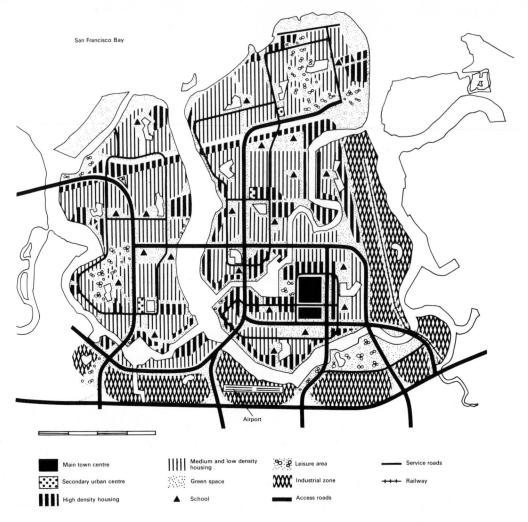

San Francisco Bay

Airport

■ Main town centre	‖‖‖‖ Medium and low density housing	Leisure area	── Service roads
Secondary urban centre	Green space	XXXXX Industrial zone	+++ Railway
‖‖‖ High density housing	▲ School	▬▬ Access roads	

Fig. 44 Redwood Shores : master plan.

Planning

One result of the weakness of the regional planning bodies is that those in charge of the new towns are given no directives aimed at fitting their projects into the pattern of regional development. The promoter usually commissions a plan from a private firm: Larry Smith & Co. for Redwood Shores; Victor Gruen & Associates for Valencia, etc. Next a master plan is commissioned from a private town planning firm: Wilsey, Ham & Blair for Foster City; The Architects Collaborative at Redwood Shores (Fig. 44); Thomas L. Sutton at Valencia (Fig. 45); Whittlesey & Conklin at Reston (Fig. 46). In Columbia, however, the

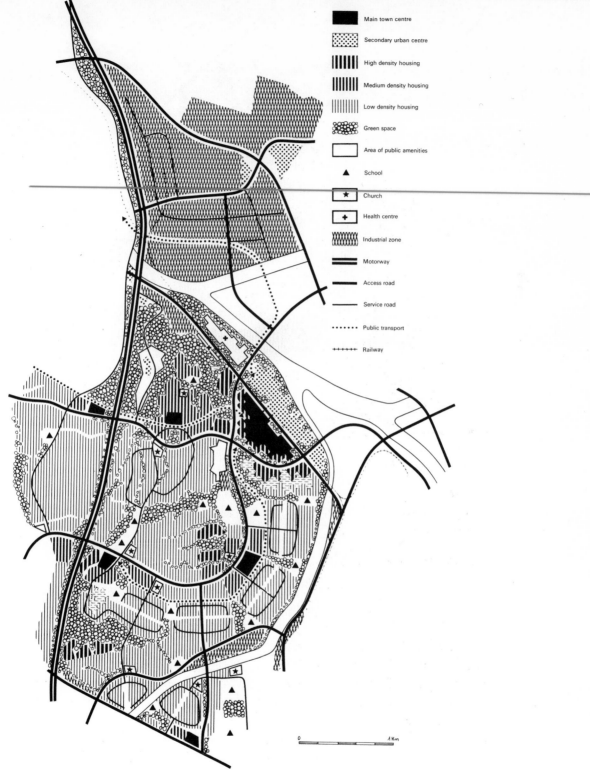

Main town centre

Secondary urban centre

High density housing

Medium density housing

Low density housing

Green space

Area of public amenities

▲ School

★ Church

✚ Health centre

Industrial zone

Motorway

Access road

Service road

Public transport

Railway

0   1 Km

Fig. 45 Valencia : master plan.

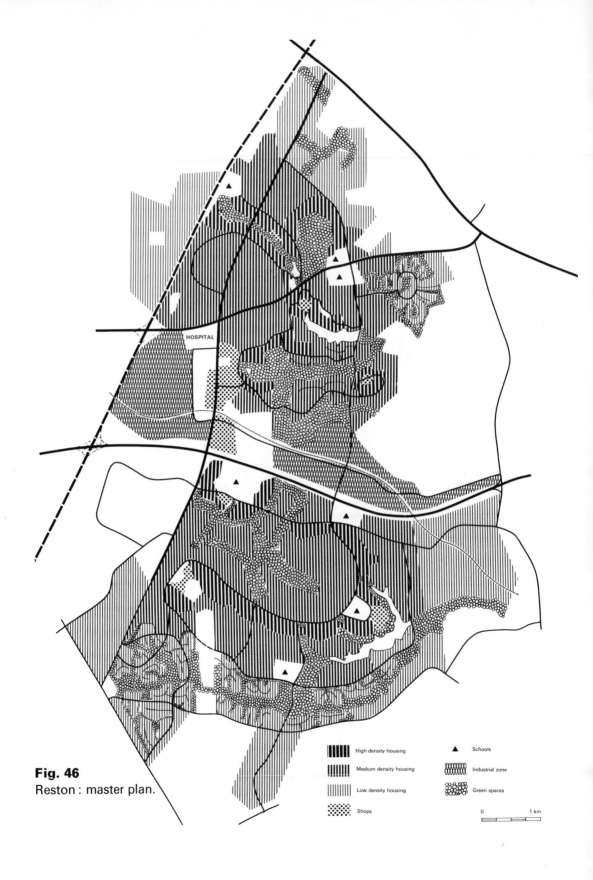

Fig. 46
Reston : master plan.

HOSPITAL

High density housing	▲	Schools
Medium density housing		Industrial zone
Low density housing		Green spaces
Shops		

0   1 km

promoter preferred to form his own staff within the Rouse Company, calling on various expert advice without losing his control of the undertaking and the co-ordination of the whole.

The master plan is usually approved by the local authorities without any trouble but is not necessarily respected by the promoter himself, who, when confronted with practical difficulties and financial problems, does not hesitate to modify the original plans. It is as if the drawing up of a development plan by an accredited firm is just an extra publicity measure on the promoter's behalf. The general and detailed plans are drawn up by various town planning or architectural concerns. There is also an extra stage, the intermediate plan, coming between the two. All these plans are, in theory, in the control of whatever local authority (town or county) has the new town on its territory.

To judge from these new towns (Reston and Redwood Shores in particular), the planning firms and the firms of contractors working on the schemes often seem out of step with each other. The actual distance often between them does not assist co-ordination: for instance, the planning firm for Redwood Shores, The Architects Collaborative, has its headquarters at Cambridge, near Boston.

The main lines of policy

The principles that guided the town planners in drawing up their schemes for the new towns have not often been stated. However, a detailed analysis of these plans shows some main lines of policy:

> The aim of a true community: development in small units (villages) in enclosed spaces, in reaction against the individualism of the American suburbs. This leads to the practice of building terraced houses instead of the usual separate plots.
>
> The intentional inclusion of leisure facilities in residential areas; the great attention given to water (Foster City and Reston), planned green spaces and recreation and sports grounds.
>
> Priority for pedestrian precincts, resulting from the first two lines of policy and unusual in a country where the motor car reigns supreme. The network of pedestrian ways links the residential quarters to the central village facilities, within 400 m (Fig. 47).
>
> A balance between public transport and private motoring. Though this may result in the reservation of space for a future public transport system, this is usually as far as it has gone. There is a large gap here between theory and practice.
>
> The attempt at a high quality environment, which often leads to the use of Mediterranean styles, with piazza, balcony, arcade and patio.

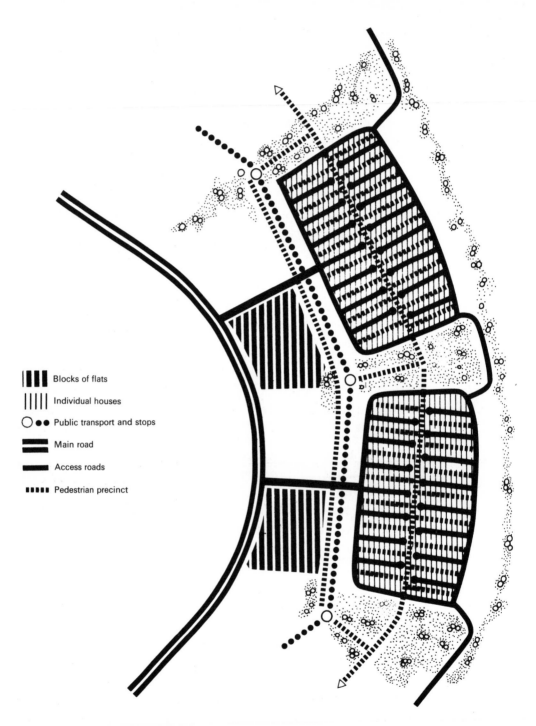

▌▐▌▐	Blocks of flats
‖‖‖	Individual houses
○ ●●	Public transport and stops
▬▬▬	Main road
▬▬▬	Access roads
▪▪▪▪▪	Pedestrian precinct

Fig. 47 Valencia : plan showing separation of traffic.

Though these ideas of town planning may not be very original, they are completely opposed to some of the natural patterns of urban development in the United States.

Plans for organization

These principles have to be applied to sites that are not always favourable: between 30 and 50 km from the great cities (Washington, San Francisco and Los Angeles), sometimes in green and wooded valleys (Columbia and Reston), sometimes flat and humid on the bay shores (Foster City and Redwood Shores), sometimes on broken, desert-type land (Valencia), the new towns are implanted wherever the promoter has found enough available space.

Some plans have conventional road systems (Valencia, Redwood Shores) while others (Foster City, Reston, Columbia) have a much freer system without gradation of types of road.

The urban pattern is made up of the road system and the siting of housing, employment and amenities. In some towns (Valencia, Redwood Shores) these zones are exactly differentiated, whereas in others (Columbia, Reston, Foster City) the pattern is freer.

The zones of employment are sometimes shared between several medium-sized areas of 20 - 60 ha near the spinal motorways (Reston, Columbia) while elsewhere larger areas are chosen (100 ha at Redwood Shores, 400 ha in the plans for Valencia) outside or on the outskirts of the town but always near the main motorways.

Tertiary employment and amenities are grouped in the town centre and in the village centres, though in practice these centres do not yet exist and detailed study of them has either not been or only just been begun (Valencia).

Employment

For the promoters of the new towns industries are desirable more for the prestige they give the site of the town (especially in the case of well-known firms) than for the possibilities of employment they afford the future inhabitants. Also, industries are important sources of revenue for the promoter (in rents) and for the local authorities (in rates). As for an eventual balance between employment and the working population, this possibility is not seriously considered and even if it could be achieved its significance would be modified by commuting from outside. For these reasons, planning of employment is only cursory: the area of industrial zones is reckoned by a fixed number *a priori* (10 000 jobs at Foster City); sometimes land unfit for other purposes is set aside for industry (marshy ground at Redwood Shores). Similarly, the planning of commercial or office areas (275 000 m^2 plus parking spaces in Valencia; 165 000 m^2 in Columbia) are more a publicity measure than an exact study of needs and possibilities. The promoter has no illusions about this and is ready to adapt his plans to whatever situation may arise.

Transport

Even though the sites of the new towns were chosen where the promoter could find enough space, he still had to ensure motorway access with, if possible, a number of approach roads providing access to the new town. Despite the stated object of public transport, there are no illusions about this and privately it is admitted to be of secondary consideration (as with the new firm in charge at Reston). Valencia is the exception: with a target population of 200 000 and the planning of a large centre, provision is made for a fast public transport system with its own track (which, however, is not included in the plans for the Los Angeles underground railway now under discussion), needed for ensuring the success of the centre and limiting the amount of parking space needed. In some towns (Columbia, Foster City, Redwood Shores) the promoter is trying to obtain a transport system for the new town from private transport companies or from the local authorities, sometimes by subsidizing them (Foster City).

The new towns have hardly any plans for internal public transport, though Columbia has a minibus service with a cheap fare instituted and subsidized by the promoter, who uses this curiosity as a publicity aid.

Car parking is fairly well provided for, though at Reston, for example, it seems that there will never be enough spaces. At present there are 1·5 garage spaces to every flat and two to every separate house.

So, for external links as much as for internal access, the new towns rely essentially on private motoring, whatever future hopes of public transport may be expressed – but not greatly believed in.

IV   The financing of the new towns

Since the new towns of the United States are building operations launched by private promoters, their financial problems are altogether different from those of the countries of eastern or western Europe. Profits, the promoters' sources of capital, the mechanics and costs of acquisition, preparing and reselling land, sale prices and rents of housing and other premises will be studied in turn.

Profits

Study of profits is of great importance to the promoters, who expect about 20 per cent profit on their investments. In Columbia, for instance, Mr Rouse, who is the director of the Rouse Company, which has already built a number of commercial centres, has installed an economic computer that can keep a check on the financial position of the operation at any particular stage. At present, the computer allows for the completion of the town in fifteen years and reckons the expenses involved and the needs of capital investment. It gives the hope of a gross profit, before taxation, of nearly $130 million in fifteen years. This economic computer has become a guide for the whole operation and no architectural decision can be taken without a reckoning of its cost and its effects on the general finances. Obviously, such a computer can have its drawbacks in estimating costs and sale prices and especially times of completion. It shows, however, a serious deficit for six or seven years, which poses the first financial problem.

Sources of capital

In practice, the financing of a new town project in the United States differs only in size from that of conventional operations. The policy of the local authorities is similar, not giving any special financial aid except occasionally for the preparation of land.

Unless the promoter already owns the land, he has to acquire it, if possible very quickly to nip any pirate operations in the bud. He then has to prepare the land, sometimes with financial aid from the local authority on whose territory it is. There are no hard and fast rules about the use of the prepared land, but usually land for individual houses in transferred to building societies who build and sell the houses while the promoter confines himself to rented property (flats, commercial premises, offices, factories, etc.). There are exceptions to this: for instance, at Irwine Ranch (near Los Angeles) individual houses are built for letting by the promoter.

Apart from private capital, the promoter has access to two sources of finance:

> Short-term loans to cover the cost of acquiring and preparing the land before the resale to building societies. These loans, by private banks, carry an interest of about 6 per cent per year. At Foster City, T. Jack Foster & Sons are borrowing at 6·75 per cent, while at Valencia the rate is only 6 per cent.
>
> Long-term loans to cover the cost of building premises for rent by the

promoter. These loans have a slightly higher rate of interest (about 7 per cent) and are usually for twenty to twenty-five years. At Reston, 6·5 per cent loans for twenty to twenty-five years have been taken out from banks and insurance companies for building flats. At Valencia, the rate is only 6 per cent over twenty-five years. These rates of interest seem very low in comparison with the promoter's future rents.

The promoters of the new towns claim to have no difficulty in obtaining these loans. However, their financial state is far from watertight, especially when they have to purchase land (as at Reston, Columbia and Foster City). When the purchase is not from one single owner in the first place (as at Foster City) prices of land rise (as at Reston and Columbia), making things more difficult for the promoter. Columbia's financial difficulties are well known and those of Reston have brought about the recent bankruptcy of the promoting company, Virginia Reston Incorporated, and its takeover by the Gulf Oil Company. Though it is obviously difficult to make accurate generalizations, it seems that the creation of a new town is a difficult operation to get under way, especially when multiple purchase of land is necessary.

The acquisition and resale of land

In some cases, the promoter does not need to acquire the land: when, for instance, a company already owning land decides to build a new town through a subsidiary company. This has happened at Valencia, where the Newhall Land and Farming Company had owned the land for over a century and transferred it to a subsidiary, the California Land Company, to build the new town. Similarly, at Redwood Shores, Leslie Properties Inc. is a subsidiary of the Leslie Salt Company, which used the land for salt pans. In other cases (such as Foster City) the promoter sells the land *en bloc* before the building starts, if possible to a single buyer (in this case the Leslie Salt Company, Foster City being immediately north of Redwood Shores). But in the most difficult cases (Reston and Columbia) the promoter has to acquire the land from multiple owners and run the risk of seeing some of them speculating on the increased value of the land once the new town is built and on the possibility of carrying out a pirate operation (such as a rival commercial centre). This financial speculation is one of the financial problems met with by the promoters of Columbia and especially Reston.

The preparation of the land is usually carried out by the promoter himself, according to need (Valencia, Reston and Columbia). The cost price of the prepared land is about $62 000 (£25 000) per hectare. In some cases, the promoter receives help from the local authorities (the town, or the county when the new town does not come under a town authority and is therefore an unincorporated area) through an improvement agency created for this purpose: this has happened at Foster City and Redwood Shores. In the case of the latter, the local town (Redwood City) issued loans (at under 6 per cent per year over forty years) and used the income to finance part of the work. The land remained in the ownership of the promoters who, however, transferred it at a lower price, because the new owners had to pay a special tax to the local authority, which enabled the loans to be repayed.

The resale of prepared land is in principle only for land intended for building houses for home ownership (the chief type of housing) while the promoter builds other premises for renting (flats, commercial premises, offices, factories). But this general principle is flexible in application, as some promoters build houses for sale or let firms build their own factories, etc. Individual plots usually range from 500 - 1000 m² and their price is calculated on a basis of £4 - 6·50 per m² over the prepared land. This makes the land relatively cheap, but, because of the low density and low cost of construction in the United States (less than £50 per m² for individual houses), they represent between a quarter and a third of the house prices (but only 10 - 15 per cent for the flats).

Prices and rents

Though building costs are low, rents are often high, nearly 10 per cent of the cost, after tax deduction, being considered normal.

The prices of houses are, as throughout the United States, fairly low. Average prices range from $25 000 - 35 000 (£10 000 - 15 000), corresponding with the price that families of upper middle incomes expect to pay for about 150 m² of floor space (five or more rooms, two bathrooms, garage for two cars, etc.). Some luxurious houses may, however, cost as much as $50 000 (£20 000), which is very expensive for the United States.

Flats only represent a small proportion of housing in the new towns. The plan for Valencia provided for a third of the housing in flats but its authors realized that this did not meet the demand and could probably not be adhered to. Rents vary from about £40 a month for a large studio flat (50 m²) to about £80 or even £120 for a four-roomed flat of over 100 m², inclusive of hot water supply and central heating. The profit on these premises is of interest because the cost of construction is covered by loans but allows for tax deduction for depreciation. The Gulf Reston Company, which took over the building of Reston in 1967, estimates the finances of a four-roomed flat as follows:

Cost of land	£625
Cost of construction	£4600 (covered by loans)
Total cost	£5225
Annual rent	£820 (15·65% of total cost)
Tax deduction for depreciation	£230 (5% of construction cost)

Rents for commercial premises are similarly calculated to bring in net profits of nearly 10 per cent (involving gross profits averaging about 20 per cent to allow for company taxes and expenses). These rents are calculated according to construction costs to ensure a fixed rate of profit and may be especially high in areas demanding special development.

Commercial rents are about \$2 - 4 (£0.80 - 1.60) per m^2 according to the type of premises and office rents are \$4 - 5 (£1.60 - 2) per m^2. For industrial premises, the price of land in Valencia is estimated at £7.50 per m^2 and the cost of construction £24 per m^2; rents are £3.75 per m^2 per year (over 10 per cent), with ten-year leases.

Costs of construction and rents are thus tailored to upper-middle-class groups. The new towns are profitable undertakings and, unlike their European counterparts, do not aim at helping to solve the housing problems of the underprivileged classes nor to break down the barriers between different social classes.

6 : Land development and new towns in Poland

In the communist countries, even more than in the West, town planning policy is part of a policy of land development, which is in turn determined by the requirements of the national economy. In this context, new towns, not counting urban developments connected with the growth of large conurbations, are an essential type of community for the establishment of new industries. Examples from Poland and later Hungary will illustrate this point. For some time the idea of new towns around large cities has also taken hold in the USSR and Czechoslovakia (the Etarea project).

I   Land development policy in Poland

In Poland there is no large capital city playing a dominant role like Paris in France, London in Great Britain, the Randstad Holland in the Netherlands or, on another scale, Copenhagen in Denmark and Stockholm in Sweden, for the city of Warsaw has a population of only 1 300 000 in a country of 32 million. War damage and later exchanges of population with neighbouring countries slowed down the rate of growth of most of the Polish towns, some of which have not yet reached their pre-war level, so that they have ample scope for natural development.

The guiding lines for a policy of land development, with town planning operations including new towns, are therefore very different in Poland from those in other countries. The main aim is to ensure the balanced economic development of the whole country, since at the end of the war 69 per cent of the population was rural, with industry concentrated along two axes: a main east-west axis in the south of the country (Upper Silesia and Cracow) and a secondary north-south axis from Cracow to Gdansk. So new industrial complexes and even economic centres were planned for the rural regions. As a corollary to this, the need arose after some years to check the growth of the larger urban areas (Warsaw, Lodz, Gdansk, Posnan, Cracow and the conurbation of Upper Silesia) and to encourage that of medium-sized towns with populations of about 100 000.

But, unlike their counterparts in other countries, the authorities in charge of land development in Poland laid the greatest stress on the economic aspects of their plans, knowing that with the country's limited resources economic plans had the best chance of success. So for the study of the optimum growth of towns the 'threshold' theory[1] was advanced and has been accepted outside Poland, while the optimum method of infrastructures advanced in the long-term plan for Warsaw sprang from the same intention.

These two principles – a balanced economic development benefiting all regions alike, and economic plans – guided the authorities in their choice of sites for development, particularly of industry. Immediately after the war the country's natural resources were as yet uncharted but the general principles could be adapted to suit future new conditions:

> The avoidance of establishing industries not directly linked to the extraction of raw materials in existing industrial regions (particularly Upper Silesia).
>
> The installation near but outside these regions of industries using these raw materials (coal), but not essential to the coalfield, to create new industrial complexes (Cracow, Czestochowa, Opole).
>
> The establishment of new industrial centres in the rural areas of the country (the area in the angle of the San and Vistula, the Wizna region and the area round Pila).
>
> The siting of industries not dependent on coal in existing or planned urban centres.

The six-year plan (1950 - 5) and subsequent plans were largely inspired by these principles. Although complete success cannot yet be claimed, it must be stressed that between 1946 and 1959 the proportion of industrial employment in the three areas of Katowice, Wroclaw and Lodz decreased from 60·7 to 42·8 per cent, while that of the most rural areas (Szczecin, Koszalin and Zielona-Gora in the north-west and Olsztyn and Bialystok in the north-east) increased from 4 to 8·4 per cent. During the same period, small towns with populations of less than 20 000 and medium-sized towns (20 000 - 200 000) developed slightly faster than the larger ones.

The Polish policy of land development seems to have been empirical in origin. In the face of war damage and the needs of modern national industries the first plans to be drawn up were local ones and it was only later that regional plans, such as that for Upper Silesia (1953), were established, and very much later (1966) that a Department of Land Development was set up, under the

[1]Boleslaw Malisz, *Zarys téorii Ksztaltowania ukladow osadniczych* (Warsaw, 1966).

National Economic Planning Committee deriving its powers from the Council of Ministers, entrusted with the detailed study of a coherent national planning policy and long-term economic plans.

This development reflects the progressive integration of physical planning within the pattern of economic planning, which is of such importance in communist countries. Such an integration is also essential for the success of town planning schemes.

At present, the responsibility for planning is shared at four administrative levels: the government (for the national policy of land use); the seventeen regions, each with its economic planning committee possessing a department for regional planning and a department of town planning, entrusted with local plans; 235 districts (out of 356), each with its town planning section; and finally the local authorities.

There are in theory three types of plan at these different levels, distinguished by their different targets: the master plans, latecomers in Poland, are very long-term plans aimed at directing development for twenty years or more and are at present in preparation experimentally at Cracow and Gdansk; medium-term plans (twenty years) to carry out the dictates of the economic plan (which itself has a target of more than twenty years); short term (five-year) plans, which carry out the different parts of the medium-term plans and are in close co-operation with the five-year economic plans.

This task of town planning was fairly well advanced by 1964, when 867 towns out of 891 had their medium-term plan, accompanied by detailed studies of the level of services proposed by the plan and the total development necessary to achieve it. The short-term plans contain details of the financial needs of the next five-year period. So, thanks to the amount and variety of work done in the Polish departments of town planning and land development, not only a large range of studies and plans but a true school of town planning and land use has gradually been developed over the last two decades. The actual results can be disappointing in comparison with the quality of the studies, despite the fact that the Polish government owns the land and, in particular, the industries that have been established. There are many problems of co-ordination that remain to be solved, not least between economic plans and actual developments, despite the fact that these have been closely studied in relation to each other.

II An example of planning: Upper Silesia

It would take too long to analyse the planning policy followed by all seventeen regions of Poland. Upper Silesia is of particular interest in this respect because it comprises the largest built-up area in the country with the most difficult planning problems and because the 1953 plan proposed a complete network of new towns there.

The coalfield of Upper Silesia has produced an industrial conurbation consisting of nineteen main towns in an area of 2400 km^2 with a population of 1 700 000 in 1950. Large-scale iron and chemical industries sprang up round the coal and zinc mines, with accompanying low grade housing. Industrial buildings and housing were often built on unstable land, atmospheric pollution was exceptionally high and, only too clearly, there had been no overall plan of development. Studies carried out from 1946 onwards led to the preparatory scheme for the 1953 regional plan, which was immediately approved by the government. Distinguishing between a central zone (fifteen communities, 700 km^2, 1 400 000 inhabitants in 1950) and an outer zone (1700 km^2, and 300 000 inhabitants), the plan proposed to give priority to the extraction of raw materials and only to allow other essential industries. Jobs in offices and public services could be introduced to employ female labour (about 75 per cent of jobs were in industry). The population should decrease over a period of twenty-five years until it reached the optimum level for the zone, necessitating the movement of 300 000 out of the central zone. But, in order to avoid unnecessary unemployment or lengthy commuting, it was proposed to rehouse this section of the population in a network of new towns to be built in the outer zone. Drawing their inspiration from the Greater London Plan of 1944 (see Chapter 1), the authors proposed in effect the creation of a ring of new towns on axes of fast transport, beyond the zones allocated for future mining activities: Pyskowice, Rokitnica, Radzionkow, Tarnowskie Góry, Grodzice and Nowa Dabrowa to the north of the central zone; Knurow, Nowe Tychy and another town to be decided on in the south. These towns were to have populations of about 30 000, while two of them – Nowe Tychy and Tarnowskie Góry – were to play more important roles, with about 100 000 inhabitants apiece, and assume some of the functions of the towns in the central zone of the conurbation.

The plan also proposed the redevelopment of the central section of the conurbation and work on infrastructures (electrification of the railways, improvement of the road network, water supply, drainage and sewers), a campaign against atmospheric pollution and the laying out of public parks.

After giving its approval to this preliminary scheme for the regional plan in 1953, the government asked for detailed proposals from the local authorities and economic agencies concerned, within the outlines of the plan and looking at least fifteen years ahead, in preparation for a complete regional plan later on. A national commission was formed to examine individually the concerns to be decentralized beyond the area of the coalfield. Unfortunately, this has proved slow work in practice because of financial difficulties.

Regional studies were carried on after 1953, but no specific administrative body was formed to carry out the plan's proposals. The study of soils and sub-soils allows a definition of different housing areas with varying possibilities, taking into account the future of the coal mines and existing or planned constructions:

> Zones with a shortage of land for building (Katowice, Gliwice, Bytom, etc.).
>
> Zones with possibilities for building but only able to cope with normal growth (Ruda Slaska, etc.).
>
> Zones with reserves of land for building (Nowe Tychy, Pyskowice, etc.).

A result of this is that, allowing for the birth rate of the population of the coalfield (20 000 a year in the central zone) and looking ahead, after the completion of the present network of new towns further sites for development will have to be sought outside the region.

The plan relies on four centres (Katowice, Bytom, Sosnowiec and Gliwice), of which Katowice has the predominant role (especially for tertiary activities), requiring the total redevelopment of its centre, including the building of high-level flats and office blocks. Redevelopment is also planned for other towns (Sosnowiec, Zabrze, Gliwice, Chorzow, Bytom, etc.). In the field of employment, a shortage of factories is not expected before 1985, but the closure of some pits in the centre will be compensated for by the opening of new pits further south and the fall in employment in the factories due to higher productivity will be compensated for by the increased variety of employment (in light industry and public services). The war on atmospheric pollution is a major problem: the electrification of the railways, the spread of district heating systems, the control of factory pollution, the re-afforestation of vast areas of waste land and the creation of parks (such as the 60 ha park of rest and culture between Katowice and Chorzow) and of an 32 000 ha green belt are the main measures decided on.

III   New towns in Poland

Their role and sites

The new towns, even when, as in Upper Silesia, they form part of a scheme for the decongestion of a large conurbation, are seen as one of many tools of a development policy aiming at an improved division of employment throughout the country.

N. Towns in Poland play 2 roles,
a) decentralization - diverse overspil pops.
+ b) like Brazilia, spread division of employment
+ wealth thought country

Three types of new town are usually recognized in Poland :[1]

> Towns aiding in the decongestion of an industrial region (especially Upper Silesia): Nowe Tychy and the other towns in the regional plan for Upper Silesia.
>
> Towns sharing in the development of new industrial complexes: for example, Nowa Huta, in the Cracow region.
>
> Towns that are part of new industrial areas: Stalowa Wola (near the confluence of the San and the Vistula).

It is obvious that economic considerations decide the choice of sites for the new towns, though in the first group there are additional social reasons – the creation of new housing areas away from the unhealthy sectors of the coalfield and sources of atmospheric pollution – and even political reasons (to minimize the separatist tendencies of Upper Silesia).

In keeping with the policy that gave rise to them, the new towns have to provide employment for their inhabitants. In the particular case of the new towns of Upper Silesia, although non-polluting industries are to be established there (especially serving the coalfield) as well as tertiary employment (administration, scientific institutes and technical schools in particular), it is readily admitted that part of the working population must work in the coalfield and that good communications will therefore be needed. The delays in carrying out the proposals of the regional plan for Upper Silesia, and especially in the construction of new railways and in the electrification of existing lines, have limited the number of new towns approved by the government and slowed down their development: Pyskowice has less than 30 000 inhabitants, Golonog (Nowa Dabrowa) hardly more than 20 000 and Kedzierzyn 30 000. Only Nowe Tychy has attained a population of 70 000 (20 000 in 1950) but its target of 120 000, originally planned for 1970, has been moved forward to 1980.

Though the creation of the network of new towns in the Upper Silesian coalfield has been delayed, the discovery of large reserves of coking coal farther south-west in the Rybnik region has led to the planning of another network of new towns and the extension of existing small towns to produce units of 30 000 - 60 000 inhabitants. Apart from Jastrzebie, which has already been started, with a present population of 25 000 out of a planned 60 000, new towns are planned at Zory, Wodzislaw, Leszczyny, etc.

The siting of these towns in the mining areas depends on transport facilities (Tychy is on a main railway line linking it with Katowice) and on the existence

---

[1]Boleslaw Malisz, *La Pologne construit des villes nouvelles* (Warsaw, Ed. 'Polonna', 1961).

of land suitable for building, if possible state-owned, which was mostly the case with the land on which Nowe Tychy was built. This town, 15 km south of Katowice, in the forests around Lake Paprocenskie, started as a new town in 1950 once the decision of the regional assembly was confirmed by the central government. A population of 100 000 was planned and later increased to 120 000.

Nowa Huta, on the other hand, is part of the development of new industrial complexes, in this instance that of Cracow, developed in conjunction with the mining concerns of Upper Silesia, although it was started in 1949 before the production of a regional plan and before Cracow had its own plan. Linked to the Lenin iron-working centre (with a predicted production of 1 500 000 tons of steel), 10 km east of Cracow on the Vistula, the new town was intended to become an autonomous town, on the pattern of the new towns in Britain (see Chapter 1). Like these, it failed in this intention and has gradually become part of the conurbation of Cracow. As B. Malisz has pointed out,[1] the distance separating Nowa Huta from Cracow was too great for the housing needs of the complex to be met by the existing town and too small for the new centre to be considered as an independent unit. Nowa Huta was looked upon as the chief element of the economic development of the Cracow region but this (probably overrated) position did not prevent the promoters of the operation from encountering considerable difficulties, particularly in the provision of essential means of communication (200 km of railway lines to link the town and the iron-working complex to the rail centre of Cracow, 200 km of track within the complex and the rebuilding of a number of stations, etc.).

Stalowa Wola is different again. The project is on a smaller scale, although it is older, dating from pre-war days. It was planned to aid the industrial development of the Rzeszow region. The town is built on a high river terrace on the left bank of the San, slightly north-east of its confluence with the Vistula, on the Rzeszow-Rozwadow railway and a main road. A population of 30 000 was planned but had only reached 7000 by 1950. The recent installation of an electrical power station and the discovery of rich deposits of sulphur at Tarnobrzeg in the vicinity of the town has accelerated its development and the preparation of a new plan for a population of 50 000.

Town planning concepts

The plans for new towns in Poland have the characteristics of Polish town planning of the 1950s and not those of today. Only the very latest – in the

[1] B. Malisz, *La Pologne construit des villes nouvelles.*

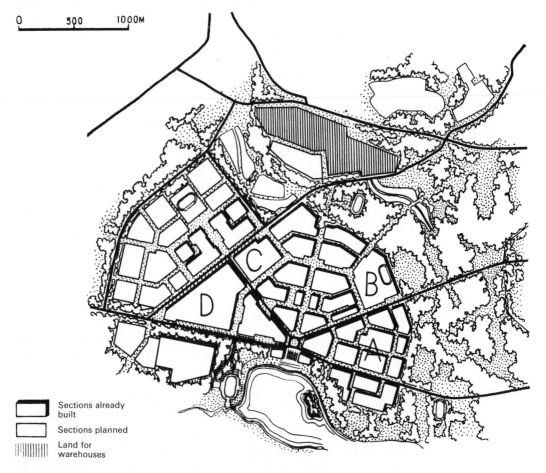

0   500   1000M

Fig. 48 Nowa Huta: distribution of land reserved for housing.

Rybnik area, for example – have been drawn up recently. At Jastrzebie natural
conditions have largely influenced the composition of the plan: the axis of the
new town is a ridge cut by several transverse valleys. The residential units are
linked to the central axis and separated from each other by the green spaces of
the valleys that merge with the surrounding forests. The centre is aligned along
the ridge and along the railway that encircles the mining area. It includes
commercial premises and various service premises, but no housing. Secondary
centres serving a 100 m radius are also planned, as well as neighbourhood
centres serving a radius of 250 m.

At Nowa Huta a competition was held for the town plan and this was won
by T. Ptaszycki with a controversial plan. This reflects a theory of town planning directly linked to the social theories of the age: the aim of the right housing

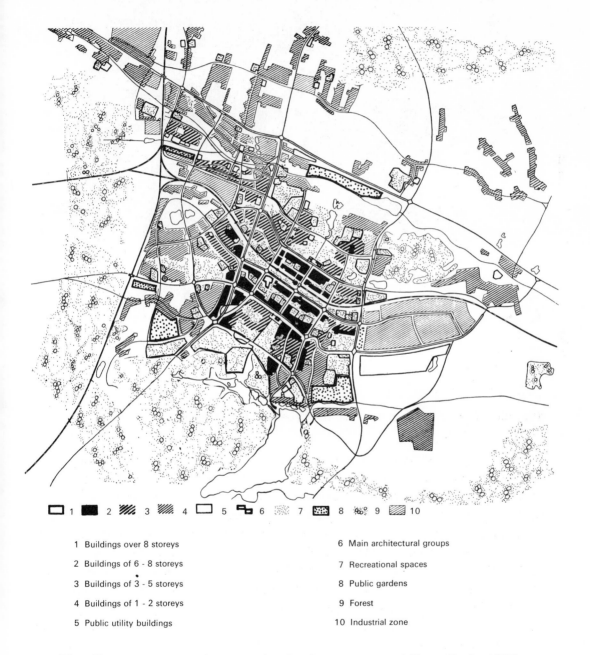

□ 1	■ 2	▨ 3	▨ 4	▭ 5	⬓ 6	▨ 7	▦ 8	⬡ 9	▨ 10

1 Buildings over 8 storeys

2 Buildings of 6 - 8 storeys

3 Buildings of 3 - 5 storeys

4 Buildings of 1 - 2 storeys

5 Public utility buildings

6 Main architectural groups

7 Recreational spaces

8 Public gardens

9 Forest

10 Industrial zone

Fig. 49 Improved development plan for the new town of Nowe Tychy 1960.

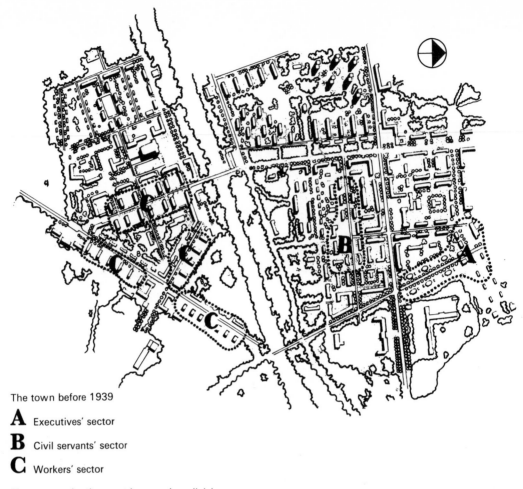

The town before 1939

A Executives' sector

B Civil servants' sector

C Workers' sector

The present development has no class divisions

Fig. 50 Stalowa Wola : detailed plan of present development.

at all social levels, with all necessary amenities, even if this results in the monotonous appearance of the town. In fact, the clarity of the scheme lies in its simplicity: the pattern is concentric, the town taking the form of a semi-circle whose centre is the main square, on the banks of the Vistula (Fig. 48).

The plan for Nowe Tychy, established as the result of another competition won by K. Wejchert and Mrs H. Adamczewska, followed a little later (drawn up in 1951 and approved, not without discussion, in 1953). The pattern is very simple, almost geometric, like that of Nowa Huta, but with a rectangular pattern. An east-west axis links sectors of individual housing (on the west, with a secondary station) to the centre (with the main station) and to the industrial zone on the east, while a north-south axis where the administrative buildings are sited links a park, on the north, to the forest and Lake Paprocenskie on the south. The main innovation was that of diverting the Katowice railway to the town centre for the benefit of commuters working in the coalfield. Four sectors, divided by the two main axes, each have a centre at the end of a rectangle. A fifth sector, on the west, consists of separate and terraced houses, while the others consist mainly of low-level flats, considered the most economic, with high-level flats (up to twelve floors) towards the centre to lend an architectonic aspect to the town (Fig. 49).

At Stalowa Wola, the original plan, dating from 1937 - 9, consists of three sectors: the old sector to the west, near the factory and beyond the railway, the workers' sector to the east of the railway track and the executives' sector on the banks of the San. The new plan, drawn up by H. Szwemin-Paterowa in 1950, proposed a cutting through the town for the road and railway, demolishing an existing village and putting the new town centre in its place. The revision of this plan, made in 1953, separated the road and railway, with both running parallel to the river, and rejected the idea of redeveloping the village (Fig. 50).

Although the available documents do not allow a detailed study of these plans, they do not appear to possess any originality.

The plans in practice

None of the plans for new towns in Poland has been put into practice as quickly as was planned. Though Nowa Huta can be said to be completed and Nowe Tychy half completed, some new towns have been delayed because of financial difficulties. The building of Nowa Huta naturally began with the sector nearest the ironworks complex, in order to house the workers employed in constructing the complex (15 000 workers in 1954) and the town (something over 10 000 workers in 1951), moving progressively towards the sector nearest Cracow (Fig. 51). Starting with small blocks of flats, the building turned more and more towards large blocks of flats, to the detriment of the green spaces. A return to less dense, more spacious and more varied constructions marked the final stages of the new town, which now has plans for an extension housing a further 30 000. Nowa Huta has essentially been an experiment in town planning: the need to build fast led at first to quick but low quality methods of construction, then to the adoption of prefabrication, with a reduction in the weight of the buildings compared to their size. These methods allowed for a fast rate of building: an average of 5000 housing units a year, with a maximum 8000 in 1954.

After several years of discussion, the building of Nowe Tychy followed a similar pattern, beginning near the old town of Tychy and spreading from west to east. By now the whole of the northern half is completed (Fig. 52). A

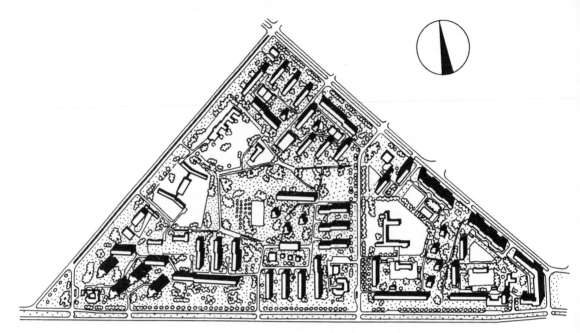

Fig. 51 Nowa Huta: detailed plan of sector D.

temporary centre with wide facilities was built in the second sector. Building methods have become more modernized, with the use of prefabrication, and construction has become more spacious and, especially, more varied. The height of the buildings increases and varies in the centre, where importance is given to the separation of traffic. The dwellings are fairly small (the average consisting of two rooms plus kitchen and bathroom) and are often crowded (with an average of 1·5 people per room) but they are well equipped with gas, district heating, etc.

The building of Stalowa Wola began in a rather disorganized fashion before the 1950 plan. The sectors that had been begun were completed by about 1955 and then building continued on either side of the railway, with model buildings and individual houses alternating with blocks of flats. The rate of building is still fairly slow: about 300 dwellings (or 600 rooms for nearly 1000 people) per year (Fig. 53).

Employment

The problem of employment varies from one new town to another. Though the majority come under plans for the industrialization of a particular region with employment and population as integral parts, those of Upper Silesia were

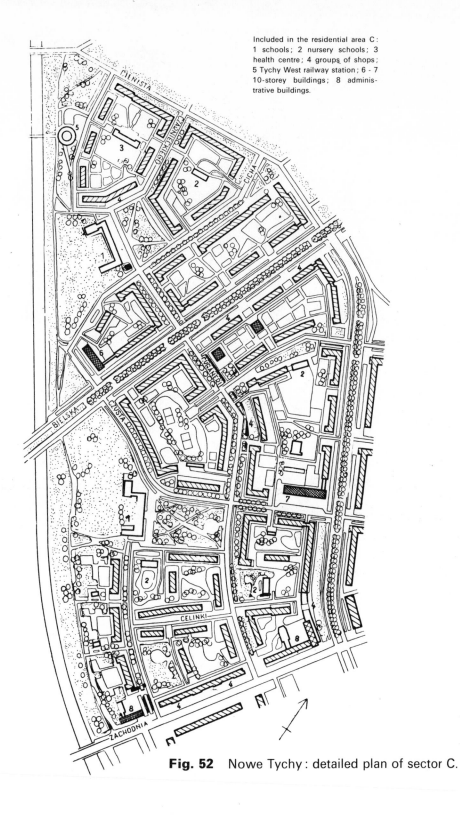

Included in the residential area C:
1 schools; 2 nursery schools; 3
health centre; 4 groups of shops;
5 Tychy West railway station; 6 - 7
10-storey buildings; 8 administrative buildings.

Fig. 52 Nowe Tychy: detailed plan of sector C.

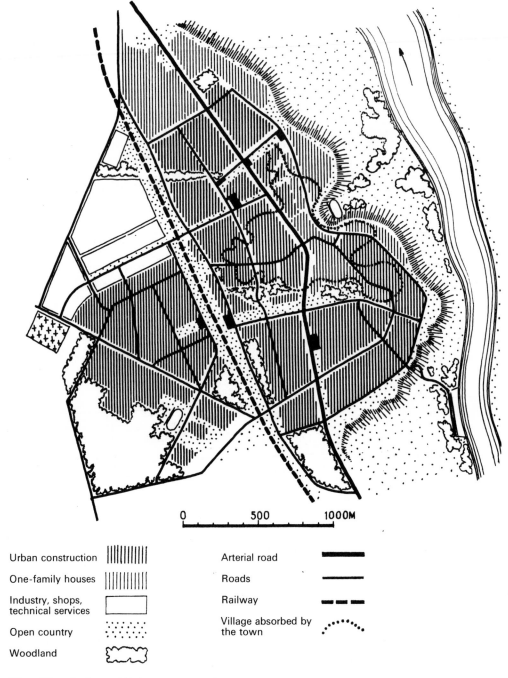

Urban construction	‖‖‖‖‖‖	Arterial road	▬▬▬▬
One-family houses	‖‖‖‖‖‖	Roads	———
Industry, shops, technical services	▭	Railway	▬ ▬ ▬
Open country	⋰⋰⋰	Village absorbed by the town	••••••
Woodland	◠◡◠◡		

Fig. 53 Stalowa Wola: present plan.

planned as satellite towns to the coalfield, to which their working populations commute daily.

Nowa Huta, contrary to its original plans, has been prevented from becoming an autonomous unit by the proximity of Cracow (10 km). However, the construction of the iron-working complex and of the town and then the working of the complex itself has created plenty of employment: 26 000 jobs in construction in 1954 and as many again in other employment, including the ironworks.

At Nowe Tychy, on the other hand, slowness in the provision of employment in the town was a drawback to the inhabitants, entailing lengthy commuting caused by the delay in carrying out railway plans, such as the rail service to local factories. It also meant a community with an unvaried class structure and an unbalanced social life. The situation has improved since 1960, after electrification of the railway in 1958 and 1963, the extension of the rail system and the creation of employment. In 1965 there were 13 606 jobs in the new town (5904 held by women workers) apportioned as follows:

	%
Agriculture and forestry	8·2
Industry	22·7
Construction	21·3
Transport and telecommunications	7·6
Commerce	14·2
Administration and finance	4·0
Services	20·5
Miscellaneous	1·5

This shows a variety of employment, even if the rate is not high enough. The notably low rate is in industry (with 3100 jobs occupying 80 ha). The number of jobs equals a little over half the working population (26 800) but 2000 of them were held by outside workers, which meant that 15 400 (57·5 per cent of the working population) were commuting elsewhere. Of these, half remained in the neighbourhood of Tychy, while the majority of the rest (39 per cent) worked in Katowice and the remaining 11 per cent elsewhere (Myslowice, Ruda Slaska, Chorzow, etc.). Despite the improvement of the rail system, the slow train service (40 km an hour) and inconvenient timetable make commuting difficult. The situation is improved by a very frequent bus service.

In comparison, Stalowa Wola is a hive of industry. In 1965 there were 21 059 jobs in the town (4844 held by women workers) for 25 859 inhabitants (11 000 of them workers). There is a great deal of commuting but this is into the town, as the town has grown too slowly to house all its workers. Many live in nearby villages some kilometres from the new town. Employment is apportioned as follows:

	Jobs	% Proportion
Industry	15 867	75
Construction	1 555	7·5
Commerce	838	4
Education, science and culture	495	2
Health, social affairs, sport	669	3
Others (including agriculture)	1 535	7·5

This is a very different employment structure from that of Nowe Tychy, reflecting the different roles of the two towns in the industrialization of the country.

Amenities

In Poland, as in all communist countries, amenities are built at the same time as housing according to standards, which, even if often low, do at least exist.

In 1960, when Nowa Huta was nearly completed (with a population of 100 000) and Stalowa Wola less far advanced (22 000), they contained the following:

	Nowa Huta	Stalowa Wola
Nursery schools	16	6
Primary schools	9	3
Secondary schools	1	0
Technical secondary schools	4	3
Children's homes	1	0
Hospitals	1 (100 beds)	1 (320 beds)
Day nurseries	0	2
Health centres	4	?
Pharmacies	5	2
Shops	212	27 600 m³
Workshops	93	7500 m³
Restaurants	20	15 200 m³
Cinemas	2 (1750 seats)	3
Theatre or entertainment hall	1 (420 seats)	`1 (900 seats)
And clubs, libraries and meeting halls, etc., in both towns		

At Nowa Huta the following were also counted:

600 000 m² of roads and footpaths
130 km of drainpipes
110 km of water pipes
85 km of district heating pipes
140 ha planted with 22 000 trees and 60 000 shrubs

The large number of amenities in Nowa Huta results from the original intention of making it an autonomous town despite the proximity of Cracow. It is not at all excessive for a population of 100 000 but some of the amenities are regarded as extravagant, such as the huge House of Culture in Stalowa Wola (including entertainment hall, cinema, clubs and libraries), which is not often in use, and the House of Sport (gymnasium, indoor swimming pool, etc.), since the preparation of the land slows down the actual construction of the town.

Nowe Tychy, on the other hand, which was planned as a satellite town and is still far from completion (with the main centre not yet built), seems under-equipped with amenities. The administrative services planned for it have not been established because of the lack of any such tradition in the town. Even the shops are slow in being built (130 out of the 143 planned for the completed sector of the town). Much of the shopping is done in the towns of the coalfield. The outlay per person on daily purchase (8350 zlotys) is lower than that of other towns (10 000 zlotys, even 15 000 or more in the large centres, such as Gliwice). Among the amenities listed for the town, the absence of secondary schools and cultural centres is notable.

Population

As with all new towns, those built in Poland since the war have a special population structure. Their growth has been rapid, as the following table shows:

Increase and predicted increase of population in three new towns

Date	Nowa Huta	Nowe Tychy	Stalowa Wola
1950	16 000	12 927	7 167
1955	82 000	26 251	17 917
1960	100 000	49 750	22 932
1965	130 000	63 300	25 859
By 1980	200 000	120 000	30 000

This rapid increase (Nowa Huta between 1950 and 1955 being an extreme example) results in a very youthful population structure, as can be seen in the following table of age structure in Nowa Huta in 1955, separating the population

Main investments completed in Nowe Tychy 1965

Sector	No. of buildings	No. of rooms	Total area of housing	Primary schools	Nursery schools	Day nurseries	Dispensaries	Shops	Restaurants	Workshops	Area of social amenities (m²)	Roads (m²)	Green spaces (m²)	Water supply (m)	Area of sector
A	58	4 591	72 162	2	2	1	1	17	3	11	12 476	32 740	71 520	2 340	18·2
B	109	6 982	111 657	1	4	2	1	40	6	31	24 156	131 660	79 485	15 030	48·3
B₁	12	712	10 668								11 615	7 038	16 497	1 210	16·1
C₁-C₂	73	5 933	105 034	1	2		1	24	2	12	14 665	28 210	65 232	3 840	25·3
C₃	28	2 055	36 855	1	1			9	1	1	4 550	15 073	23 303	1 760	15·5
E₃	30	2 385	42 618	1	1			9		3	5 055	15 030	12 090	2 510	17·7
E₄-E₅	14	1 571	26 026	1	1		1	7		5	5 683	9 470	2 587	1 715	13·6
D₁	16	2 983	49 877	1	1			20		4	7 068	20 700	31 639	1 820	18·5
Separate houses	32	365	7 081	1						3	3 600	4 050	2 600	1 100	
E₂	14	1 737	27 390	1				4			4 872	7 732	8 890	630	10·4
F	8	1 189	16 233								2 380	10 937		3 450	28·0
Total	394	30 503	505 601	10	12	3	4	130	12	70	96 120	282 640	313 843	35 405	211·6

Age structure of the population of Nowa Huta in 1955

Age	New sectors	Workers' hostels	Former villages
0- 2	12·3	1·8	6·6
3- 6	14·0	1·0	8·5
7-13	9·4	0·4	11·7
14-17	4·9	4·8	8·1
18-19	2·3	16·5	3·6
20-24	10·2	27·1	10·4
25-29	15·7	22·4	7·1
30-34	12·3	9·3	7·4
35-39	5·0	3·6	4·9
40-49	8·3	9·3	12·9
50-59	3·4	3·3	10·6
60+	2·2	0·5	8·2
	100·0	100·0	100·0
Total			

Age structure of Nowe Tychy compared with those of other new towns in Poland and Czechoslovakia and the towns of the Katowice area

Age	Nowe Tychy	Towns of the Katowice area	Nowa Huta	Ostrov (Czech)	Czech new towns
	1958	1960	1958	1962	1959
0-4	17·9	10·1	16·5	18·0	12·7
5-9	14·9	10·3	10·7	10·3	16·4
10-14	7·4	8·4	5·3	6·6	10·5
15-19	4·9	7·0	5·7	4·6	5·6
20-24	6·9	7·6	12·5	17·1	3·8
25-29	13·5	8·5	16·5	17·5	9·0
30-34	12·7	8·2	11·9	10·4	12·2
35-39	8·6	7·3	6·0	5·9	11·9
40-44	3·4	4·7	3·6	4·2	4·7
45-49	3·3	6·2	3·5	1·8	5·6
50-54	2·2	6·3	2·8	1·2	3·0
55-59	1·5	5·4	1·9	0·7	2·0
60-64	1·2	3·9	1·3	0·5	1·2
65-69	0·7	2·7 ⎫	0·9	0·5	0·5
70-74	0·5 ⎫	⎬		0·5	0·4
75+	0·4 ⎭	3·4 ⎭	0·9	0·2	0·5
Total	100·0	100·0	100·0	100·0	100·0

of the former villages, the workers' hostels (communal housing for workers in the iron-working complex, gradually being converted into normal housing) and the new sectors. In 1958, 37·5 per cent of the population was under 18 (compared with 33 per cent for the country as a whole), 58·2 per cent aged 18-59 and 4·3 per cent over 60, still giving a more youthful than average population. The population of Nowe Tychy is more youthful still.

This very youthful structure has its effects on the planning of amenities. For instance, to avoid a future surplus of school buildings it has been decided to use these for morning and afternoon shifts of schoolchildren and for adult education in the evenings.

The growth of the population obviously results mainly from new arrivals, though normal increase is also large. As the following table shows, it accounts for a third of the growth of Nowe Tychy up to 1962.

The growth of Nowe Tychy 1956-1962

Date	Total increase	Natural increase	%	New arrivals	%
1956	4532	947	20·9	3585	79·1
1957	4627	1100	23·8	3527	76·2
1958	5215	1179	22·6	4036	77·4
1959	5280	1172	22·2	4108	77·8
1960	3845	1074	27·9	2771	72·1
1961	4150	957	23·1	3193	76·9
1962	2700	927	34·3	1773	65·7

The birth rate decreases fairly quickly once people are settled in the new town (faster than for the country as a whole) but the death rate is low and even decreasing.

Population rates for Nowe Tychy and the other towns of the Katowice area

	Nowe Tychy				Other towns			
Year	Births	Deaths	Natural increase	Marriage rate	Births	Deaths	Natural increase	Marriage rate
1956	37·1	7·0	30·1	7·4	23·6	9·1	14·5	9·6
1957	38·3	7·2	31·1	8·5	23·0	9·6	13·4	10·1
1958	35·3	6·3	29·0	8·3	22·7	8·7	14·0	10·0
1959	32·3	6·7	25·6	8·2	21·2	9·1	12·1	9·6
1960	28·0	5·4	27·6	8·5	18·7	7·9	10·8	8·8
1961	23·1	4·7	18·4	7·5	16·8	7·8	9·0	8·7
1962	22·4	4·9	17·5	5·9	16·2	7·9	8·3	8·2

The population census also gives some indications of the geographical origins of the population of the new towns. For instance, at Nowa Huta in 1955, half the population originated from the Cracow area (halved between the city and the rest of the region), 20 per cent from the Katowice area, 5 per cent from the Rzeszow and Kielce area and 20 per cent from the rest of the country and abroad. At Nowe Tychy, two-thirds of the population originate from the Katowice area, half of these from the coalfield (a quarter from Katowice and a quarter from the Tychy district).

Households are usually large, partly due to the high birth rate and the youthful population structure:

Size of households at Nowe Tychy, in the other towns of the region and at Havirov

Size of household	Nowe Tychy	Other towns of the region	Havirov (Czechoslovakia)
1	3·2	18·5	1·4
2	11·7	22·5	9·7
3	25·2	22·2	25·0
4	30·2	20·6	39·9
5	18·3		17·4
6	7·2	16·2	9·6
7 and over	4·2		
	100·0	100·0	100·0
Average size	3·88	3·01	3·91

There is an almost 30 per cent difference between the town and the other towns of the Katowice region. This number of large families no doubt explains the fairly low employment rate (35 per cent of the total population compared with 39·7 per cent in the other towns of the region), due particularly to the low rate of female employment (18 per cent compared with 25·8 per cent). The predominance of jobs in industry in Nowe Tychy also has its effect. The proportion of the resident working population in different jobs is shown in the table on p. 214.

Also, besides the almost complete absence of self-employed workers (craftsmen, etc.), there are few skilled workers but many unskilled workers and managerial staff.

The working population of Nowe Tychy according to type of employment

Type of employment	Men	Women	Total
Agriculture	0·6	0·3	0·5
Mining	45·7	12·4	36·9
Industry	18·7	17·7	18·5
Construction	13·8	8·9	12·5
Transport	3·6	3·9	3·7
Commerce	3·2	15·9	6·6
Administration	2·2	3·7	2·4
Services	8·0	27·7	13·3
Others	4·2	9·5	5·6
Total	100·0	100·0	100·0

The new towns of Poland possess all the characteristics of a youthful population, often accentuated by its rapid construction, with a slow rate of expansion, made up of large households recently installed but mainly originating from the same region.

Social life

Such an unbalanced population structure is not conducive to the creation of vitality in its social life, whatever cultural facilities may have been provided. Though Nowa Huta prides itself on the possession of one of the finest theatres in Poland, this is mainly frequented by people from Cracow or elsewhere. Nowe Tychy has a poor social life for the same reasons. It is hoped to remedy this situation by more varied jobs and the creation of cultural institutions such as the Silesian university (though this project has not yet materialized).

Conclusion: present trends

The new towns of Poland are disappointing in many respects to the western observer, particularly in the field of town planning, but what must not be forgotten is the progress they have made compared to traditional forms of construction in the country. The dwellings may be small (with two main rooms on the average) and their standard of construction poor but they are becoming progressively larger and they provide a good standard of living.

The new towns policy drawn up about 1950 has not been carried out in detail. Some towns have had a delayed start (Nowe Tychy, Stalowa Wola), others have been abandoned; others again (Nowe Huta) have grown at such an excessive rate that they have joined up with the neighbouring city of Cracow. Among the causes of failure to reach their targets are the delay in the building of the rail network, which hindered the provision of local employment (Nowe Tychy), and especially the lack of a single co-ordinating body in charge of planning, like the British development corporations (see Chapter 1), and a special system of finance for the new towns. Buildings in accordance with the original plan, is carried out by three groups of promoters: the national industries, the co-operatives and the local People's Council, whose respective roles vary considerably from one town to another. Because of the problems of financing the new towns, town planners in Poland now prefer town extensions that can rely on existing infrastructures. It is obvious, however, that such a policy is limited and that, whatever forms of planning are retained, amenities for the new population will have to be financed: it is not at all certain that the new towns would not prove the more economic in the long run.

At any rate, the present policy of Polish town planners favours the extension of small and particularly medium-sized towns. Many of these have already grown rapidly since 1950 (sometimes to the detriment of new towns like Ruda Slaska and Wodzislaw in Upper Silesia). Others have undergone planned increases due to the establishment of large industries (Joworzno, Oswiecim) or the exploitation of newly discovered raw materials: Tarnobrzeg (copper) or Turoszow (lignite), etc.

Plock, 120 km north-west of Warsaw on the Vistula, owes its development to a huge industrial complex whose site was decided in 1959 in connection with the oil pipeline from the USSR to East Germany, which enabled a large refinery to be built with a planned capacity of 10 million tons by 1970.

The population (28 500 in 1946; 55 000 in 1965) should more than double to 120 000 by 1980. Even this rate of growth will not be enough to house all the workers in the oil and chemical complex, which will tend to slow down the provision of other types of employment and increase commuting between neighbouring villages and the complex. The development of Plock comes within the planning framework of the Vistula valley and the market town of Wyszogrod, between Plock and Warsaw, should house a population of 30 000 by 1980, thanks to the establishment of a large cellulose store employing 6000 workers.

Oswiecim lies to the east of the Upper Silesian basin and has developed rapidly from a population of under 10 000 in 1950 to nearly 40 000 at the present time, thanks to the development of the chemical industry. It will probably reach a population of 80 000 by 1980.

Polish town planners seem to have followed in the steps of their British counterparts (see Chapter 1), though perhaps at a different pace. After the first wave of new towns around 1950, they concentrated on the extension of existing towns, thinking these less costly, at least in the short term. They may well return, like the British, to proposals for further and larger new towns.

7: Land development and new towns in Hungary

As Hungary is a communist country, planning is of paramount importance both in the economic field and, increasingly, in construction. After the war economic considerations led to the establishment of industries without regard to their site, with new towns growing up as an afterthought. It was then seen to be necessary to formulate an overall policy as a framework for regional economic planning, with the result that a national plan for land development was drawn up in 1963, becoming official after some revision and serving as a framework for regional planning and for the outlines of town planning.

I A policy of land development and regional planning

The planning system

Hungary possesses two high authorities in the field of physical planning: the National Planning Bureau, concerned with the policy of land use, and the Ministry of Construction and Town Planning for regional and town planning.

In practice, the drawing up of plans is mainly carried out by the Hungarian Institute of Town and Country Planning, usually known as the Budapest Institute of Town Planning (Varosépitési Tervezö Vallalat – VATI). The town planning section of the Ministry of Construction is responsible for keeping a check on the plans drawn up by the Institute, whether on a national scale (especially for land use), for regional or for town planning. The task of town planning is shared between the Budapest Institute of Town Planning and five other town planning institutes sited in the main provincial towns (Miskolc, Debrecen, Pecs, Györ and Szeged). The Budapest Institute deals with over half the country, while the five provincial institutes only deal with the outlying parts of the country. They are, like the Budapest Institute, government bodies and each of the twenty-four districts also has its planning bureau to deal with small-scale town planning. The city of Budapest stands outside this general pattern with a special body of its own: the Institute of Studies for the City of Budapest (Budapesti Varosépitési Tervezö Vallalat – BUVATI), entrusted with the plans for the city and the region.

The government examines and approves the regional plans and those of Budapest and the five large provincial cities, while less important matters are the responsibility of the National Planning Bureau and the Ministry of Construction. The master plans for other towns are submitted to the department council for approval and plans for country towns to their district council, while other overall or detailed plans are approved by the town council through its executive council. The plans once approved have force of law but before approval they can be disputed by a third party.

For some years Hungary has had a complete set of plans at all levels. A development plan for the whole country was drawn up in 1963 by the Budapest Institute of Planning and, though not approved by the government, it follows the main lines of the official policy. It is now being revised and will probably soon be approved. The overall or detailed regional plans are now drawn up on lines laid down in the national plan and town plans have to be in accord with both national and regional plans. To this effect, a document called 'town interconnections' is sent by the Budapest Institute of Planning to whoever is in charge of the town plan. The Institute, like its provincial counterparts, also keeps a check on local plans: this is the role of the fifteen town planners in charge of the Budapest Institute and their provincial counterparts.

These two plans are drawn up in co-ordination with economic plans, which have so far been five-year plans. In 1967, however, a policy of long-term (fifteen-year) plans was instituted. The land development plan is the basis for the long-term economic plan and the Budapest Institute works in close collaboration with those preparing it.

The 1963 land development plan[1]

The land development plan was in preparation from 1957 onwards and published in 1963, mainly in the form of two sets of maps. The first studied in great detail existing conditions, mainly from data furnished by the 1960 census: raw materials, transport systems, the general economy, productivity, topography, population, commercial facilities, social institutions, etc. It emphasized the low level of community life outside Budapest. The four largest provincial cities (Miskolc, Györ, Debrecen and Pecs) had between 100 000 and 160 000 inhabitants, while the Budapest conurbation had 2 million. Industrial activity was concentrated in the northern third of the country (77 per cent of workmen), while the rest of the country was entirely agricultural, with a third of the country's working population on the land.

[1]The principles of this are to be found in the work of Karoly Perczel and György Gerle, *Regionális Tervezés es a Magyar Településhálózat* (Budapest, Akadémiai Kiadó, 1966).

The second set contains the proposals of the plan summarized in four maps. The first shows the proposed planning framework, based on the creation of eight regional centres, which, together, could balance the importance of Budapest. These consist of the five main cities in the country (Miskolc, Györ, Pecs, Debrecen and Szeged) as well as Nyiregyhaza, Szolnok and Szekesfehervar, transport centres situated more in the interior. The development of these eight towns is obviously a long-term undertaking (with no stated target in the plan) linked to the aims and implementation of the economic plans. These eight towns, as well as Budapest, would form the centres of new economic regions not corresponding to the existing twenty-four departments. The planning framework of the country would be completed by seventy-two other towns, known as regional subcentres, and by a further thirty or forty towns without any particular regional role. The creation of the eight 'balancing centres' also involved the extension of small neighbouring market-towns with populations of 10 000 - 20 000, rather than the creation of new towns. Finally, the plan proposed the setting up of a network of 910 rural centres to play the same part as the 120 or so towns as district centres for a number of villages (with some thousands of inhabitants). Where it was undesirable to use agricultural land for extensive building (in the great Hungarian plain, for example), the building of new villages was planned. This policy has already been partly put into force: twenty-five of the proposed seventy-two subregional centres have had industries established as planned and some experimental villages centres have been created.[1]

The second map shows predicted population figures for 1980, allowing for present tendencies and the aims of the plan. In this respect, it should be stressed that because of the country's low birth rate (linked to the legalization of abortion) the natural population increase is very low (less than 3 per cent or 25 000 a year since 1965) and the population growth of the towns is mainly a result of a rural exodus (60 per cent of the population was rural in 1960).

The third map shows proposed transport systems and new infrastructures, especially for railways by-passing Budapest and providing direct links between the 'balancing centres'.

The fourth map shows the proposed policy for the siting of industry. This is based on the prohibition of new industries in the Budapest conurbation, apart from the development of some existing industries. This proposal forms the backbone of the whole development plan, aimed at helping to check the growth of Budapest, and it is based on legislation dating from 1960, which distinguishes three categories of industry:

[1]Karoly Perczel (Budapest Institute of Planning), *Le plan de développement du réseau des agglomérations de Hongrie*, from a conference held at Pecs, 6 June 1967.

Existing industries capable of expansion, specifically linked to Budapest,
not creating any nuisance and with premises in first-rate condition.
Their future development presumes that they will prejudice neither
the general industrial policy nor the development of the Budapest
region. To this category may be added existing industries capable of
a particular and limited expansion: those in course of construction
or at an advanced state of preparation or which cannot be split up.
Industries continuing to function with their present capacity but incapable of expansion through the provision of new premises: not
causing any nuisance, their existence in Budapest advantageous, but
equally capable of carrying on their work in the provinces. This
category can renew and modernize plant but can only build socio-
cultural facilities or storerooms.
Industries whose development should be cut down immediately or by
degrees: out-of-date industries, creating a nuisance, not specifically
linked to Budapest and being able to function equally well in the
provinces. These cannot carry out any expansion, not even modernization, except as safety measures.

This legislation has so far only been moderately successful. Certainly a
number of industries have been established in the provinces and the few
exceptions have had government approval. The proportion of workers in the
Budapest conurbation decreased from 43 per cent in 1960 to 40 per cent by 1967
but the growth of employment in Budapest has at the same time continued:
almost a quarter of the new jobs in industry are now in the Budapest conurbation, even though the state controls almost the whole of industry, as shown
by the following figures at the end of 1964:

Employment in state industry	1 319 521	(84·9%)
Employment in co-operatives	175 066	(11·3%)
Employment in private industry	59 764	(3·8%)
Total industrial employment	1 554 351	(100·0%)

The following measures, however, are taken by the state: building for
industries leaving Budapest has priority. After 1 January 1968, within the
framework of the new economic structure, each industrial firm draws up
independent financial plans, only receiving directives from the economic plan.
Also, the state makes grants to the departmental councils of the development
areas to be used as subsidies for the establishment of industries: this concerns
the east and south of the country, apart from the already industrialized con-

urbations of Pecs and Miskolc. Though state industries seem guided on the whole by these provisions, the small co-operative industries remain free to choose their sites: their share of industrial employment, though still small, is on the increase.

It should also be mentioned that the departure of industries from Budapest is not usually accompanied by an exodus of manpower. There has been a particular attempt to attract managerial workers and skilled workers but these prefer to remain in Budapest, so that it is often necessary to get them to accompany the industry temporarily until they have trained their successors in the new provincial units.

Finally, it may be noted that the Hungarians, repeating the mistake of the British and French, have neglected the development of tertiary employment. This explains the continued growth of Budapest (from an increase of 17 000 in 1966 to 36 000 in 1967) despite a natural decrease of population.

The map of industry in the 1963 plan also shows the main concentrations of industry to be expanded or created. The choice of sites takes account of the presence of raw materials, transport infrastructures, the nature of the sites and the need to plan complementary industries to ensure variety of employment. All this requires large centres: the 'balancing centres'.

The 1963 plan gave official status to a policy of land development hinging on the limitation of Budapest's growth and on the creation of eight 'balancing centres' in the provinces. While still unofficial, this policy had already been put into force through the directives issued to local town planners by the regional planning service of VATI (the 'town interconnections'). Legislative and financial provisions wield a similar influence: grants to departmental councils for the establishment of industries will run into several million fiorints from 1970 onwards.

II Regional plans

The Budapest Institute of Town and Country Planning also carries out regional plans of various types:

> Regional studies, providing the basic data for regional projects.
> Regional projects showing the most effective use of the land.
> Regional development plans stemming from the national economic plans and dealing either with a particular industry or a particular question (tourism or the control of a river, for example).

There may be several plans for the same region, dealing with different aspects of regional development (industry and agriculture, for example) and co-ordination between these various plans is ensured by the fact that they are carried out by the same body.

Regional planning did not really begin until 1958 (apart from a first hesitant abortive attempt in 1949). The plans have still to be revised and in some places completely new ones are preferred. Like the national development plan, the regional plans do not set any time limit but they are all long-term (up to the end of the century) and the government gives approval to target figures in terms of the five-year economic plans. These regional plans, together with the national development plan, help to establish directives for more detailed town plans. The new long-term (fifteen-year) economic plans may, however, entail the revision of the aims of physical planning.

The particular case of the Budapest region

The capital (with a population of 1 844 000 in 1960 and an area of 525 km²) has its own town planning institute, BUVATI, which has also been entrusted by the Ministry of Construction with the majority of the plans for the Budapest region (with a 1960 population of 3 217 000 and an area of 11 900 km²).

The 1959 plan for Budapest and its neighbourhood was mainly concerned with town planning and covered an area of 2175 km² with a population of 2 170 000 in 1960. A regional plan covering a larger area is nearly completed and should soon be approved by the government.

The 1959 plan, like the regional plan, is based on the idea of checking the growth of the capital. Rather than advocating the decentralization of industry into the provinces, however, it laid stress on dispersal within the region. This did not meet with unanimous approval, even though its authors pointed to existing infrastructures and the possibilities of other economies as justification. Regarding the organization of housing, BUVATI proposes the creation of a ring of ten satellite towns with populations of about 40 000 about 40 km from the centre by the extension of existing small towns and the creation of centres with plenty of employment and amenities capable of absorbing commuters from outside the conurbation and of acting as subregional centres. The building of dormitory cities outside the built-up area, about 20 km from the centre, was also proposed but has not so far been put into practice. Large housing estates within the boundaries of the conurbation are preferred. The 1959 plan, which also laid down the policy of the categorization of industries in Budapest, contains a motorway plan (an internal ring road on the west and five radial motorways, of which the easternmost one is already in existence), a rail plan (based on a line by-passing Budapest on the south) and a plan for an underground railway (whose construction was interrupted in 1953 but resumed in 1964, with its first stretch due to be opened in 1970).

III   New towns

In Hungary, as in the other communist countries, new towns are built for different reasons from those of western Europe and *a fortiori* those of the United States, being concerned with aiding the country's development by providing housing for workers taking part in the industrialization of the country.

The sites of the new towns are obviously a direct result of this aim but there are many other aspects, such as planning, employment, social life, administration and finance.

The choice of sites

The creation of new towns has followed the establishment of industries and not vice versa. The four earliest – Dunapentèle,[1] Komlo, Kazincbarcika and Oroszlany – were part of the original economic plans and they were sited in areas of low population. This low population density near the industries then being established was what created the need to build the new towns.[2]

Dunaujvaros (formerly Dunapentèle and later Sztalinvaros) is linked to the iron-working complex started in 1949 (and today the largest in Hungary), the Danube providing water as well as transport for Russian iron ore from the Black Sea and coking coal from the Pecs basin in the south of the country. The town is on the banks of the Danube, 70 km south of Budapest on a 6300 ha plateau 50 m above the river, near islands forming a natural harbour. It is in the middle of a rural area and on the site of a former Roman fort. This position, chosen as a result of many studies, is by no means perfect: witness the subsidence caused by the bed of clay on the loess plateau, necessitating the later reinforcement of the foot of the cliff overhanging the river.

Komlo dates from 1950 and is situated in the south of the country, in the coalfield of the Pecs area, on the site of a former mining village now completely absorbed by the new town. Its development is linked with that of Dunaujvaros, whose iron-workings use the coking coal it produces.

[1] Known as Sztalinvaros from 1951-56 and 1957-61 and as Dunaujvaros since 1961.
[2] T. Z. Garab, 'Les villes socialistes de Hongrie', *Documentation sur l'Europe Centrale*, vol. IV, No. 3, May-June 1966 (Louvain, Institut de Recherches de l'Europe centrale).

Oroszlany, dating from the same period, is connected with the coal mines 50 km west of Budapest and with the thermal power station using the coal.

Varpalota (90 km south-west of Budapest on the road to Graz) is connected with the extraction of bauxite in the Bakony mountains and of lignite, which has made possible the building of a thermal power station for use in the treatment of the bauxite.

Ajka (150 km south-west of Budapest) is in a comparable position to that of Varpalota: the extraction of bauxite and lignite (with a thermal power station), which was begun between the wars, was developed after the building of the new town in 1951.

Kazoncbarcika (22 km north-west of Miskolc) is the sixth new town in Hungary to be built in 1950 - 1 and owes its existence to a chemical fertilizer works linked to the coal mines for the extraction of gas used in the chemical industry. Water (from the river Sajo) and coal were on the spot but not enough gas could be extracted, so that gas from Debrecen and Romania and from imported coal has had to be used.

It was not until 1955 that another new town – Tiszapalkonya – was created, on an almost virgin site, 30 km south-east of Miskolc at the junction of the Sajo and Tisza rivers, to house workers in the chemical industry (glass and fertilizers) and in the thermal power station.

The latest, Szashalombatta, built in 1961, is also linked with a thermal power station (serving Budapest) and an oil refinery. It is 30 km south of the capital, at the end of the pipeline bringing oil from across the Danube.

Planning

When the new towns were built, Hungary did not have a long tradition of town planning. The Soviet model, the only one ideologically acceptable, was ununreliable. The new towns could and did serve as experiments but were not always successful, especially architecturally. The official policy proclaimed was that of the garden city: space, sunlight and greenery. But the priority given to blocks of flats built and designed on lines reminiscent of the French *grands ensembles* limited the number of open spaces and parks so generously provided in theory.

Several general principles can be distinguished, however. To start with, the new towns were planned for both industrial and residential areas,[1] sometimes very close to each other, as at Dunaujvaros, where there are only a few hundred

[1]Markos Gyorgy, *Les nouvelles villes industrielles socialistes* (*Magyar orozag Gazdasagi Földrajza*) (Budapest, 1962).

metres between the iron-works and the residential sector. In the second phase of building the original new towns, a green belt was planted to separate the two (Dunaujvaros, Tiszapalkonya, etc.). To begin with, the need for an urban centre was denied, as it was thought to benefit those living near the centre at the expense of those on the outskirts. This idea, however, was soon abandoned, although space for the centre was not reserved and built on until the town was nearly completed. Priority was given to housing, at the expense of accompanying amenities, which were often late in being built and of insufficient quantity.

The plans are prepared in accordance with usual custom in Hungary. The main town plan is drawn up by the Budapest Planning Institute or by one of the five provincial institutes, according to the whereabouts of the new town, in tune with the data of the economic development plan. It decides the outlines of the proposed area, the position of the main installations, etc. The principle of neighbourhood centres (with about 5000 inhabitants) needing one primary school is generally adopted. Detailed plans show the type and position of different buildings. Building regulations determine the height of the buildings, their spacing and density. There must not be more than 700 people to the hectare and the distance between the buildings must, on average, be double their height.[1]

An innovation has been introduced recently: the experimental period of two or three years, during which the plan is tried out. The comparison between the results of this trial period and theoretical calculations may entail its revision and help to prepare the final, official plan.[2]

These plans can also be revised or added to. This has been necessitated by the unexpected increase of population in the earlier new towns (such as Dunaujvaros) and even in those not yet completed (such as Tiszapalkonya). This method also allows for the modification of the conventional character of the original plan.[3]

The town plans prepared by the Budapest Institute of Planning or one of the five provincial institutes are submitted for the approval of the municipal council and then the departmental council. However, when the new towns do not yet rank as towns, the plans are approved by the Ministry of Construction. The general plans follow the same procedure and the detailed plans may be

[1]*New Towns in Hungary*, an article in English published by the Hungarian government (undated).

[2]Eva Nemes, 'Foyers pratiques, confortables et beaux', *Commerce extérieur hongrois*, No. 4, 1964.

[3]Dr Imre Perenyi, 'Cinquante ans d'urbanisme socialiste', *Varosépités*, No. 5, October 1967.

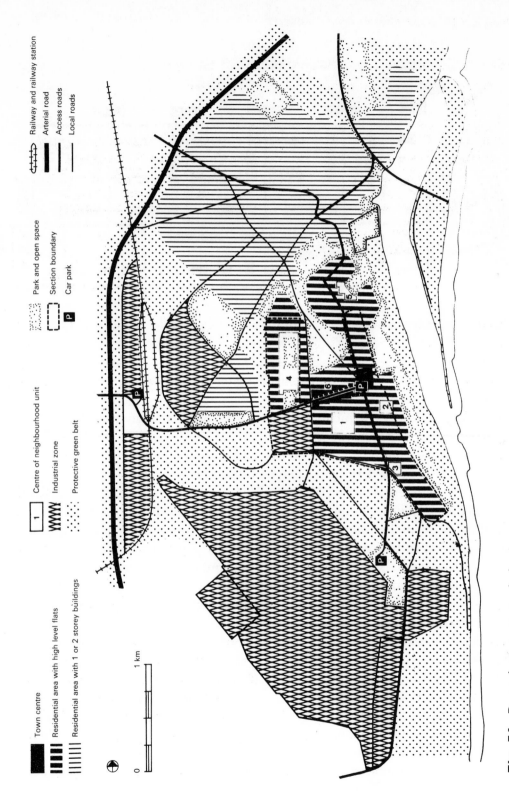

Fig. 54 Dunaujvaros: general plan.

Town centre

Residential area with high level flats

Residential area with 1 or 2 storey buildings

1 Centre of neighbourhood unit

Industrial zone

Protective green belt

Park and open space

Section boundary

P Car park

Railway and railway station

Arterial road

Access roads

Local roads

0   1 km

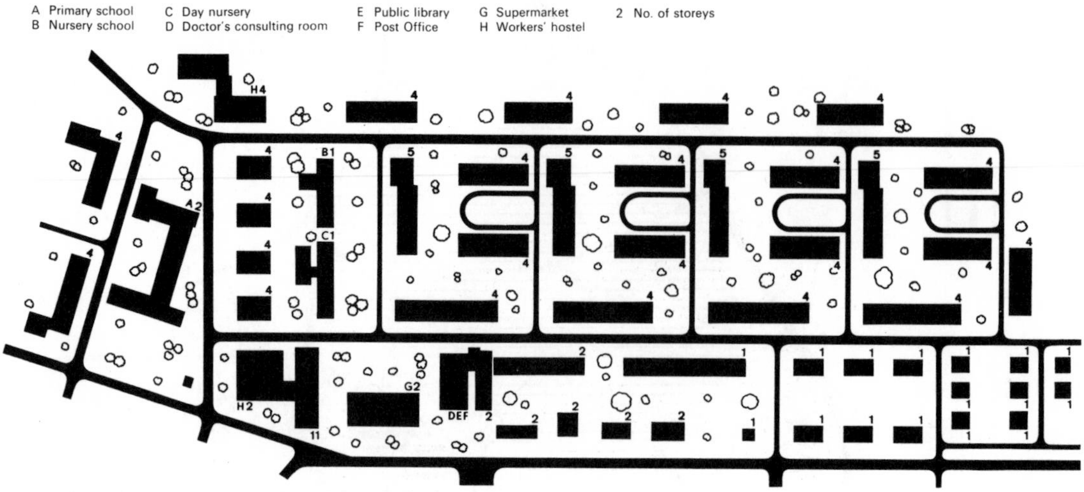

A Primary school   C Day nursery   E Public library   G Supermarket   2 No. of storeys
B Nursery school   D Doctor's consulting room F Post Office   H Workers' hostel

Fig. 55   Dunaujvaros : detailed plan of the third neighbourhood unit.

drawn up by one of the planning institutes or by a special department in the new town.

Dunaujvaros differs in many respects. The original plan was the work of Mr Tibor Weiner and was carried on after his death in 1965 by the Budapest Institute of Planning, which revised the master plan in 1966 in accordance with regulations. There used to be a village of 4000 inhabitants to the north of the town's site, which is bounded by the river on the east, the village on the north, the line of the motorway on the north-west, the railway on the west and the iron-working complex on the south (Fig. 54). The extension now planned on the north-west to house 75 000 - 80 000 (at first planned for 45 000) could not be carried beyond these boundaries without building beyond the river or the railway, which would not be desirable. An extension of the iron-working complex is the only possibility and the redevelopment of the former village is also planned (Fig. 55).

At Kazincbarcika, a chemical centre incorporated in the regional plans of 1948 and 1962 within the Ojd-Miskolc combine, the plan was drawn up by the Budapest Institute of Planning in 1956 (five years after building had begun), but only in provisional terms. A fresh plan has now been prepared at Miskolc, the major town of the region, by the regional planning institute, which has also carried out overall plans. A total population of 45 000 - 50 000 is planned for, half of which (23 000) is already in residence.

Tiszapalkonya, founded in 1955, had its plan approved by the departmental

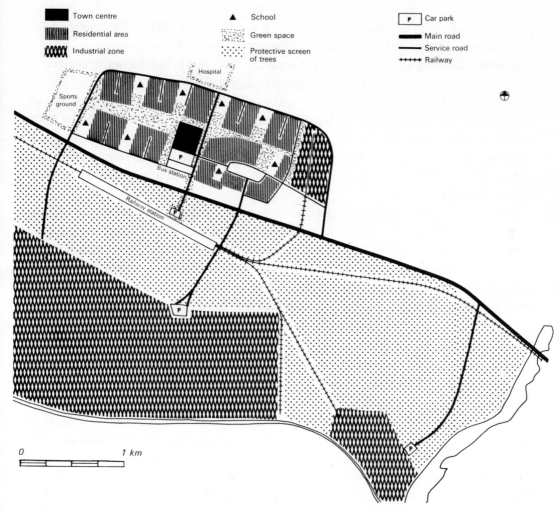

Fig. 56 Tiszapalkonya : general plan 1965.

council in 1956. The new plan of 1965 was submitted to the departmental council and to the Ministry of Construction. The original plan was for a single sector with 2500 dwellings. The new plan is for four comparable units along two axes enclosing a central zone of green spaces and amenities. This plan can be very flexible, as the number of planned sectors could easily be increased on a linear pattern (Fig. 56). Plans are for a population of 40 000, while the originally planned population of 10 000 is already installed. The status of town was acquired on 31 March 1966.[1]

[1]Dr Albert Kovacs, 'Tiszaszederkeny', an article appearing in the periodical *Budapest*, No. 11, November 1967.

At Szashalombatta, planned for a population of 30 000, the master plan
(1 : 5 000, like the plans of all the Hungarian towns) was drawn up by the
Budapest Planning Institute (a multidepartmental body led by an architect in
collaboration with an engineer). The pattern is very simple: one sector of blocks
of flats and one sector of houses (including the former village). 300 people per
hectare are planned for the 50 ha of blocks of flats, or 15 000 people in 5000
dwellings (800 of them already built) and 50 people per hectare on the 35 ha
of houses (1750 people). There will be later extensions on the north-west,
where 50 ha will be used for blocks of flats. Another, denser sector of houses
is also planned.

This planning has received criticism from many sources, including the official
press, with subsequent replies from those in charge.[1] Apart from the lack of
amenities, the new towns are attacked for the monotony of their construction
and the standardized character of their planning. These criticisms may seem
justified to the western observer but the new towns will give the Hungarian
town planners an opportunity to improve their methods.

Housing

Housing in the new towns consists essentially of small blocks of flats such as
are to be found elsewhere. The average size of the dwellings continues to increase but is at present 50 m^2: two rooms with bathroom and kitchen. There is
a low proportion of individual housing but, especially at the start, plenty of
rooms for workers in special hostels. These were introduced after 1956 to fulfil
a demand and reduce public expenditure.

Housing is allocated to the families of workers in the town (especially in
industry) but the occupants are not ejected if they change their jobs: the
position is similar to that of the new towns in Britain (see Chapter 1). A special
area where the prepared land can be resold to private buyers is available for
building individual houses.

At Dunaujvaros in 1960 the following had been built:

  24 per cent of dwellings with one and a half rooms

  68 per cent of dwellings with two and a half rooms

  8 per cent of dwellings with three rooms

or on average 1·85 rooms per dwelling (with an area of 47 m^2). At present the
average dwelling has two rooms and an area of 53 m^2. Though there are few
rooms, they are usually much larger than those of the French housing estates.

[1] Dr Lajos Filkey, 'The architectural problems of Dunaujvaros', *Varosépités*, No. 5,
October 1967.

At Szashalombatta, two and a half roomed flats are being built (60 m^2: the two main rooms of 18·5 and 15 m^2) and one and a half roomed flats of 45 m^2 with the main room 18·5 m^2 and the smaller room 11 m^2.

In the realm of construction, the first development was of poor quality and already seems dilapidated after fifteen years. Prefabrication is now used more and more (as at Tiszapalkonya, for example) but even where traditional building methods are used plans are standardized for reasons of economy. There is an obvious link between the uniformity of the preliminary plans and the monotonous character of the resulting towns. At first, buildings were not more than five storeys high but high-level flats appeared after 1957.

The housing usually has modern comforts: running water, bathroom, kitchen, district heating (except for the earliest housing), electricity and, in most of the towns, town gas and main drainage. The rooms in hostels, for workers without families, are planned for two to four occupants and the hostels have communal baths, refectories, etc. They are gradually replacing the temporary hutments dating from the beginning of the town's construction.

The new towns neverthless have a permanent housing crisis. For one thing, construction does not keep pace with the creation of employment and, for another, the dwellings are very small. Also, the shortage of public amenity buildings aggravates the situation by the temporary use of housing instead. In 1964 there were 1435 families on the waiting list for housing at Oroszlany. But the situation continues to improve and the time is now well past when multiple occupation was the rule, as it was only ten years ago.

Amenities

When the new towns were first built, the hurry to build housing was such that amenities were either neglected or carried out without any organization. At Dunaujvaros, for instance, a school of twenty classes was opened in 1951 although there were only enough pupils for two! Some years later, there was still only this one school, by then quite insufficient for the numbers attending.

Later on, attempts were made to fit amenities to the requirements of the resident population, where free spaces allowed. Norms were laid down but not always adhered to. They are as follows for a sector of 5000 inhabitants:[1]

One primary school of 16 classes (8 years).
Two nursery schools of 50 places each.
Two nurseries of 40 places each.
Two sets of medical consulting rooms.
Two pharmacies.

[1]*New Towns in Hungary*, published in English by the Hungarian government.

Amenities in the New Towns

Amenity / Population in 1964	Dunaujvaros 40 500	Kazinbarcika 23 000 (18 000 in 1961)	Komlo 26 900 (26 700 in 1961)	Oroszlany 18 100	Tiszapalkonya 10 000	Szazhalombatta 5000[2]
Primary schools	7 (7000 pupils)	2[1] (2000 pupils)[1] (16 classes)	13 (6000 pupils)	3 (3000 pupils)	2[2]	1
Technical schools	1 (metallurgy & mechanical construction)	1 (chemical industry)	1 (mining industry)	1 (mining industry)	0	
Training schools	1 (industrial)	0	1 (mining)	1 (mining)	0	
Secondary schools	1	1 under construction (16 classes)	1 (8 classes)	0	0	1 under construction
Nursery schools	12} 2300			6} 420	2} 280	1
Day nurseries	9} children			1} children	2} children[2]	1
Hospitals	1 (450 beds) opened 1965	1 temporary (150 beds), 1 under construction (400 beds)	1 (110 beds)[1]	0	0	1 (40 beds)[2]
Maternity homes	1 (100 beds)	1		1 (25 beds)	0	0
Consulting rooms	10 (120 doctors)		8[1] (11 doctors)[1]	15	1	
Dispensaries	1	3	0	1	1	1[2]
Pharmacies	4		1	2	0	
Sanatoria	0	0	1 (100 beds)	0	0	0
Swimming pools	1 (large pool)	0	1	1 (33 m pool)	0	0
Sports stadia	1	0	1	1	0	0
Luna park	1	0	0	1	0	0
Hotel/restaurant	1	1	1			1[2]
Libraries	3 (120 000 books)	1 (43 000 books)	1	1 (20 000 books)	0	0
Museums	1	0	1	0	0	0
Houses of culture	1 large & several small	1	2	6	1 under construction	1[2]
Theatres	1 planned	0	1 planned	0	0	0
Cinemas	2 (2 more planned)	0	0	1 (500 seats)	1 temporary (280 seats)	0

To these are added, for the whole town, a cinema (430 - 600 seats for 1000 residents), a cultural centre (theatre: 40 - 50 seats for 1000 residents), a secondary school (two classes for 2000 dwellings), a town hall, post office, fire station, shopping centre and local shops and workshops. To these, of course, must be added infrastructures (roads, water supply, electricity and gas supplies, drainage, heating, telephone service) and green spaces ($3 \cdot 5$ - 10 m^2 per person). As shown in the table, these norms are not always adhered to.

Employment

Data on employment are difficult to obtain, especially as the last census was taken as long ago as 1960. We have seen that the new towns were created to serve large industrial installations. The structure of employment in each is very unbalanced.

Dunaujvaros was built to house the workers of the largest iron-working complex in Hungary. This, covering 300 ha south of the city, consists of:

An ore concentration plant.
A coking plant.
Two blast furnaces producing 600 000 tons of cast iron yearly.
Four Martin furnaces producing 300 000 tons of steel yearly.
A hot rolling mill producing 450 000 tons of sheet metal a year.
A cold rolling mill producing 90 000 tons of sheet metal a year.
A thermal power station.
A chemicals factory.
A factory making fireproof bricks.
An engineering works.

The whole complex employs nearly 12 000 workers.

But this complex does not absorb all the industry in the town. In particular, there is a cellulose factory and a paper mill (employing 900 workers), a textile mill (with 300 women workers), a workshop making men's suits (1000 women workers), a factory making children's shoes (100 women workers), a shirt-maker's (450 workers), a factory for prefabricated building units, a dairy, etc. Altogether, there are almost 17 000 jobs in industry. However, in 1960 industry only absorbed a little over half of the working population:

Industry	9017	(50%)
Construction	2042	(11%)
Transport and telecommunications	1159	(7%)
Commerce	1049	(6%)
Services and administration	3483	(19%)
Agriculture	1244	(7%)
	17 994	(100%)

Since 1960 the relative importance of agriculture (corresponding to the former village) has obviously diminished. There are not many jobs in administration and services but, apart from the town hall and party headquarters (the first to be built) there is a large office block.

Kazincbarcika was planned for the chemical combine, which produces over 300 000 tons of nitrate fertilizers and plastics. Other large sources of employment are the thermal power station and a coal screening plant. Altogether, there are 8000 jobs in industry out of a total 13 000.

Komlo is above all a mining town (with over 8000 miners), producing 1·2 million tons of coal in 1960. It remains a mining town in appearance and few other industries have taken root.

Oroszlany (mining and thermal power station) is in a similar situation. At Varpalota, the extraction of lignite and bauxite, the thermal power station and the manufacture of aluminium are the main industries. The same is true of Ajka.

At Tiszapalkonya the link between the residential sectors and the factories (a chemical combine, producing 700 000 tons of nitrate fertilizers in 1968, paint, varnish, resins, etc., and a thermal power station) is accentuated by the direction of the roads, which, despite the protective green belt against pollution, give a clear view of the group of industrial buildings. The present 3500 jobs in this large industrial complex will be later increased by a large oil and chemical factory. The town also houses at present about 1000 building workers employed in the construction of the town and the factories. Employment in services, commerce, crafts and service industries is still very limited.

Szashalombatta, the latest new town, is linked to the oil refinery and the electricity station. There are already 1000 jobs at the refinery and 500 at the electricity works. Service industries are planned (bakery, dairy, ice-cream factory, mineral water factory, etc.). It is reckoned that eventually the two large industries will employ 40 per cent of the working population, service industries 35 per cent and commerce, agriculture, etc., the remaining 25 per cent.

Traffic and transport

The question of transport did not play a large part either in the choice of site or in the planning of the new towns. The traffic system does not derive from any original plan. It is only at Szashalombatta (the latest new town) that any separation of traffic has been attempted. One cannot but note, however, the generous proportions of some of the roads (such as the main avenue of Dunaujvaros) and some of the squares, planned mainly for purposes of prestige.

Rail and road links are not always good. Though Szashalombatta is near a motorway linking it with Budapest and is on the Budapest-Pecs railway (with about one train an hour), Dunaujvaros, on the other hand, is at some distance from the main line and a special line has been laid, with one through train a day to Budapest.

Tiszapalkonya is some way from the Miskolc-Debrecen railway (with six trains a day and a forty-five minute journey for the 30 km to Miskolc). Kazincbarcika is also linked to Miskolc (22 km away) by slow trains (a thirty minute journey, eight trains a day in each direction) and by bus. Bus services play the main role in all the new towns, especially for serving neighbouring villages where many of the industrial workers still live.

The larger towns have internal transport systems. Dunaujvaros has an internal bus system with twenty-four routes. Buses run every few minutes in the rush hour and between ten minutes and half an hour in slack periods.

At Kazincbarcika, a study of commuting was made by a special department in Budapest. At present, the internal system consists of six bus routes with an infrequent service (buses only at peak hours or hourly), which is run by a state concern. The question of parking has not occupied the town planners until recently. At present, one open parking space per dwelling is the rule for future planning, but this has not been so in the past and in some places extra areas are reserved outside new constructions to make up the deficit. The norm of one parking space per dwelling does not correspond with actuality: at Tiszapalkonya, for instance, 40 per cent of the spaces are planned for external sites, 30 per cent in commercial parks and 30 per cent in individual parking spaces but only 30 per cent of the total has been carried out (mainly in external sites and 150 individual parking spaces): but so far there are only 200 private cars.

Commuting can be an important problem, especially at first, taking place into the town and only to a negligible extent in the opposite direction, and lessening when housing is ready for workers' families. It is reckoned that 4500 workers commute to Dunaujvaros from neighbouring villages (or some even to Budapest), 1000 to Szashalombatta and 1000 to Tiszapalkonya, etc.

Population

The population growth of the new towns has been fairly irregular, linked to the rate of construction of housing and especially to successive extensions of the industrial complexes to which they are related. It has not reached 5000 a year in the first years, except at Dunaujvaros, and has rarely exceeded 2000 a year elsewhere. This is nevertheless a fast enough rate for an unbalanced population structure.

The population growth of the new towns has been as follows:

Town	Population						Present predicted population
	1949	1954	1.1.1960	1.1.1962	1.1.1964	1967	
Dunaujvaros	3 949	27 507	31 048	37 415	40 530	46 000	75 000-80 000
Komlo	5 932	18 875	24 850	26 513	26 892		30 000
Oroszlany	3 740	7 153	13 074	16 639	18 119		25 000
Varpalota	11 065		21 197				25 000
Ajka	8 307		15 362				20 000
Kazincbarcika	5 053	12 026	15 585	19 571	23 338	31 000	40 000
Tiszapalkonya			2 548	3 074	11 000	13 000	40 000
Szashalombatta					3 000	8 000	25 000-30 000
Total	43 000		127 000	145 000	165 000	190 000	280 000-290 000

The population structure is a very youthful one: in the 1965 census the average age was under 29 at Dunaujvaros and Oroszlany and 25 at Tiszapalkonya. The average age at Kazincbarcika was 17.

As the following table relating to the population of Dunaujvaros in 1960 shows, there is also a considerable imbalance between the sexes, mainly caused by the influx of unmarried workers housed in special buildings (hutments and later workers' hostels).

Population structure of Dunaujvaros 1960

Age	Men	Women	Total
0-4	1 618	1 478	3 096
5-9	1 719	1 764	3 483
10-14	1 151	1 080	2 231
15-19	1 275	988	2 263
20-29	4 383	3 253	7 636
30-39	3 397	2 613	6 010
40-49	1 553	1 114	2 667
50-54	668	456	1 124
55-59	503	405	908
60+	719	839	1 558
Total	16 986	13 990	30 976

This imbalance is to be found in the population structure of all the new towns: 78·1 per cent of the population in 1960 was under 40 (compared with 62·2 per cent for the country as a whole), with an average of 120 men to every 100 women.

This youthful population structure explains the very low death rate (about 2 - 4 per 1000) in the new towns and the average birth rate of about 12 - 15 per 1000. This last is higher than the national average (legal abortion having reduced the birth rate considerably over the last decade), while at the same time being low for a town with a very youthful structure. This can be explained by the presence of so many young unmarried workers. The natural excess of births over deaths (at present 8 per 1000, after being 10 per 1000 for some years) is responsible for a large proportion of the population increase of the new towns (17 per cent from 1949 to 1960, 35 per cent at Dunaujvaros since 1960).

The average size of households is large, especially at first: at Tiszapalkonya it is over four, having approached five. At Dunaujvaros in 1960 there were 3·9 people per dwelling (2·1 per room). At Kazincbarcika there are 4·26, corresponding to over two people per room, typical of all the new towns and of the country as a whole, where households are smaller on the average but the dwellings also smaller. Geographic origins differ greatly from one town to another but an important element is the rural population, coming especially from the over-populated great Hungarian plain. The nature of the employment also has its influence: at Dunaujvaros many of the newcomers are from the northern regions of Hungary where there were already iron-works. At Kazincbarcika, the newcomers are mainly from the east of the country, the least industrialized region: they often arrived to work on the construction of factories and the town and were later employed in the factories, while the managers, on the other hand, came from other industrial centres throughout the country. The same is true at Tiszapalkonya, where the newcomers of rural origin seem the most numerous. Nowhere does the Budapest conurbation play a large part in peopling the new towns.

The geographical mobility of the population is twofold, with families permanently housed on the one hand and temporary unmarried workers on the other. Figures from four towns for 1963 show that temporary immigration is much higher than temporary emigration, even for nearly completed towns like Komlo, showing that a large proportion settle in the new towns. The rate of departures (temporary or final) equals about 5 per cent of the population and of arrivals 15 per cent (20 per cent at Oroszlany and only 13 per cent at Kazincbarcika). These movements concern young adults in particular.

Mobility of population in four new towns 1963

Town	Permanent arrivals	Temporary arrivals	Total arrivals	Permanent departures	Temporary departures	Total departures	Balance
Dunaujvaros	2110	4556	6666	1056	715	1771	4895
Komlo	1050	2375	3425	1254	488	1742	1683
Kazincbarcika	2008	3251	3259	706	423	1129	4100
Oroszlany	1288	2939	4227	693	361	1054	3173

Some of those leaving one town settle in other more recent new towns, such as Szashalombatta. This is especially the case with specialized workers and managers. Others leave a new town for economic reasons, such as the mining crisis that drove miners out of Kazincbarcika. Also, building workers who have not settled follow where there is new work. The amount of voluntary departures is very small among households already occupying a dwelling in the new towns because they would not find the equivalent elsewhere. Internal mobility is fairly low because the housing shortage makes it impossible to give a larger dwelling to every expanding household. Sometimes, also, earlier households wish to occupy newer housing, as at Tiszapalkonya, where district heating did not exist at the beginning. But, in theory, at least, they are not entitled to any priority.

Social life

The new towns in Hungary were not simply exercises in industrial organization with town planning as a secondary consideration. In Hungary they are known as 'socialist towns', expressing the hope of a new spirit arising in Dunaujvaros and the other new towns.

In this respect, achievement was very far at first from aim. The settlement in temporary housing of a large population of workers without their families, first in building and mining and later in industry, will certainly create a 'pioneering spirit', but in the worst sense: excessive frequenting of cafés, an atmosphere of brutality, a high crime rate, the frequent prostitution of young girls from the country, etc. In short, the new towns acquired a bad reputation.[1] The gradual settlement of families was not enough to alter this atmosphere. The housing priority given to skilled workers and managers at the expense of the earlier arrivals, the building workers, created psychological tension and the lack of amenities inhibited any cultural life for a long time. This situation improved considerably later on: Dunaujvaros comes second in the country for the use of libraries and we have seen the efforts made in the provision of cultural buildings, theatres, cinemas, libraries, etc. Television (more than 5000 sets in Dunaujvaros) has developed rapidly, increasing leisure interests but lessening social intercourse among the population.

After a difficult start, life in the new towns is growing more like that of other towns in Hungary, with one difference: the part played by education, especially adult education. At Dunaujvaros about 300 adults attend evening classes at the advanced metallurgical technical school[2] (with a similar number

[1]T. Z. Garab, op. cit.
[2]Endre Varkonyi, 'Dunaujvaros', *Hungarian Review*, No. 8, 1960.

of adolescents attending classes at this school after normal school hours) and the new town is well on its way to outshining the medieval centre at Szekesfehervar: first-rate theatre companies and concerts are frequent in the new town.[1]

Administration and finance

The question of administration and finance is obviously very different in communist countries from that in western Europe or the United States. In Hungary the creation of new towns is demanded by large national organizations responsible for different branches of employment.

Whether these are industrial organizations, national construction organizations or *ad hoc* organizations, the state is always in charge and finances the operation directly or indirectly. Nevertheless, various administrative methods were tried before the new towns were considered large enough for the municipal councils to take over and direct their development as in the other towns in the country.

Dunaujvaros is a special case: the Company for Investment in Heavy Industry was entrusted with the development of the iron-working complex and the town during the first phase. This body, directly dependent on the Ministry of Heavy Industry, worked on the spot and was only concerned with Dunaujvaros, an operation of national importance. It employed over fifty people, mainly professionals: architects, engineers, financial experts, etc. In co-operation with the architect Tibor Weiner, who drew up the plans for the town, it settled the allocation of government funds assigned for the development of Dunaujvaros after consultation with the government departments concerned.

In 1950 a new local authority was created, but the role of the municipal council remained limited up to 1957 (by which time the town had a population of 29 000) when it was entrusted with the further development of the new town. For this task, the municipal council relies on a Planning Bureau and a Department of Building and Transport. The former, which prepares detailed plans, consists of a staff of seventeen (two architectural engineers, one lawyer, seven technicians and seven clerical staff). The latter, whose job it is to direct and control the operation, has a staff of twelve (two architectural engineers, five technicians, five clerical staff). The Projects Bureau carries out plans that extend to the surroundings of the town and has a staff of over forty, including

---

[1]Zolyar Halasz, *Un coup d'oeil sur la Hongrie*, paper in French published by the Hungarian government (1962).

eight architectural engineers, fourteen technicians, draughtsmen, etc. The municipal council is also in charge of this bureau. Tibor Weiner, who had drawn up the original master plan for the Company for Investment in Heavy Industry, held the post of chief planner until his death in 1965. He was succeeded by one of the chief architects of the Budapest Planning Institute, but this post is unprecedented in Hungary and is due to be discontinued. Since 1957 investments connected with the iron-working complex have been his concern, with the help of the appropriate ministry and sometimes of other ministries (particularly the Ministry of Light Industry).

Kazincbarcika was also developed at the instigation of the Ministry of Heavy Industry, at least to begin with. It had a local body responsible for the development of the industrial complex and the new town, with a staff of nearly 200, but, unlike that of Dunaujvaros, it extended its powers far beyond the town. In 1954, the municipal council of the new local authority was elected and in 1960 it took over the task of completing the town (industrial investments remaining in the hands of the appropriate national companies). The town has a small building department (with a staff of six), but studies are carried out and plans are drawn up at departmental level (in Miskolc) as they are for the other towns of the department. So, unlike Dunaujvaros, the main role is played by the department and not the town itself.

In 1966 Tiszapalkonya became a new local authority and was in Kazincbarcika's present position: the departmental Planning Bureau drew up the plans and the town had only a very small building bureau with a staff of two. Previously, the factories and then, after 1965, the department were in charge of the town's development.

At Szashalombatta the situation is different: here a construction organization from Budapest, the Institute for Housing Planning (Lakoe Pulet Tervezon Vallalat) draws up the general plans and detailed plans, with a staff of five especially concerned with the new town.

In the field of finance, the funds are always public but are dispensed in different ways. In Dunaujvaros, the various ministries concerned finance industrial investments. Amenities are financed by the ministries concerned through the town, which is responsible for organizing them, if necessary through special municipal societies. Day nurseries, nursery schools and primary schools are the responsibility of the cultural department of the municipal council, which is also in charge of libraries, cultural buildings and assembly halls. Secondary schools are the responsibility of the cultural department of the departmental council; training schools that of the Ministry of Employment; metallurgical further technical schools that of the Ministry of Heavy Industry.

Cinemas are run by a special body at departmental level. Hospitals and dispensaries are the responsibility of the town (department of health), and so is commerce (department of commerce). There is one body in charge of retail business (where the staffs are wage-earners except for some small private businesses), one for bakeries, one for restaurants and one for large stores. Profits go into the national purse that financed these investments in the first place. There is also a co-operative concern running some businesses.

In the matter of housing, the following are differentiated:

> Housing built by the state for letting (about 50 per cent of all housing in Kazincbarcika, for example).
>
> Housing built for home-ownership by co-operatives. The original deposit is low (10 - 15 per cent of the cost) and the remainder is on a long-term (twenty to twenty-five years) interest-free loan. This type of housing makes up about 45 per cent of the total at Kazincbarcika.
>
> Housing built privately (individual houses) with state aid (long-term loans with moderate interest varying according to the financial position of the household).
>
> Housing privately built without state aid for non-wage-earning families with high incomes.

These last two categories, which account for half the housing in the country as a whole, play a very small role in the new towns (5 per cent in Kazincbarcika). To these must be added housing built by banks and sold with loans (this category of high quality housing does not exist in the new towns) and special housing provided on very easy terms to the occupants of rebuilt slums. In the new towns other than Kazincbarcika the proportion of rented housing is lower and that of co-operative and individual housing higher.

In these circumstances, the question of finance is simple, being just one item of national expenditure. The local authority and the department organize the amenities for which they are responsible with the help of government grants (according to their populations) and local taxation. This consists merely of a municipal rate – said to be for construction and development – which is levied on income other than the main salary. The question of the financial balance of the operation does not arise but it is obvious that government income from rents and repayments of loans bears no relation to the investments carried out (7000 million fiorints (£125 million) for the town of Dunaujvaros between 1950 and 1967, not including the factories). The financial mechanism was, however, altered on 1 January 1968, in connection with the overhaul of the whole Hungarian economy, and more responsibility was given at the local level. Each department became responsible for the building on its territory, financing it with its own funds and those still emanating from the government. This increase in autonomy will be a help to the successful development of the new towns. The reluctance to build adequate centres in the first new towns was unfortunate, but the reform will soon make finances available for a start on the centre of Tiszapalkonya. Infrastructural systems are also being carried out in advance there instead of only keeping pace with current needs.

Conclusion

The start of the new towns in 1950 already seems old history to the Hungarian planners. The latest new town – Szashalombatta – was started as long ago as 1961. Nowadays town planning in Hungary is faced with other problems, the main ones being a redevelopment of old towns and of villages (rural housing is mainly of very poor quality in Hungary), the development of housing estates on the outskirts of towns and the building of new villages on the Hungarian plain. At present these various questions are being studied at the economic level (though all would seem equally important) to decide on priorities in investments. The new towns still seem to suffer from the results of the administrative and financial disorganization that attended their creation and they are regarded as costly experiments. This seems all the more ingenuous since it relies for its main argument on the fact that the new towns demand structural provision that is unnecessary in the case of redevelopment or urban extensions where existing amenities may suffice. This is to make illogical comparisons. It is in fact obvious that the use of existing amenities lowers the level of service to the populations previously catered for by them and that the same new amenities will be necessitated in the long run to preserve the same or a higher level of services, allowing for greater problems of construction as well.

The pessimism of the authorities with regard to the new towns is particularly surprising when one considers the alternative of large extensions of small towns, in the Budapest region in particular, where a similar investment in amenities will be necessary.

The new towns in Hungary do not, admittedly, strike the outside observer as town planning efforts of exceptional quality like the garden city of Tapiola or some sectors of the suburbs of Stockholm (see Chapter 2). Nevertheless, the comfortable housing, the care given to landscaping (parks, gardens, tree-lined avenues), the balance ensured between employment and population, even at the cost of an imbalance of employment (the lack of jobs in the tertiary sector) whose effects will be felt by the next generation, the variety of cultural amenities, even if late on the scene, all combine to make these new towns the most successful outcome of national town planning seeking to create its own tradition.

It may well be asked whether the Hungarian planners, by renouncing the new towns in favour of extensions to small existing towns, are not depriving themselves of a trump card in their planning policy, whose aim is the checking of Budapest's growth and the development of balancing centres in the provinces. Recent developments are, in fact, hardly reassuring: though the share of industrial employment concentrated in Budapest has decreased, it has increased in actual amount and the population increase of the city and its environs has not been halted (no doubt because of the disproportionate increase of tertiary employment in the capital), despite a drop in the birth rate.

8 : An attempted synthesis

The analysis, country by country, of new towns either completed, in course of construction, or still at the planning stage, shows, besides some similarities, considerable differences. This makes the exact definition of a new town, attempted at the beginning of this study, a difficult matter. In an attempt to arrive at a satisfactory definition, some of the elements of the new towns that have been studied will be analysed:

> Site
> Size
> Conception of zones and distribution of housing
> The role of the centre
> Provision of employment
> The administrative and financial framework

This attempt at synthesis will also make it possible to see what changes are taking place in each of these spheres.

I   The siting of new towns

The choice of site is the first that faces the promoters of new towns, and it cannot be taken in isolation. The following may, therefore, be differentiated:

> New towns established outside urban areas.
> New towns established within an urban area but not in continuity with the existing built-up area.
> New towns established as continuations of existing built-up areas.

Independent new towns

In many countries the official development policy aims at ensuring the balanced development of all regions of the country. Some of these regions being very rural (as in Hungary) or sparsely populated (as in Siberia or central Brazil), the creation of new towns seems one means of putting this policy into practice.

In this case, their sites are usually chosen for economic reasons and the availability of raw materials.

This situation is common in eastern Europe. Many new towns in the USSR, particularly in Siberia, meet the demand for the creation of industrial centres, especially where there is a supply of raw materials (coal, iron or oil). In Poland the usual aim is also to ensure a balance of employment throughout the country and Stalowa Wola is a typical example of a new town set up in an unindustrialized area. Though Nowa Huta is sited in the neighbourhood of Cracow, its creation reflects the wish to create a new industrial complex based on iron-working in that part of the country. There are similar examples in Hungary, new towns having been set up to house the workers in industrial complexes purposely created outside traditionally industrialized zones. Dunaujvaros exists for the iron-working complex established on the great plain of Hungary, on the banks of the Danube, which affords transport of coal from Pecs and of iron ore from Russia. Komlo and Oroszlany are linked with coal mining and Ajka and Varpolata with the extraction of bauxite; Kazincbarcika and Tiszapalkonya are linked to chemical combines and Szashalombatta, site of the country's large oil refinery, is at the mouth of the oil pipeline.

Similar reasons sometimes hold sway even in western Europe. In West Germany, for instance,[1] Salzgitter (Lower Saxony), Marl (North Rhine Westphalia) and Kaufbeuren (Bavaria) were founded, the first in 1942 and the other two in 1946, to allow the creation of metallurgical industries. At Salzgitter (with a population of over 120 000) iron ore from the Harz mountains is worked. Marl (population 100 000) was set up in conjunction with the northerly movement of the centre of coal mining in the Ruhr. So, twenty years later, was Wulfen, which is now being built[2] and is to house a population of 50 000. In 1937 Wolfsburg (Lower Saxony) was founded in conjunction with the Volkswagen works. In Italy the plans made for the Mezzogiorno will probably lead to the decision to build new towns. Even in Great Britain, though the new town movement sprang from the desire to decrease the congestion of London's built-up area, many new towns have later been sited in the interests of national development, such as the wish to check the economic decline of the north of England (Newton Aycliffe, Washington, Peterlee) or to revitalize mining areas (Telford, Cwmbran). There have sometimes been joint objectives, as at Skel-

[1]Manlia Budinis, 'Les villes nouvelles de la République fédérale allemande', *Revue géographique de l'Est*, No. 3, 1964.
[2]Erich Zahn, Eberhard Avras, Fritz Eggeling and Karl Eduard Grosche, 'Planning Neue Stadt Wulfen', *Architektur Wettebewerke*, 1965.

mersdale and later Runcorn, outside Liverpool, to ease the congestion in the great Irish Sea port and to create new economic centres.

A final case is that of new capitals established away from large urban areas, either to accelerate the economic growth of the regions where they are sited or to sidestep political rivalry between several large cities or regions of the country (Canberra, Washington), or for these two reasons at once (Brasilia), or as the result of territorial changes (Chandigarh, new capital of the Punjab, the former capital, Lahore, now being part of Pakistan).

New towns built near but separate from a large city

One of the main objectives of any national planning policy is to provide against the concentration of men and jobs in a single built-up area – or conurbation – whose unwieldy size is feared and whose increased development would be at the expense of the other towns in the country. This policy has been put into practice over the last two decades in Great Britain, France and the Netherlands in particular, in connection with the built-up areas of London and Paris and the conurbation of western Holland, but has assumed different aspects in different places. In Great Britain the purpose affirmed for a quarter of a century has not only been to stabilize the population of the London region but to lower the density of its central area by moving a part of its population into new planned developments, the new towns in particular, on the edge of the urban region and separated from the existing built-up area by a green belt. The largest of the new towns and the major extensions of existing towns now planned are about 100 km from London. In the Paris region, on the other hand, until recently, the limiting definition of the edge of the built-up area led to large-scale building operations on the rare open spaces within the restricted built-up area. In the Netherlands the growth of the great cities making up the Randstad Holland has for some years been directed towards the outside of the ring-shaped conurbation.

The Greater London Plan established by Sir Patrick Abercrombie, with its green belt and ring of new towns beyond, has influenced town planning in Europe for the last twenty years. Even if this pattern is not copied, it is still referred to. For example, it is now inspiring the Hungarian town planners working on the plan for the Budapest region, who propose a ring of medium-sized satellite towns (with populations of about 40 000) some 40 km from the centre.

Some of the new towns in Poland, especially in Upper Silesia (Nowe Tychy, etc.) were similarly founded to aid the decongestion and partial redevelopment of very different urban regions. The theoretical project of Etarea in Czechoslovakia is 20 km from the centre of Prague. In France it seems that the master plans being prepared for the highly urbanized provincial regions are tending towards new towns separated from the main built-up area (the valley of the lower Seine and the new towns east of Lyon).

New towns continuous with built-up areas

The desire, stressed by British town planners, to retain an undeveloped area between the original built-up area and the new towns does not receive universal approbation. One school of town planning as prominent as that of London, that of Stockholm, prefers on the contrary, starting with the 1952 plan, to site planned urban development along radial lines served by public transport and continuous with the parent city. This is an altogether different conception of the role of the new towns, conceived on a different scale and seen as part of a single built-up area. The wish to limit commuting times between these new residential zones and the original centre militates against the creation of a buffer area. A similar principle guided the authors of the Copenhagen 'finger plan' (1947). At Helsinki the Finnish town planners will make use of a very similar pattern (1960) to that carried out for Stockholm.

Apart from the Scandinavian countries, these principles have inspired Dutch town planners until recently. In Amsterdam the new sectors on the west, south and north, and now on the south-east, have also been planned in continuity with the original built-up area, the latest planned to rely on an underground railway system similar to that of Stockholm. In Rotterdam new sectors like Pendrecht, Hoogvliet, Capelle, etc., are planned on the same lines. The same is to be found in West Germany at Sennestadt (population 20 000), founded in North Rhine Westphalia in 1954 to absorb the overspill population of Bielefeld, and Nordweststadt, built near Frankfurt.

This type of continuity is necessary to small-scale operations incapable of providing enough amenities and satisfactory balance of employment on their own: the notion of urban unity, rejected in Great Britain, then becomes of prime importance.

Continuity has also been adopted for the new towns of the Paris region, as set out in the master plan of 1965. There are two chief reasons for this: first and foremost, the belief that the unity of the region, especially where employment is concerned, is a trump card that it would be foolish to relinquish; second, the wish to limit commuting times, which the British experiment has shown to be the inevitable lot of a not inconsiderable portion of the population.

Lastly, though no general rules can be distinguished in the New Communities of the USA, since these are sited where there is available land, they are built as close as possible to large built-up areas.

II The size of the new towns

It is obvious that the siting of new towns cannot be independent of their size, which is the second main decision to be made in advance. In this respect, there are considerable differences between one country and another for various reasons:

> New capitals cannot have their size fixed *a priori*, since, if they function successfully, they are bound to increase rapidly, as Washington did (doubling its expected size in less than thirty years). Where a target is fixed (as for a population of 500 000 for Brasilia), it can only be for one stage at a time.
>
> Towns sited to aid the industrial development of rural or sparsely populated regions have a fixed population in relation to the productive capacities of the new industries, altering in time with their development and the future creation of ancillary employment (Nowa Huta, Dunaujvaros, etc.).
>
> The size of new towns founded to check the growth of large built-up areas depends on:
>> the size of the built-up area;
>> its rate of growth;
>> the proportion of this growth to be absorbed by the new towns;
>> the number of the new towns.

This amounts to the fact that, all things being equal, new towns may be of greatest size in large urban regions (London, Paris, etc.), in regions undergoing rapid growth (Paris, Milan, Stockholm, etc.) or where independent planning rests on solid foundations (Stockholm, Amsterdam, etc.) and is channelled into a limited number of operations (the principle of the preliminary plan for the Copenhagen region in 1961). But the influence of these four factors can produce a great variety of situations in actuality. In Great Britain, the Abercrombie Plan is based on the hypothesis of a stabilized population in the London region, so that the role of the new towns was only to absorb one section of the overspill from the densely populated inner area. It was thought possible at that time to attain this objective by creating a limited number (eight) of new towns of fairly small size (populations of 20 000 - 60 000 according to the Reith Commission's report in 1946). In the Netherlands, on the other hand, despite the fact that the largest built-up areas (Amsterdam, Rotterdam, The Hague) were only a tenth the size of the London region, it was decided to concentrate urban development in the same way: to the south at Rotterdam (Hoogvliet and later Pendrecht), to the west, then to the south and finally the south-east of Amsterdam, with scope for large-scale developments (a population of 135 000 at West Amsterdam; 110 000 planned for Amsterdam South-East; 200 000 at Capelle, north-east of Rotterdam).

In Stockholm the scheme set out by the 1952 plan is based on the idea of small-scale units (populations of 10 000 - 20 000) strung round stations of an underground railway line, the group of units on the same line forming a new town with a population of 50 000 or more, served by a centre established in one of the units (Vällingby, Farsta, Skärholmen, etc.).

Among all these contradictory choices, it seems that the present tendency in nearly all European countries is to increase the size of planned urban developments.

We have seen that with all the earliest developments it was impossible to ensure a satisfactory balance and sufficient diversity of employment, except where, as in Great Britain, the developments were on a large enough scale. Some firms – particularly offices – were reluctant to establish themselves in small or medium-sized units, whose name had not yet gained any prestige, where manpower was limited, where there was a lack of ancillary services and where they felt cut off from the world of information, ideas and business. Also, the new centres seemed to have their commercial function overdeveloped at the expense of those of administration, culture, leisure, etc. Various studies concerned with the development of the first new towns have shown that a large population was necessary to the existence of some amenities and that a large enough town was a prime condition for the success of a centre performing many functions and, as a result, of a genuine community spirit in the town.

This change of theory led Danish town planners (in the preliminary plan of 1961) to propose the absorption of the capital's growth in city sectors (not seen as new towns independent of the capital), with populations of 250 000, their development (successive, not simultaneous) taking about ten years each. At the same period, town planners working on the regional plan for Stockholm (first edition 1958, second edition 1967) proposed the creation of a fresh batch of new sectors: these, built round the stations of a fast suburban railway line, would absorb populations of 40 000 - 50 000 and would be grouped to form genuine new towns with populations of 200 000 with a large urban centre. At Helsinki, Heikki Van Hertzen, creator of the garden city of Tapiola (population

17 000), suggests the creation of a line of new towns along the coast with populations of about 100 000, with Tapiola as the initial nucleus of the first of them. In the Netherlands the new towns under construction – such as Lelystad, at the heart of the polder zone – or being planned – a new town north-west of Amsterdam and the towns of Spijkenisse and Hellevoetsluis south and south-west of Rotterdam – will have populations of about 100 000 each. The theoretical project of Etarea (Czechoslovakia) provides for an eventual population of 135 000. In Great Britain itself the new regional studies for the south-east (1964 and 1967) have adopted the idea of major extensions of medium-sized towns, involving the doubling of their present populations of 50 000 - 100 000 (Ipswich, Northampton, Peterborough, etc.) and the creation of new towns with populations of about 250 000 (Milton Keynes) or more (a new town between Portsmouth and Southampton).

It is interesting to note that this tendency is not the result of a violent change but of slow development. In Great Britain the population target for the new towns has been constantly raised. Whereas, according to the recommendations of the Reith Commission it should not exceed 60 000, higher figures are now accepted and have been raised to over 120 000 for Harlow, Stevenage and Basildon. Similarly, in Sweden the populations of the neighbourhood units built round the underground railway stations and, as a result, of the urban centres serving groups of these units, have steadily increased from 10 000 to 25 000 apiece.

In France, after the experience of the *grands ensembles* and the priority development areas (ZUP), the present tendency in the Paris region (master plan of 1965) as much as in the provinces (master plan of the valley of the lower Seine, 1967; master plans of the OREAM in course of preparation) is to plan new towns on a large scale. In the Paris region it is reckoned that the new urban centres that form their nuclei can be planned to serve populations of at least 500 000.

III   Conception of zones and distribution of housing

The new towns in Britain, fruit of a long process of planning set in train by Ebenezer Howard, have served as models to most of the urban developments of the last twenty years, even where – in Sweden or Hungary, for example – the solutions adopted seem very different.

The new towns in Britain all aim at being garden cities. Their development is based on two principles:

A rigorous zoning ensuring the complete separation of residential zones, industrial zones (on the outskirts) and the central business zone (shops, amenities and business concerns).

The arrangement of housing in neighbourhood units with populations of 5000 - 10 000, with their own amenities and their own secondary centre, separated from each other and from the other zones by wide stretches of greenery.

The idea of the neighbourhood unit, in various forms, is incorporated in the plans of almost all the new towns in Europe. In Stockholm they are to be seen in the sectors built round the underground railway stations, the sectors themselves cut into smaller sections by the road system. The garden city of Tapiola is divided into three neighbourhood units of a little over 5000 inhabitants each, each with its secondary shopping centre and its own amenities (schools, etc.). Even the new districts of Amsterdam, which impress the visitor with their unity and continuity to a remarkable extent, are divided into neighbourhood units of 20 000 inhabitants on the average, either delimited by the main road system (as in Amsterdam West) or built round the underground railway stations after the Stockholm pattern (as in Amsterdam South-East). In Hungary the neighbourhood unit usually corresponds to the area served by one primary school (5000 inhabitants) but sometimes exceeds this figure (up to 10 000 at Tiszapalkonya or in the recent sectors of Dunaujvaros). Town planners in Poland prefer much larger sectors: populations of about 20 000 at Nowa Huta and Nowe Tychy.

In the United States the search for a living community has led town planners to provide 'villages' very similar in conception to the neighbourhood units of the traditional garden city.

There are fewer cases where this idea has been rejected but the unrealized project of Hook in England and the town of Cumbernauld in Scotland are the most typical examples. Adopting for the latter the principles proposed unsuccessfully for Hook, the town planner H. Wilson planned a continuous elongated residential zone to absorb an initial population of 50 000. When, however, the population target was raised to 70 000, traditional neighbourhood units had to be added to the original plan. At Lelystad, Van Eesteren's plan is based on an urban fabric in which a geometric road network separates the different sectors. At Albertslund the sectors are composed of the same type of prefabricated housing, the transition from one type to another marking the divisions.

The principle of almost complete zoning has been adopted nearly everywhere in the last twenty years. This can be explained by the reaction against the haphazard town development of the nineteenth and early twentieth centuries and, though it is not confined to the new towns, these offer it a particularly favourable setting, as they are starting from scratch. In the new towns in Britain, the industrial zones (later to absorb ancillary services) were placed in the master plans on the outskirts of the town, on a favourable site from the point of view of transport and prevailing winds (because of smoke). The new urban developments in Sweden do not include much industry, but what there is is grouped for preference in special zones, such as Johannelund, near Vällingby. Similarly, at Tapiola an industrial zone was planned between two neighbourhood units from which it is separated by belts of woodland. In every instance, small-scale industries or craftsman's workshops can be incorporated in the urban fabric, in, for example, small zones of service industries. In eastern Europe, the contrast between residential and industrial zones takes on a symbolic, even monumental character, such as the entrance to the iron-working complex of Nowa Huta (Poland) or of Dunaujvaros (Hungary) or the factory chimneys of Tiszapalkonya (Hungary). Nevertheless, a wooded zone always separated the industrial complex from the residential zones to lessen atmospheric pollution. The urban centre represents another major element of zoning against which there seems to be a present reaction (particularly in the ideas of Victor Gruen), though it is difficult to see how the new ideas can be put into practice. For instance, a detailed study of industrial establishments shows that very few of them could be incorporated in the urban fabric. As for offices, rare in new towns at the moment, these tend to prefer sites in the centres (the new towns in Britain, Farsta, Tapiola) or in special zones (Råcksta near Vällingby in Sweden, Slotermeer in Amsterdam West). As for the slight overlapping of activities in the urban centres, and it is only slight, it must be stated that the peripheral centres in the United States hardly appear to conform to the ideas of Mr Gruen. Those that come nearest are the new Scandinavian centres (Vällingby, Farsta, Skärholmen, Tapiola).

There is a far greater difference between the new towns as regards the respective roles of individual dwellings and blocks of flats. The former have a clear predominance in the new towns in Britain (over 80 per cent with this proportion tending to increase) and in the United States, as well as in Albertslund in Denmark (80 per cent). The latter are predominant in the new towns in Sweden (85 per cent), in Tapiola (80 per cent), in the new sectors in the Netherlands (about 80 per cent) and in the new towns of eastern Europe. It is of interest to note that, despite this contrast, the characteristics of zoning are often very similar.

IV   The role of urban centres

A well-known characteristic of new towns is the importance given to the main centre, which is the first of a graded system of usually three levels. The secondary level is formed by the centres of neighbourhood units or local sectors. In Harlow (north of London) the centre of a sector serves a population of about 20 000 and includes twenty to thirty shops and some amenities, while each neighbourhood unit (population 5000) has several general stores. Secondary centres are often of less importance in Great Britain. In Cumbernauld the principle has been rejected and there are only a few scattered shops outside the main centre. In the suburbs of Stockholm secondary centres are established at the centre of neighbourhood units, near the underground railway stations. They include several stores, a primary school, some amenities, etc., but do not compete with the main centres.

There is a universal desire to create centres with many functions, but this aim has only been partially achieved. It is true that the centres of the new towns in Britain, the larger centres of the Stockholm suburbs and even that of Tapiola have managed to bring together, apart from shops, private services, administrative services, some educational establishments, offices, religious and cultural buildings and leisure facilities (meeting hall, cinema, bowling alley, etc.). But even so their commercial function is predominant, helped by the arrangement of the centre, and the life of the centre is governed by the opening times of the shops and their number of customers.

It is this, as we have seen, that has been mainly responsible for turning British and Scandinavian and now French town planners to plans for larger new towns with larger centres that can become true centres of town life.

The need to mix the different functions of the centre to avoid too much zoning does not seem to be recognized. It must be realized, however, that the centres of existing new towns have only partly coped with this problem and that older towns do not offer any solution to it. It will certainly be necessary, when planning large-scale new towns, to provide the maximum flexibility so that changes can be made and original projects altered in the light of further experience and new contingencies. But, while accepting this principle of flexibility, it is not so easy to see how it can be put into practice.

V   The provision of employment

In every country the aim is to provide employment for the population of the new towns as far as possible. This principle, however, is interpreted very differently from one place to another. Where new towns are founded outside urban regions to encourage the industrialization of underdeveloped areas, there are always enough jobs for their inhabitants. In fact the opposite is the problem: how to provide enough housing to keep pace with the rate of employment, as in the new towns of Poland and Hungary. To begin with, special workers' cities are built and workers also live in nearby villages. Even after ten or twenty years, a proportion of jobs is occupied by workers living in nearby rural zones and the population of the town is unbalanced because of the presence of a number of unmarried workers.

In Great Britain the balance between employment and the working population was one of the basic principles of the new towns. It is realized through the link introduced between the obtaining of a job in the new town and the allocation of housing: to obtain the latter, it was necessary to show that one worked in the new town, but if one later changed jobs one did not have to give up one's house. As a result, commuting was not completely suppressed, especially when the second generation arrived at working age: in Harlow 20 per cent of the working population has jobs outside the new town, even though there is an approximate balance of numbers between employment and the working population.

Elsewhere, the aim has been merely to provide as many jobs as possible on the spot, without seeking an exact balance. This holds good for Albertslund (Denmark) and Tapiola (Finland), for the new sectors of the Stockholm suburbs, for those of Amsterdam or Rotterdam and for the New Communities of the United States. In all these the problem is very different from that of Britain. The different scale of the built-up areas in Scandinavia and the Netherlands (about a tenth the size of London) does not make the dispersal of industry such a pressing matter; distances between the new towns and the centre are much less and the small size of these new towns makes them less attractive to business concerns. In some places, like Stockholm, employment is deliberately concentrated in the centre. Nowhere is there any balance in numbers between jobs and the working population. In the new towns of Scandinavia there is usually one job for every two workers (Vällingby, Tapiola). But, allowing for those jobs occupied by non-residents, only one out of three inhabitants of the new sectors works on the spot. In the Paris region as good a balance as possible is being sought between employment and the working population, while leaving each inhabitant of the new towns free to work on the spot (which demands a variety of employment) or elsewhere.

Besides the balance of numbers, in fact, there is the question of types of employment. These should be as varied as possible, both to ensure the creation of a balanced population and to enable all, especially new young workers, to find a job in the town. Even the new towns in Britain have come to grief on this point: two-thirds of all jobs, even in the towns round London, are in industry. This has given rise to a mutilated social structure (few in the professional class but also few from the underprivileged classes) and to employment problems for the young (particularly young girls) who would like to find office jobs.

This aim of ensuring a variety of employment has played a large part in the recent tendency to increase the size of new towns. It is considered that, for one thing, there would be more firms offering a wider choice to those seeking jobs and that, for another, businesses – especially offices – would install themselves more readily if they knew they could find a wide range of services, other firms of a similar nature and attractive amenities (university, cultural facilities, etc.).

Many questions remain unanswered: what firms will decide to settle in the new towns of the Paris region, of Lyon or elsewhere in the provinces? Present firms, unable to influence either type of premises or types of worker, cannot provide an answer, which will mainly be reached empirically by study of the first large-scale new towns.

VI The administrative and financial framework

The new towns also differ very much from each other on the administrative level. Great Britain was the only country to adopt special legislation for the development of its new towns. The New Towns Act of 1946 came into being thanks to the very favourable political climate of the post-war era. The development corporations set up in each new town proved to be extremely efficient tools. On one hand, they ensured the unity of the planning, building and administration of the new towns (though Crawley and Hemel Hempstead, once they were finished, were run by a special organization, the New Towns Commission); on the other, after some early difficulties with local authorities, they provided administrative backing to Government aid, which was not granted to other local authorities. The administrative bodies of the new towns in France appear to have far more limited powers.

Elsewhere, the solutions arrived at vary greatly and do not follow any general rule. In Amsterdam, Rotterdam and Stockholm the city itself builds new sectors on land it has previously acquired, though this is only possible because of the extent of their territory. When this becomes completely urbanized, as it is at present, the city can only extend itself farther by agreement with the suburban authorities whose land it has acquired for building on. These authorities are in fact the official planning bodies. In Denmark the small local authority of Hestederne has been responsible for the new town of Albertslund. The same thing happens in Germany: municipal authorities have created the four large new towns of Salzgitter, Marl, Wolfsburg and Kaufbeuren (sharing responsibility with the Volkswagen company in the case of Wolfsburg). Construction is entrusted to building societies which are often non-profit-making (co-operative societies in Albertslund, municipal societies in Stockholm, etc.).

In the particular case of Tapiola, a private non-profit-making society, the Housing Foundation, was put in charge of the famous garden city.

Private companies build new towns in many countries. This is obviously the case in the United States, but has also taken place in Germany, as at Sennestadt, the overspill town for Bielefeld.

In eastern Europe, on the other hand, the state is directly responsible for creating the new towns, sometimes through administrative bodies such as the large companies running the industries for which the town has been founded.

This variety of administrative organization is reflected in the answers found to questions of finance. Great Britain, in the 1946 New Towns Act, was the only country to institute a special financial system for the new towns. This enables the development corporations to borrow the sum necessary for developing the new towns at a moderate rate of interest (about 5 per cent on the average) over a very long period (sixty years) with a system of deferred repayment that eases the initial stage. This very advantageous financial system has enabled the development corporations to make a profit by the end of fifteen years. As businesses bear the cost of the new town's general amenities through the rents they pay the development corporation for land or premises, rents for housing are able to be very moderate.

Elsewhere traditional methods have been used to finance the new towns. While in Sweden and the Netherlands the wide powers exercised by the cities responsible for these new sectors make the co-ordination of housing and amenities fairly easy, this is not the case in Denmark or Finland. In Finland the financing of amenities by the Housing Foundation, with hardly any help from the rural municipality (Espoo) on whose territory the garden city of Tapiola is built, has been particularly difficult. No satisfactory answer to this question has been found so far in France.

These few examples may suffice to underline the importance of an *ad hoc* administrative framework and method of finance in new towns, as such legislation provides the best opportunity for a successful operation.

VII Different types of new town

The study of some of the characteristics of new towns in different countries makes it possible to differentiate types of new town in an attempt to reach a satisfactory definition of the term.

The first category is made up of towns built outside urban regions for economic reasons, either because of the presence of raw materials or to create a new industrial centre in a rural area or for political reasons, such as the creation of a new capital.

The second category is formed by new towns aiming at the creation of a complete urban life, with housing, employment, education, leisure activities, commerce, etc. The new towns in Britain and the new towns planned in France come into this category, as do the new town projects in the Netherlands (Lelystad, Hellevoetsluis, etc.) and the town sectors of Copenhagen. This group is, however, very heterogeneous. In Great Britain it includes at one and the same time the earliest new towns, which were supposed to be self-sufficient and autonomous but have not managed to be either, new towns (such as Milton Keynes or South Hampshire) planned for several hundred thousand inhabitants, 100 km or more from London, and the major extensions of medium-sized towns for populations of 100 000 - 200 000 by the end of the century. On the other hand, the new towns planned for the Paris region, which will be continuous with the built-up area and large in size (with populations of 300 000 - 500 000, plus the population of the new urban centre's zone of influence), providing as wide a choice as possible of employment and amenities, do not wish to be autonomous but to be part of an urban region that is unified but not centralized. This same conception is to be found with the town sectors of Copenhagen.

The third category is formed by the new sectors planned as extensions of a city or as its satellites. This principle is accepted in Stockholm, where the new towns built in conjunction with the underground railway system have no pretensions to autonomy. A similar conception has inspired town planners in the Netherlands over the last twenty years until lack of developable space drove them to plan genuine new towns further away, towards the exterior of the Randstad Holland (to the north and north-east of Amsterdam and to the south of Rotterdam). Tapiola (Finland), Albertslund (Denmark), Sennestadt and Nordweststadt (Germany) and the new towns of the United States also come into this category, for which the term 'satellite town' seems more suitable than 'new town'. Some of the French ZUP (Le Mirail, Caen-Hérouville) would also seem to come into this category.

Finally, mention must be made of large-scale building operations within existing built-up areas, the French *grands ensembles* being a typical example, which certainly cannot qualify as new towns but rather as city satellites.

Conclusion

At the end of this study of new towns in various countries[1] much remains unanswered. It seems that the term 'new town' should be reserved for those urban communities able to exercise a complete range of urban functions, which excludes not only the *grands ensembles* but also new sectors created to aid the growth of a built-up area to which they remain closely linked and on whose centre they remain largely dependent.

But what kinds of new town do regional master plans propose for the next generation? It should be possible to profit from the best examples. In Britain, the most valuable lesson is undoubtedly the remarkable success of the methods practised since 1946, two years after the publication of the Greater London Plan, which formulated them in theory. A simple and efficient administrative framework was created; a special system of finance, unique and very advantageous, was planned and British town planners had only to prepare their plans and carry them out, without being too much worried by the practical difficulties so common elsewhere (Denmark, Finland, etc.).

Scandinavia illustrates particularly the possibility of operations of high architectural quality, illustrated especially by Tapiola and some sectors of the suburbs of Stockholm, such as Hässelby Strand, at a relatively low cost. It is a mistake, made all too often by architects, to assume that low-cost building (especially for state-aided housing with ceiling prices) must necessarily be of low quality. The Scandinavian town planners and architects can give proof, if it is required, that these are matters of taste rather than of cost.

The new towns of Britain, the Netherlands and Sweden show that it is possible for housing and amenities to keep pace with each other. This is certainly easier where there is a single body in charge of the whole operation, whether a development corporation or a municipality with wide powers. Nevertheless, the observer cannot forget the lesson of the new sectors of Stockholm, where the underground railway was installed at the same time as the first residents, but several months or even years ahead of the opening of the shopping centres. The town and railway had been planned in conjunction and therefore kept pace with each other. Delay in rail services to new towns could well be fatal, dissuading people and businesses alike from settling there.

[1]Unfortunately time did not allow the inclusion of the USSR.

Besides these obvious lessons, much else remains in doubt:

How fast should new towns be built? Could the maximum rate of 2000 dwellings a year in some of the towns round London be much exceeded? Depending on this, how much of the overspill of large built-up areas could be absorbed by the new towns?

What types of employment should be provided in the new towns? Allowing that production industries are willing to be dispersed into new towns, there is still uncertainty about offices and services. At present these tend to remain in the centre, except for some research establishments. These, though, are the jobs due to increase most in the future, so that if the overall number of jobs in the centre is to remain relatively stable it will be necessary to site many jobs apart from production outside the centres, which assumes the wider choice of site that has already begun.

What will the population structure of the new towns be? This question naturally follows the previous one. A youthful population can be expected, as in all new residential areas, its ageing slowed by residential mobility (introducing new young households), with the highest and lowest social classes barely represented: the first because few suitable jobs for them will be created in the new town and, especially, because they will not choose to live there except for exceptional aesthetic reasons (as in Tapiola, where architects, artists, etc., have congregated); the second because the new town will include few families without breadwinners and few low-paid jobs, these being found particularly in declining industries, which will not be established in the new towns. The creation of a social life will be especially difficult, as it has been in the *grands ensembles* of France, the new towns in Britain and the satellite towns of Sweden. Also, it will not be easy to secure the participation of the inhabitants in the life and organization of the town.

What will the form and organization of the new urban centres be? If one can make a rough guess at their composition, this will largely consist of experimental organization in the matter of zoning: what elements are naturally linked? – which give rise to a true community spirit? – which of these are part of the image of the town as seen by its inhabitants? And many more questions, to which the study of existing new towns provides no answer and for which further studies will be necessary.

Experience so far leaves many important questions without a satisfactory answer. Will one be provided by the creation of the new towns now planned for France and elsewhere, with the risks and guesswork that this implies? If so, it seems that there are two necessary conditions: one, that access should be available from the start to relevant documents, statistics, etc.; the other, that the new towns should not all be cast in the same mould, so that different results can be compared later on. Meanwhile, more detailed studies of particular aspects, applying to old towns as well as new, can help town planners to make the decisions that will shape the future of the new towns and the way of life of the citizens of tomorrow.

Bibliography

I GREAT BRITAIN

1: General policy of town and country planning

ABERCROMBIE, PATRICK *Great London Plan 1944*. London, HMSO, 1945. pp. 221.

Control of Office and Industrial Development Act 1965. London HMSO, 5 August 1965. pp. 30.

COPPOCK, J. T. and PRINCE, HUGH C. *Greater London*. London, Faber & Faber, 1964. pp. 405.

DEPARTMENT OF ECONOMIC AFFAIRS *The North West: A Regional Study*. London, HMSO, 1965. pp. 178.

DEPARTMENT OF ECONOMIC AFFAIRS *The West Midlands: A Regional Study*. London, HMSO, 1965. pp. 115.

FIRST SECRETARY OF STATE FOR ECONOMIC AFFAIRS *The National Plan*. London, HMSO, September 1965. pp. xviii + 204 + 239 + 31.

FOLEY, DONALD L. *Controlling London's Growth: Planning the Great Wen 1940-1960*. Berkeley, University of California, 1963. pp. xvi + 224.

FORSHAW, J. H. and ABERCROMBIE, PATRICK *County of London Plan*. London, Macmillan, 1963. pp. xii + 188.

HALL, PETER *London 2000*. London, Faber & Faber, 1963. pp. 220.

LONDON COUNTY COUNCIL *Administrative County of London: Development Plan 1951: Analysis*. London, LCC, 1951. pp. xvii + 325.

MERLIN, P. and GUERTIN, P. 'Urbanisme en région de Londres et aménagement du territoire', *Cahiers de l'IAURP*, **8**, June 1967.

MINISTRY OF HOUSING AND LOCAL GOVERNMENT *The South East Study 1961-1981*. London, HMSO, 1964. pp. xv + 146.

MINISTRY OF HOUSING AND LOCAL GOVERNMENT *A Strategy for the South East: A First Report by the South East Economic Planning Council*. London, HMSO, 1967. pp. 100.

MOINDROT, CLAUDE *L'aménagement du territoire en Grande-Bretagne*. Caen, Association des Publications de la Faculté des Lettres et Sciences humaines de l'Université de Caen, 1967. pp. 299, maps.

MOSER, C. A. and SCOTT, WOLF *British Towns: A Statistical Study of their Social and Economic Differences*. Edinburgh and London, Oliver & Boyd, 1961 (Centre for Urban Studies Report 2).

PLANNING ADVISORY GROUP *The Future of Development Plans*. London, HMSO, 1965. pp. vi + 62.

ROUILLER, JEAN-EUDES *L'évolution du rôle et des circonscriptions des collectivités locales en Angleterre*. Paris, District de la Région de Paris, March 1964.

ROYAL COMMISSION ON THE DISTRIBUTION OF THE INDUSTRIAL POPULATION *Report presented to Parliament by Command of His Majesty January 1940*. London, HMSO, 1963. pp. x + 320.

TOWN AND COUNTRY PLANNING ASSOCIATION *The Paper Metropolis: A Study of London's Office Growth*. London, TCPA, March 1962. pp. 88.

THE ECONOMIST INTELLIGENCE UNIT *A Survey of Factors Governing the Location of Offices in the London Area*. Prepared for the Location of Offices Bureau, January 1964. pp. 180.

WHITTLE, WILFRED, LIGHAM, BERNARD and SHAKESPEARE, L. W. *Moving out of London*. Manchester, *The Manchester Guardian* and *Evening News*, 1964. pp. 59.

2: Planning in the London region (excluding existing new towns)

BUCHANAN, COLIN, & PARTNERS *South Hampshire Study*. A study made for the records of the Ministry of Housing and Local Government, in 3 vols: 1 *Report on the Feasibility of Major Urban Growth*, pp. 156; 2.1 *The Area, Its People and Activities*, pp. 318; 2.2 *Methods and Policies*, pp. 173. London, HMSO, 1966.

BUCHANAN, COLIN, & PARTNERS *Ashford Study: Consultants' Proposals for Designation*. A report to the Ministry of Housing and Local Government. London, HMSO, 1967. pp. 87.

BUCHANAN, COLIN, & PARTNERS *Llantrisant: Prospects for Urban Growth*. Cardiff, HMSO, 1969.

BUCKINGHAMSHIRE COUNTY COUNCIL *Town and Country Planning Act 1962: County Development Plan: Amendment 1961*, North Bucks New City. Comprehensive Development Area and Designation. 2 vols: 1 *Written Statement*, pp. 6; 2 *Report*, pp. 9 + 5. Undated.

EATON, R. J. *North Bucks New City Monorail*. North Bucks New City, 1 March 1965. pp. 16.

IPSWICH COUNTY BOROUGH *A Planning Study for Town Development*. Study made for the Ministry of Housing and Local Government. London, HMSO, 1964. pp. 108.

MERLIN, P. and GUERTIN, P. *see under* (1).

MINISTRY OF HOUSING AND LOCAL GOVERNMENT *Northampton, Bedford and North Bucks Study: An Assessment of Interrelated Growth*. London, HMSO, 1965. pp. 86.

MINISTRY OF HOUSING AND LOCAL GOVERNMENT *A New City: A Study of Urban Development in an Area including Newbury, Swindon and Didcot*. London, HMSO, March 1966. pp. 99.

MINISTRY OF HOUSING AND LOCAL GOVERNMENT *Expansion of Ipswich: Comparative Costs: Consultants' Supplementary Report*. London, HMSO, 1967. pp. 23.

New Towns Come of Age. A special issue of *Town and Country Planning*. January-February 1968. pp. 134.

New Towns Statistics. Town and Country Planning (annual report on the new towns). January 1966. pp. 37-43.

Official Architecture and Planning, 30 (10), p. 46, 'Expanding towns in the regional context'.

SHANKLAND, COX & ASSOCIATES *Expansion of Ipswich: Designation Proposals: Consultants' Study of the Town in its Sub-region*. London, HMSO, 1966. pp. 88.

STONE, P. A. *Housing, Town Development, Land and Costs*. London, Estate Gazette. pp. xvi-154.

TECHNICAL PANEL, LONDON *Population, Employment and Transport in the London Region: Report on the situation up to 1971, with proposals*. Standing Conference on London Regional Planning, 25 November 1964, Agenda item 8, LRP 340. pp. 34.

TECHNICAL PANEL, LONDON (BENNETT, HUBERT) *Office Employment in the Conference Area*. Standing Conference on London Regional Planning, 8 July 1964, Agenda item 16, LRP 279. pp. 8.

TECHNICAL PANEL, LONDON (BENNETT, HUBERT) *The South East Study 1961-1981 and the White Paper South East England*. Standing Conference on London Regional Planning, 22 April 1964, Agenda item 17, LRP 240. pp. 12.

TOWN AND COUNTRY PLANNING ASSOCIATION *The Government's South East Study*. London, TCPA, 29 April 1964. pp. 46.

WELLS, HENRY W. *Peterborough: An Expansion Study 1963*. London, Graphic Press, 1964. pp. 79, maps.

3: The new towns

BENNETT, SIR THOMAS *Crawley New Town 1958*. Address to representatives of official and other organizations. Crawley CDC, 29 March 1958. pp. 16.

BURNS, WILFRED *New Towns for Old. The Technique of Urban Renewal*. London, L. Hill, 1963. pp. 233.

COHEN, BENJAMIN, LIET-VEAU, GEORGES and VALAT, JEANNE 'Une expérience à suivre, les villes nouvelles anglaises'. *Annales de l'Institut technique du Bâtiment et des Travaux publics*, **207-208**, March-April 1966.

Crawley New Town Master Plan. Undated.

CUMBERNAULD DEVELOPMENT CORPORATION *Cumbernauld New Town: Preliminary Planning Proposals*. 3 vols: 1 *Preliminary Planning Proposals*, April 1958, pp. 36, duplicated; 2 *Planning Proposals, First Revision: an addendum report to the preliminary planning proposals*, May 1959, pp. 14; 3 *Planning Proposals, Second Revision: second addendum report to the preliminary planning proposals*, January 1962, pp. 34.

CUMBERNAULD DEVELOPMENT CORPORATION *Economic Assessment of Main Roads* (addendum). June 1961, February 1964. pp. 15 + 3.

CUMBERNAULD DEVELOPMENT CORPORATION *Origin Destination Survey Procedure as adopted in the Traffic Forecast for Cumbernauld New Town*. November 1962. pp. 7.

CUMBERNAULD DEVELOPMENT CORPORATION (ROSS, WILLIAM) *Ninth Annual Report for the Year Ended 31 March 1965*. 1965, duplicated. pp. 28.

DEPARTMENT OF HEALTH FOR SCOTLAND (REITH, J. C. W.) *Interim Report of the New Towns Committee*. London, HMSO, March 1946. pp. 68.

DUFF, A. C. *Britain's New Towns: An Experiment in Living*. London, Pall Mall Press, 1961. pp. 108.

GIBBERD, FREDERICK *Harlow New Town*. 2nd ed. Epping and Loughton, West Essex Press, August 1952. pp. 28.

GIBBERD, FREDERICK *Harlow Expansion Survey*. A report to the Ministry of Housing and Local Government on the possibility of expanding Harlow. Harlow CDC, March 1963.

HARLOW DEVELOPMENT CORPORATION *New Town Population Survey 1961*. London, The Economist Intelligence Unit, January 1962. pp. 11.

HARLOW DEVELOPMENT CORPORATION *Population Projection Report (1961 Survey)*. London, The Economist Intelligence Unit, April 1962. pp. 10.

HARLOW DEVELOPMENT CORPORATION *New Town Population Survey: Technical Report on Projections*. London, The Economist Intelligence Unit, June 1964. pp. 5.

HARLOW DEVELOPMENT CORPORATION *New Town Population Survey 1964*. London, The Economist Intelligence Unit, January 1965. pp. 25.

HOWARD, SIR EBENEZER *Garden Cities of Tomorrow*. London, Faber & Faber, new ed., 1965 (the first ed. was published in 1898 under a different title).

LABALLE *Les villes nouvelles en Grande-Bretagne: Contribution essentielle à la politique d'aménagement du territoire*. Undated. pp. 40.

LLEWELYN-DAVIES, LORD 'Villes nouvelles: l'expérience britannique'. *Political and Parliamentary Review*, No. 800, June 1969. pp. 85-96.

LONDON COUNTY COUNCIL *The Planning of a New Town*. London, 1961. pp. 182.

MERLIN, P. and GUERTIN, P. 'Villes nouvelles en Grande-Bretagne'. *Cahiers de l'IAURP*, **8**, June 1967. pp. 94.

MERLIN, P. 'Les villes nouvelles en Grande-Bretagne'. *Annales de Géographie,* May-June 1968. pp. 278-95.

MINISTRY OF HOUSING AND LOCAL GOVERNMENT *The New Towns of England and Wales: Review of Progress*. Report ch. VII, 'New Towns'. London, 1960. pp. 44.

MUGGLI, HUGO W. *Greater London und seine New Towns*. Basel, Verlag Halbing & Lichtenhabn, 1968. pp. 164.

New Towns Act. 9 & 10 Geo 6, ch. 68. London, HMSO, 1964. pp. 46.

Northern Architect, March 1969, pp. 27-48, 'Six new towns'.

OSBORN, FREDERIC J. and WHITTICK, ARNOLD *The New Towns: The Answer to Megagalopolis*. Introd. by LEWIS MUMFORD. London. L. Hill, 1963. pp. 376.

PINCHEMEL, GENEVIÈVE and PHILIPPE 'Les villes nouvelles britanniques': 1 *La vie urbaine*, October-December 1958, No. 4, pp. 252-85; 2 *La vie urbaine*, January-March 1959, No. 1, pp. 11-51.

ROSNER, R. *Neue Städte in England*. 1962. pp. 158.

ROUILLIER, JEAN-EUDES *Les méthodes employées dans la réalisation des 'villes nouvelles' en Angleterre*. Paris, District de la région de Paris, February 1964. pp. 30.

RUNCORN DEVELOPMENT CORPORATION *Runcorn New Town*. 1967. pp. 136.

STRATHCLYDE UNIVERSITY *Cumbernauld: A Household Survey and Report*. Cumbernauld Development Corporation, 1967.

SUQUET-BONNAUD, ANTOINETTE *Une expérience hardie en matière d'urbanisme: les villes nouvelles en Grande-Bretagne*. Paper presented to the Musée Social, town planning and housing section. Paris, Musée Social, 1 June 1961, duplicated.

THOMAS, RAY *London's New Towns: A Study of Self-contained and Balanced Communities*. Political and Economic Planning publications, **35**, April 1969. pp. 373-473.

THOMAS, WYNDHAM *The Lessons of the New Towns*. Aberdeen, Scottish Housing and Town Planning Council, 3 October 1963, duplicated. pp. 10.

TOWN AND COUNTRY PLANNING ASSOCIATION *New Towns Come of Age. Town and Country Planning*, special ed., 1968.

TOWN AND COUNTRY PLANNING ASSOCIATION *New Towns*. An exhibition arranged in collaboration with the fifteen new town development corporations. London, Royal Academy Galleries, 1959. pp. 59.

Town and Country Planning. Statistical data on the new towns in each January number.

II SCANDINAVIA

1: The Copenhagen region

(a) Town planning in the Copenhagen region

Betaenkning] vedrørende partiel byudviklingsplan, N2 for Københavnsegnens byudviklingsområde, afgiv. den 2 maj 1951, af det af boligministeren den 6 Oktober 1949 nedsatte byudviklingsudvalg for Københavnsegnen. Copenhagen, J. H. Schultz, 1951, 1951. pp. 39.

Copenhagen Regional Plan: A Summary of the Preliminary Proposal 1948-1949. July 1949.

København. Skiste tilen generalplan. Summary. Copenhagen, Stadsingeniorens Direktorat, 1954. pp. 32.

MALLING, V. 'Plan for a green belt (how it was conceived and carried out)'. *Planning Outlook*, **4** (1). pp. 38-40.

MERLIN, P. with GUERTIN, P. 'Urbanisme à Copenhague, Stockholm, Helsinki'. *Cahiers de l'IAURP*, 9, October 1967. pp. 60.

Principskitse til Engsplan for byudviklingen Indtil 1980 i København, Frederiksborg Og Roskilde amter. Copenhagen, Engsplansekretariatet for Storkøbenhavn, December 1960. pp. 32.

Report of the Technical Committee appointed to examine the preliminary outline for the Copenhagen Metropolitan Region. Copenhagen, Regional Planning Office, December 1961. pp. 22.

(b) Town planning legislation in Denmark

MERLIN, P. with GUERTIN, P. *see under* (1a).

NATIONAL PLANNING COMMITTEE *National Zoning of Denmark 1962: The Background.* Introduction. Copenhagen, November 1962, duplicated. pp. 15.

Town Planning Act (Act No. 181, 29 April 1938, as amended by Act No. 211, 23 April 1949, and Act No. 63, 21 February 1962). Undated, duplicated. pp. 14.

Zoneplan 1962 for Denmark. 3rd ed. Copenhagen. S. I. Moller, 16 August 1962. pp. 48.

(c) Planning of the new towns of the Copenhagen region

Albertslund Syd, Teknisk projekt til gårdhuse og raekkehuse. 1965. pp. 32.

Forslag til vej- og stiplan. Bilag A. Vejnettets detailudforming. Copenhagen, Planlaegringsudvalget, July 1963. pp. 34.

MERLIN, P. with GUERTIN, P. 'Villes nouvelles en Scandinavie'. *Cahiers de l'IAURP*, **9**, October 1967. pp. 64.

2: The Stockholm region

(a) Town planning in the Stockholm region

L'aménagement urbain dans les pays nordiques. M. Göran Sidenbladh, 1965, duplicated. pp. 12.

General Plan för Stockholm. Stockholm, K. L. Beckman, 1952. pp. 472.

RYDEN, LARS, LINDBERG, INGEMAR and PERSSON, LARS *Skärholmens Centrum. Utredning rörande dimensioneringen av det planerade stadsdelgruppcentret i Skärholmen.* Varby baserad bl. a påerfarenhater från Farsta centrum, Stockholm, January 1963. pp. 3 + 33.

STOCKHOLM CHAMBER OF COMMERCE *Les centres commerciaux suédois: Expériences et réalisations*. 1965. pp. 39.
SWEDISH PLANNING INSTITUTE *Swedish Planning of Town Centres*. Exhibition catalogue. Stockholm, undated. pp. 54.

3: The Helsinki region

(a) *Town planning in the Helsinki region*

HELSINGIN YLEISKAAVAEHDOTUS *Laaditu asemakaavaosatolla*. Tilgmaniin Kirjapaino Helsinki, 1960. pp. 80.
LÀURILA, PEKKA, HELPINEN, HARTO and SÖDERLUND, JAN 'Helsingin Keskustasuunnitelma'. *Helsingfors Centrumplan*. 1965. pp. 62.
MERLIN, P. with GUERTIN, P. *see under* (1a).
VAN HERTZEN, HEIKKI 'Planning problems in the province of Uusimaa: seven towns' plan and its underlying principles'. *New Towns Seminar* (Working Session IV), 14 August 1965. pp. 7.

(b) *Planning of the new towns in the Helsinki region*

HANNUS, ARNO 'Government organisation, land use controls, financing and taxation as related to new town development'. *European New Towns Seminar* (Working Session II), 13 August 1965. pp. 20.
MERLIN, P. with GUERTIN, P. *see under* (1c).
Tapiolan Puutarhakaupunki 1951-1965. *Tietoja suosituimmista asuntotyypeistä ja asumiskustannukista*. Undated. pp. 24.
Uusima 2010. 1966. pp. 145.
VAN HERTZEN, HEIKKI 'Planning, design and management of Tapiola'. *New Towns Seminar* (Working Session I), 12 August 1965. pp. 11.
VAN HERTZEN, HEIKKI 'Practical problems of new town development'. *New Towns Seminar* (Working Session III), 13 August 1965. pp. 6.

III THE NETHERLANDS

1: National planning policy

BLIJSTRA, R. *L'urbanisme aux Pay-Bas depuis 1900*. Amsterdam, P. N. Van Kempen, undated pp. 58.
BURKE, G. L. *Greenheart Metropolis: Planning the Western Netherlands*. London, Melbourne and Toronto, Macmillan, 1966. pp. 172.
GOVERNMENT PLANNING DEPARTMENT *Rapport relatif à l'aménagement du territoire aux Pays-Bas*. Abridged. ed. The Hague, 1960. pp. 73.
GOVERNMENT PLANNING DEPARTMENT and MINISTRY OF HOUSING *L'aménagement du territoire aux Pays-Bas*, I: *Aperçu général*. The Hague, September 1962. pp. 41.
GOVERNMENT PLANNING DEPARTMENT and MINISTRY OF RECONSTRUCTION AND

TOWN PLANNING *L'aménagement de l'espace aux Pays-Bas*. The Hague, January 1951. pp. 27.

MAUREL, A. 'Loisirs aux Pays-Bas'. *Cahiers de l'IAURP*, **12-13**, December 1968. pp. 52.

MERLIN, P. 'Aménagement du territoire et urbanisme aux Pays-Bas'. *Cahiers de l'IAURP*, October 1967. pp. 93.

MINISTRY OF HOUSING AND CONSTRUCTION *Le logement aux Pays-Bas*. The Hague, 1964. p. 70.

NETHERLANDS GOVERNMENT PHYSICAL PLANNING SERVICE (WITSEN, J.) *National Physical Planning in the Netherlands*. Conference at Helsinki, 26 November 1965. pp. 18.

NETHERLANDS GOVERNMENT PHYSICAL PLANNING SERVICE *Second Report on Physical Planning in the Netherlands* (condensed ed.). 2 vols: Part I *Main Outline of National Physical Planning Policy*, pp. 50; Part II *Future Pattern of Development*, pp. 86. The Hague, 1966.

RUTGERS, J. *Dienst van Stadsontwikkeling en wederopbuow Rotterdam Municipal. Real Estate Policy in the Netherlands*. Conference at Brussels at the Belgian National Housing Institute, 13 November 1959. pp. 19.

SPITS, A. *Les travaux du delta*. Amsterdam, September 1962. pp. 43.

2: Amsterdam

AMSTERDAM BUREAU OF INFORMATION *Amsterdam, capitale des Pays-Bas*. 1965. pp. 63.

CITY OF AMSTERDAM PLANNING DEPARTMENT *Grondslagen voor de Stedebouwkundige ont wikkeling van Amsterdam Algemeinen Vitbreitdingsplan*. Amsterdam, 1935. pp. 169.

CITY OF AMSTERDAM PLANNING DEPARTMENT *Développement urbain et le service des terrains d'Amsterdam*. Amsterdam, May 1967. pp. 39.

CITY OF AMSTERDAM PLANNING DEPARTMENT *Amsterdam Zuid-Vost*. Amsterdam, undated. pp. 15.

CITY OF AMSTERDAM PLANNING DEPARTMENT *Beknopte nota van Toolichting bij het structuurplan 1:25,000 van de agglomeratie Amsterdam, Zuid en Zuidoost*. Amsterdam, undated. pp. 16.

MERLIN, P. *see under* (1).

MULDER, J. H. *Moments décisifs dans le développement urbanistique d'Amsterdam*. Amsterdam, Planning Department, undated. pp. 11.

PROVINCIALE PLANOLOGISCHE DIENST NOORD HOLLAND, *Drie miljoen Noord Hollanders*. Haarlem, 1967.

VAN WALRAVEN, ALBERTUS 'Amsterdam'. Extract from *Urbanistica*, No. 38. Turin, March 1963. pp. 32.

3: Rotterdam

Loop der Bevolking van Rotterdam binnen zihn huidige gemeentegrens tijdvak 1830-1966. Rotterdam, Town Hall, 1966.

Magasins et centres commerciaux dans le nouveau Rotterdam. Rotterdam, Town Hall, November 1962. pp. 6.

MERLIN, P. *see under* (1).

REINHARDT, HANS *The Story of Rotterdam. The City of Today and Tomorrow*. Rotterdam, Town Hall, 1955. pp. 49.

4: The development of the Zuider Zee area

BOARD OF THE ZUYDERZEE WORKS *A Structure Plan for the Southern Ijsselmeerpolders*. The Hague, 1965. pp. 32.

DEPARTMENT FOR THE ZUIDER ZEE *La genèse et le développement du polder Flevoland-Est*. Publication No. 20. The Hague, April 1961. pp. 11.

DEPARTMENT FOR THE ZUIDER ZEE *Genèse et développement du polder Flevoland-Sud*. Publication No. 21. The Hague, April 1961. pp. 8.

DEPARTMENT FOR THE ZUIDER ZEE *La clôture du Zuiderzée*. Publication No. 14. The Hague, May 1962 (new ed.). pp. 13.

MERLIN, P. *see under* (1).

MINISTRY OF TRANSPORT AND THE WATERSTAAT *Du poisson à la moisson*. The Hague, undated. pp. 116.

SOCIETY OF DUTCH ARCHITECTS *Planification et création d'un milieu: Expérience dans les polders du lac Yssel*. Undated. pp. 95.

SPITS, A. *Terres nouvelles: Les travaux du Zuiderzée*. Amsterdam, August 1962. pp. 55.

VAN EESTEREN, C. *Stedebouwkundige plan voor Lelystad*. The Hague, Ministrie van Verkeer en Waterstaat, undated. pp. 111.

IV FRANCE

Bâtir, N. 402, December 1967, pp. 35-48, 'Toulouse-Mirail, ville nouvelle de 100,000 habitants'.

Cahiers de l'IAURP., 15, May 1969, pp. 72, 'Évry: Centre urbain nouveau et ville nouvelle'.

CLERC, PAUL *Grands ensembles, banlieues nouvelles*. Enquête démographique et psychosociologique, INED, Travaux et documents, Cahier No. 49, Presses Universitaires de France, 1967.

La vie des ménages de quatre nouveaux ensembles de la région parisienne 1962-1963. 3 vols. pp. 170, 234, 46. Paris, Équipe d'Observation sociologique de la Compagnie d'Études industrielles et d'Aménagement du territoire (CINAM) pour le compte du ministère de la Construction.

MERLIN, P. *Pourquoi des villes nouvelles?* Mission d'études de la ville nouvelle du Vaudreuil, April 1969. pp. 33.

MERLIN, P. *Les villes nouvelles en région parisienne*. Promotions, October 1969.

Projet de schéme d'aménagement de la Basse-Seine. Mission d'Etudes Basse-Seine, March 1968.

Recueil de textes législatifs et réglementaires sur l'urbanisme. Paris, Journeaux officiels, 1967. pp. 1235 + xxxv.

Revue *Les cahiers de l'IAURP*.

Revue *Les cahiers de l'OREAM* (Lyon-Saint-Étienne).

Revue *Les feuillets de l'OREAM Lorraine* (Nancy-Metz-Thionville).

Schéma directeur d'aménagement et d'urbanisme de la région de Paris. District de la région de Paris, 1965. pp. 220.

Schéma directeur d'aménagement et d'urbanisme de la région de Paris. Délégation générale au District de la région de Paris, 1965. 3 vols: 1, pp. 261; 2 *Avis et rapports du Comité d'Aménagement de la région parisienne et du Comité consultatif économique et social de la région de Paris*, pp. 210; 3 (1) *Avis et rapport du Conseil d'Administration du district de la région de Paris*, pp. 223; 3 (2) *Avis et rapport du Conseil d'Administration du district de la région de Paris*, pp. 224-472.

V   THE UNITED STATES

1: Regional planning policies

ASSOCIATION OF BAY AREA GOVERNMENTS *Preliminary Regional Plan for the San Francisco Bay Region*. Berkeley, November 1966. pp. 52.
BOSTON REDEVELOPMENT AUTHORITY *1965-1975: General Plan for the City of Boston and the Regional Core*. Undated. pp. 162.
CITY PLANNING COMMISSION *Staten Island Development Policies, Programs and Priorities*. Comprehensive planning report. June 1966. pp. 66.
LOS ANGELES CITY PLANNING DEPARTMENT *The Los Angeles Economy: Selected Statistics and Projections*. November 1966. pp. 52.
MERLIN, P. 'Plantification régionale des métropoles des États-Unis', *Cahiers de l'IAURP*, **15**, May 1969. pp. 32.
NARDIN, H. 'Urbanisme et rénovation urbaine dans les grandes villes des États-Unis', *Cahiers de l'IAURP*, **15**, May 1969. pp. 30.
NATIONAL CAPITAL PLANNING COMMISSION *A Plan for the Year 2000: The Nation's Capital*. June 1961, pp. 113.
NATIONAL CAPITAL PLANNING COMMISSION *The Proposed Comprehensive Plan for the National Capital*. February 1967. pp. 230.
PHILADELPHIA CITY PLANNING COMMISSION *Comprehensive Plan for the City of Philadelphia*. 1960. pp. 103.
PHILADELPHIA CITY PLANNING COMMISSION *Capital Program, 1967-1972: City of Philadelphia*. December 1966. pp. 281.
Planning for the Los Angeles Metropolis. Discussion paper. June 1967. pp. 32.
REGIONAL PLAN ASSOCIATION *The Region's Growth*. May 1967. pp. 143.
REGIONAL PLAN ASSOCIATION *Exploration of Alternative Regional Planning Policies*. Working paper. Undated. pp. 19.
Regional Plan News, November 1964, No. 75, pp. 14, 'The second regional plan'.
Regional Plan News, May 1965, No. 78, pp. 14, 'A Center for the suburbs'.

2: New towns

Architectural Record, June 1966, 'Redwood Shores. Framework for a new kind of living'.
Architecture d'aujourd'hui, No. 132, June-July 1967, pp. 88-9.
CALIFORNIA LAND CO. *Valencia: Proposed Land Use Plan*.
Design of a City: Foster City. 1965.
Foster City Report, **5** (1). Foster City, San Mateo County, Calif., Summer 1967.
General Development Plan: Columbia (Maryland). A new city by community research and development corporation. January 1966.

MARYLAND NATIONAL CAPITAL PARK AND PLANNING COMMISSION *Master Plan for Germantown*. October 1966. pp. 45.
NARDIN, H. and MERLIN, P. with RICHARD, P. 'Villes nouvelles aux États-Unis'. *Cahiers de l'IAURP*, 15, May 1969. pp. 32.
Reston Master Plan: Fairfax County. Virginia.
ROUSE COMPANY, THE *A New City: Columbia*. 1966. pp. 32.
VICTOR GRUEN ASSOCIATES *Transportation for Valencia*. Undated. pp. 36.

VI POLAND

ADAMCZEWSKA, M. *Wplyw realizacji na przemiany planu miasta* (*The Carrying Out of a Plan*). Warsaw, 1964.
Architecture d'aujourd'hui: No. 62, 1955; No. 80, 1958; No. 118, 1964.
CIBOROWSKI, A. *L'Urbanisme polonais 1945-1965*. Warsaw, 1956.
City and Regional Planning in Poland. Cornell University Press, New York, 1965.
FOURQUIER, A. and J. 'Planification et urbanisme en Pologne'. *Cahiers de l'IAURP*, November 1968. pp. 167 + 119.
GUZICKA, J. 'Zespol miejski Nowej Huty i rola w rozwoju Krekowa' ('Nowa Huta and its influence on the Development of Cracow'). *Miasto*, No. 11, November 1966.
KNOBELSDORF *Tychy: Ludnosc nowego miasta satelitarnego* (*The Population of a New Town*). Katowice, 1966.
MALISZ, B. *La Pologne construit des villes nouvelles*. Warsaw, 1961.
MALISZ, B. *Zarys teorii ksztaltowania ukladow osnadniczycho Arkady* (*An Outline of a Theory of the Formation of Housing Systems*). Warsaw, 1966.
MALISZ, B. *Physical Planning for the Development of Satellite and New Towns*. Warsaw, Institut urbanistyki i architektury, 1966.
OSABANIA, MAREK *Nowe Tychy Miasto satelita*. Katowice, 1966.
Statystyka Miast i osiedli 1945-1965 (*Statistics of Towns and Built-up Areas*). Warsaw, 1967.
Urbanistica, No. 25-26, 1960; No. 34, 1961.
WICZYNSKI, A. and DZICWONSKI, M. *Problemy miast szybko rozwijajacych sie* (*The Problem of Rapidly Developing Towns*). Warsaw, OITEB, 1964.

VII HUNGARY

1: National and regional planning

INSTITUT HONGROIS POUR L'URBANISME ET L'AMÉNAGEMENT DU TERRITOIRE *Recherches de l'aménagement régional en Hongrie*. A report prepared for the UN Economic Committee of Housing and Town Planning. 1964. pp. 22.
Kategorizalasi (*elövrasik*) (*Industries in Budapest*). pp. 4.
MERLIN, P. 'Aménagement du territoire et villes nouvelles en Hongrie'. *Cahiers de l'IAURP*, March 1968. pp. 82.

NOVAK, P. and ZSITVA, T. 'Uj. Általames rendezési terveink' ('General planning'). *Magyar Epitömüveszet*, 1962, No. 1. pp. 19-22.

PERCZEL, KAROLY 'A regionalis tervezés a város rendezés és az épitészet' ('The regional plan, town planning and architecture'). *Magyar Epitömüveszet*, 1962, No. 1. pp. 10-12.

PERCZEL, KAROLY *Le plan de développement du réseau des agglomérations en Hongrie.* Translation of a paper delivered to the conference at Pecs, 6 June 1967. pp. 5.

PERCZEL, KAROLY and GERLE, GYÖRGY *Regionanális tervezés es a Magyar településhalozat.* Budapest, Akadémiai Kiedó, 1966. pp. 445.

2: Housing

MERLIN, P. *see under* (1).

MINISTRY OF CONSTRUCTION AND URBAN DEVELOPMENT *Architecture et construction en Hongrie.* Budapest, 1965. pp. 24.

MINISTRY OF CONSTRUCTION AND URBAN DEVELOPMENT *Politique de logement en Hongrie.* Budapest, 1967. pp. 40.

3: Planning in the Budapest region

BUDAPESTI VAROSÉPITÉSZI TERVEZÖ VALLALAT (BUVATI) *A Budapesti regio vizsgálatai* (*Studies of the Budapest Region*). Budapest, 1958.

BUVATI *A Budapesti regio rendezési terve Iresz* (*Development Plan for the Budapest Region*). Budapest, 1959.

GARAB, T. Z. *Les nouveaux centres d'habitation à Budapest.* Documentation sur l'Europe centrale, Louvain, 5 (6), November-December 1967. pp. 311-27.

HEIM, ERNÖ and PREISICH, GABOR 'Budapest es környéke általanos rendezési terve' ('General Development Plan for Budapest and its Surroundings'). *Magyar Epitömüveszet*, 1962, No. 1. pp. 4-9.

MERLIN, P. *see under* (1).

PREISICH, GABOR, FODOL, LASZLO, GYORFFY, LAJO and SZABO, KALMAN 'A Budapesti Belvaros rendezési' ('Development Plan for the City of Budapest'). *Varosépités*, No. 3, June 1966. pp. 3-19.

4: The new towns

ACZEL-KOVATS, TAMAS 'Les villes de demain'. *La vie hongroise*, 1, April 1958. pp. 11-13.

BOROS, F. *Geographical Aspects of Dunaujvaros.* Papers of the symposium on the effects of industrialization on the agricultural population in the European socialist countries. Budapest, 18-22 October 1967. pp. 118-27.

GARAB, T. Z. *Les villes socialistes de Hongrie.* Documentation sur l'Europe centrale, Louvain, 4 (3), May-June 1966. pp. 171-207.

HALASZ, ZOLTAN *Un coup d'oeil sur la Hongrie* (pp. 99-107). Pannonia, Budapest. pp. 112.

KOVACS, ALBERT 'Tiszaszederkeny', *Budapest*, November 1967, No. 11. pp. 24-5.

MERLIN, P. *see under* (1).

New Towns in Hungary. Published in English by the Hungarian government. Undated.

VARKONYI, ENDRE 'Dunaujvaros'. *Hungarian Review*, 1966, No. 8. pp. 6-9.

VIII OTHER COUNTRIES

1: Germany

Architektur Wettbewerbe, 1965, 'Planning Wulfen New Town'.
BUDINIS, MANLIO 'Les villes nouvelles de la République fédérale allemande'. *Revue géographique de l'Est*, 3, 1964. pp. 229-60.
Fachzeischrift für architektur und bautechnik, 1, 1966, 'Deutsche Bauzeitung'.

2: Italy

Quadro di riferimento per la pianificazione territoriale nel mezzogiorno d'Italia. Rome, April 1965.
TEKNE (Società per azione) *Consulenze e progrettazioni technico organizzative: Piano territoriale di coordinamento della Puglia*. Milan, 28 June 1967. pp. 113.
Urbanistica 50-51, October 1967, 'Rivista trimestriale dell'istituto nazionale di urbanistica'.

3: Czechoslovakia

Casabella 313, 'Pianificazione urbane e territoriale in Cecoslovacchia' (article by J. HRUZA). pp. 12-122.
CITY OF PRAGUE PLANNING INSTITUTE *Etarea: Étude du milieu humain dans la ville.* Government Committee for Technology in Czechoslovakia, 1967. pp. 64.
L'Architecture française, May-June 1968, pp. 42–7, 'Etarea: Ville satellite de Prague: Étude du milieu urbain dans la ville'.
Urbanistickà prirucka, 1957, pp. 665, 'Stavba Mest A Vesnic'.

4: Yugoslavia

INSTITUTE OF TOWN PLANNING AND ARCHITECTURE *Skopje*. Summary of the report on master plan 8. Skopje, October 1965. pp. 46.

IX GENERAL BIBLIOGRAPHY

AIA Journal, undated, 'Stockholm, Tapiola, Cumbernauld'.
Bulletin du PCM, No. 2, February 1967, pp. 104, 'Rapport de mission sur le développement urbain en Europe du Nord'.
INTERNATIONAL CITY MANAGERS' ASSOCIATION *New Towns: A New Dimension of Urbanism*. November 1966. pp. 54.
Le Monde articles 'Cités sans passé a l'étranger'. 7, 8, 9, 10, 11-12, 13 October 1964.

Index